DON'T SELL STOCKS ON MONDAY

Yale Hirsch

Facts On File Publications

New York, New York • Oxford, England

Don't Sell Stocks on Monday

Hirsch, Yale.
Don't sell stocks on Monday.
Includes index.
1. Stocks. I. Title.
HG4661.H57 1985   332.63'22   83-20814
ISBN 0-8160-1044-7

Printed in the United States of America

10 9 8 7 6 5 4 3 2 1

Composition and design by Brill & Waldstein

To my wife Davida and to Betty Ross. Their encouragement, determination and assistance enabled me to bring this project to completion.

CONTENTS

INTRODUCTION

"Stocks will fluctuate" was J.P. Morgan's classic retort when he was asked about the future course of the stock market.

This well-known remark is often quoted by writers and professors with a wink-of-the-eye implying that the only prediction one can truly make about the market is that it will either go up, down or sideways. Many investors wholeheartedly believe that no one ever really knows which way the market will go.

Nothing could be further from the truth! During the past nineteen years I have made many exceptionally accurate forecasts in the annual *Stock Trader's Almanac,* which I have written and published since 1968. These forecasts were based on thousands of hours of research into recurring patterns. I learned that while stocks do indeed fluctuate, they do so in well-defined, often predictable patterns which recur too frequently to be the result of chance or coincidence.

You too can forecast market trends with accuracy and confidence once you understand:

1. How our quadrennial elections of presidents unequivocally affect the economy and the stock market, just as the moon affects the tides.

2. That there is significant market bias at certain times of the day, week, month, and year.

3. How the passage of the Twentieth Amendment to the United States Constitution inadvertently fathered the January Barometer, which has a super track record for indicating the market trend each year.

4. Just how important it is to be somewhat of a contrarian.

Many investors have made fortunes following the political cycle. You can be certain that money managers who control hundreds of billions of dollars are also political cycle watchers. Sharp people are not likely to ignore a pattern that has been working like a charm for decades.

Even if you are the type of investor who pays scant attention to cycles, indicators, and patterns, your investment survival in some future market could hinge on your interpretation of one of the recurring patterns found within these pages. One of the most intriguing and important patterns is the symbiotic relationship between Washington and Wall Street.

Aside from the potential profitability in seasonal patterns, there's also the pure joy of seeing the market very often do just what you expected.

Most of the forecasting secrets I have developed or acquired are revealed here. Nothing has been held back.

When you study and review the documentation, charts, and tables, be sure to trust your own common sense. Remember, nothing is guaranteed. If something has worked ten times out of ten and then misses, its record becomes ten out of eleven. Most of all, if something has been working (some pattern, premise, or device) and everyone seems to know about it, you had better adapt a contrary stance, pronto.

To give you an idea of what you'll find out about in these pages, here are fourteen forecasting secrets right off the bat. All will be fully documented later.

FORECASTING SECRET #1:
HOW TO PREDICT A BULL OR A BEAR MARKET YEAR

The January Barometer which I popularized in the *Stock Trader's Almanac* provides the tip-off. It's incredible how consistent the Barometer has been since 1950. In thirty of the last thirty-five years, the market for the entire year in essence has followed the Standard & Poor's composite index, rising for the year when the index was up in January and dropping for the year when the index was down.

Chapter 8 explains the probable reason why and provides statistical tables for the past thirty-five years showing you market performance in January both chronologically and by rank (highest gain first).

If you want an even quicker forecast, turn to January's "Early Warning" system (page 104) to see how you can often get a glimpse of what lies ahead by watching the market's action during the first five trading days of the month.

Both forecasting methods have an accuracy of about 85%. Since its inception in the 1930s, the January Barometer has been 100 % accurate in odd years.

FORECASTING SECRET #2:
THE MONTH MOST LIKELY TO GIVE YOU THE
BIGGEST GAIN IN THE DOW JONES INDUSTRIALS

April is the clear-cut winner. Turn to page 40 and you'll find out why. You'll also see which is the second best month (this may come as a complete surprise), and how each of the other ten months in the year fare.

You'll also find out how mutual funds, pension funds, and other institutions affect the market, what their trading patterns are, and signals that alert you to the near-term future direction of the market at various times of the year.

FORECASTING SECRET #3:
THE BEST TIME TO BUY "BARGAIN STOCKS"

Shrewd market observers have noted that many depressed issues sell at bargain levels near the close of each year as tax-conscious investors rid their portfolios of these losers for tax purposes. What happens to them then is revealed in the interesting table on page 162.

Stocks that hit new lows for the year around December 15 sharply outperform the rest of the market by mid-February of the following year. Furthermore, because of the "January Effect," S&P low-priced stocks have gained an outstanding 500% more than the S&P 500 in twenty-eight of the last thirty Januarys.

FORECASTING SECRET #4:
THE BEST TIME TO BUY GOLD STOCKS

There is an intriguing seasonal price behavior pattern evident in gold stocks. The fourth quarter in each of the years since 1963 has tended to produce attractive buying opportunities in golds such as Homestake (U.S.A.), Campbell Red Lake and Dome Mines (Canada), and ASA Ltd. (South African fund).

These stocks tend to hit seasonal highs the following spring or summer. Catching the highs and lows of ASA in a recent period would have produced an average annual gain of about 88%. Also take note that gold's three latest six-year cycles indicate a giant move could be forthcoming for gold stocks (p. 154).

FORECASTING SECRET #5:
THE TWO-DAY "SURE THING" FOR TRADERS

The day before and the day after Thanksgiving combined have gained almost nine Dow points on average for nineteen straight years, without a loss. In thirty-three years there was only one five-point loss and one loss of less than a point (p. 157).

FORECASTING SECRET #6:
THE BEST MONTH TO BUY STOCKS
IF YOU'RE LOOKING FOR SHORT-TERM GAINS

October, without a doubt, has been the best buying month for short-term traders over the past thirty-five years. The chief reason has been that most major market declines seem to choose this time of year to turn around (see The Market Turnaround Calendar, page 123).

In one-, two-, three-, and six-month time periods, October ranks number one as best buying time, with November second and December third.

FORECASTING SECRET #7:
WORST MONTH OF PAST TWO DECADES

In recent years, the market gets clobbered in May with monotonous regularity. Starting in 1965, May has been up only five times and down sixteen times for a net loss of 345.82 Dow points. May 1984 saw a loss of over sixty-five Dow points. There ought to be a sign on Wall Street— WARNING: INVESTING IN MAY MIGHT BE HAZARDOUS TO YOUR WEALTH! (See p. 130.)

FORECASTING SECRET #8:
BEST DAYS OF THE MONTH

The stock market rises more often (60.8%) on the second trading day of the month than on any other. And a period of five consecutive trading days—the last, first, second, third and fourth—distinctly outperforms the rest of the days of the month.

In a 398-month study (May 1952-June 1985) the market was up 57.6% of the time on these five bullish days, compared to an average of 50.2% for the remaining sixteen trading days of a typical month (p. 28).

FORECASTING SECRET #9:
BEST DAY OF THE WEEK TO BUY STOCK

A most unusual phenomenon in the stock market is the startling contrast between the first and last trading days of the week.

A tabulation of all the trading days in the last thirty-two years reveals that Mondays rise about 43% of the time while Fridays are up 58% of the time. While the market was gaining 930 Dow points during those thirty-two years, Mondays alone were losing an astounding 1,565 points (p. 19). My advice: DON'T SELL STOCKS ON MONDAY, buy them! Always buy into weakness.

If Friday is a down day, Monday is even more likely to be down. During the same period, 73.2% of the Mondays saw a drop after a down Friday.

FORECASTING SECRET #10:
INVESTMENT POSTURE FOR FEBRUARY

January is often a time for sharp moves, and February is a time for consolidation. If January is up, remain fully invested; if down, consider a move to the sidelines (p. 115).

Aerospace companies tend to start rising late summer in anticipation of the annual U.S. budget in January and top out thereafter.

FORECASTING SECRET #11:
WHEN TO BUY AUTO STOCKS

Auto stocks (General Motors, Ford, Chrysler) tend to be strong in the summer and fall, weak in the winter and spring. These stocks should be traded more often than held—buy when they are depressed and sell when they shoot up in price. Note: auto stocks in the past have tended to turn down just as new models were being introduced. Always remember the old adage: Buy straw hats in winter (p. 115).

FORECASTING SECRET #12:
THE SANTA CLAUS RALLY

December markets are often blah markets that tend to go nowhere, although you can often make substantial profits from depressed bargains you pick up around the middle of the month (Forecasting Secret #3).

But one short period at the end of the month almost always proves rewarding. Santa Claus comes to Wall Street almost every year with a short, sweet respectable rally. In the past thirty-three years he has appeared twenty-six times. The rally occurs within the last five days of the year and the first two in January.

When Santa doesn't call, beware. Five of the years he failed to show up preceded bear markets (p. 163).

FORECASTING SECRET #13:
WHEN TO PROFIT FROM AIRLINES AND SOFT DRINKS

In contrast to auto stocks, airlines and soft drinks usually tend to bottom out by late fall and peak in early spring. Buy them in September-October, take profits in March-April (p. 136).

FORECASTING SECRET #14:
THE WORST TIME TO JUMP INTO THE MARKET

On those occasions when the Dow average leaps twenty to thirty points for the day, the volume of shares traded invariably booms in the next day's opening hour, accompanied by a further rise in the Dow. Don't be caught in the morning's euphoria, as the market will likely give up most of the day's gain and more by the afternoon (p. 15).

1
BEST HOURS OF THE DAY

A TYPICAL DAY IN THE MARKET

Each day in the market is a new ball game. A bullish news item might move the market up, a bearish one, down. Sometimes the market is unaffected by either. Stocks some days inch upwards throughout the day, while other times it's down, down, down.

Most hourly fluctuations seem to be random movements. However, it is not uncommon for sharp moves in the last hour or two to continue in the same direction the following morning. Also, by examining the hourly prices of the Dow Jones industrial average over the last 22 years (excluding 1969, when the market closed earlier, and the last seven months of 1968, when the market operated on a four-day week), a definite composite pattern emerges.

The "typical" market day opens flat and rises slightly in the next hour. Weakness sets in around noon as professionals go to lunch. After rallying towards 2:00 P.M., the market drifts downward the rest of the afternoon.

One might look at Figure 1 and think that the market spends a good deal more time declining than rising, and he would be right. What is the reason for this paradox, as we all know from experience that the market does have an upward bias over the years? Suppose the market, as measured by the Dow, has a strong opening and is up five points at the start of the day. Then with each hourly reading it gives up half a point at a time, right through to the closing bell. What we wind up with is an opening increase and six hourly decreases. However, what counts most is that the Dow Jones average has gained two points for the day.

The decision of the New York Stock Exchange to begin one half hour earlier starting September 30, 1985 may affect future trading patterns slightly.

7

FIGURE 1

MARKET PERFORMANCE EACH HOUR OF THE DAY

(November 1963-June 1985)

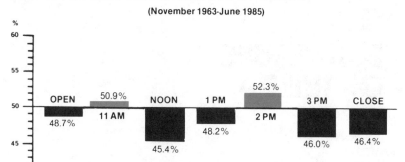

Based on number of times Dow Jones industrial average increased over previous hour

A TRADER'S HOURLY DIARY

The introduction of stock index futures in 1982 ushered in a new era by providing the perfect vehicle for trading certain recurring short-term patterns. While a floor trader on the NYSE, Justin Mamis learned a number of the market's peculiarities that occur at certain hours of the day. He relates them in his book, *How To Buy.** Some excerpts follow:

WHAT TIME OF DAY TO BUY

The market has its own intra-day cycle that it adheres to with consistency.The opening phase lasts from thirty to forty-five minutes. If the market has opened lower, once the selling is out of the way, prices will try to rebound. If the market has opened higher, there'll be a spate of profit-taking and a downside dip. In-and-out traders often use such a turn to take profits in a market that has been strong; as soon as TICK begins to falter, they sell. Similarly, if they want to buy, they wait, before stepping in, until an upturn in TICK shows that the selling has run its course.

Mid-day is always a difficult time. Do not trust mid-day rallies; they are isolated, often deceptive and frequently fizzle thereafter. Similarly, don't trust rallies that start too soon in the afternoon. They usually peter out.

Watch for the action during the "magic twenty minutes," between 2:20 p.m. and 2:40 p.m. NYSE time. If prices have been rallying before hand, and then ease back during that twenty-minute period, the likelihood is then great that the last hour of trading will be strong, so it is a good time to buy. Similarly, if prices have been fading, a little rally during those "magic twenty minutes" is a warning—and perhaps a chance to sell —since the market will then customarily slide again with greater vigor toward the close of trading.

* Farrar, Straus Giroux, 19 Union Square West, NY, NY 10003

Don't hold us to that precise time on the clock. Sometimes the shift in tenor takes place a little earlier, but it tends to encompass that time span and to last just about twenty minutes.

Never buy weakness near the close, because the odds are that you can do at least as well on the next day's opening. However, when the market is just starting a new move, it pays to buy strength near the close, even if prices are already up a point or more on the day. What you are doing is anticipating a gap opening up the next day.

TABLE 1

PERFORMANCE EACH HOUR THROUGH THE YEARS

PERIOD	OPEN	11AM	NOON	1 PM	2 PM	3 PM	CLOSE
1963-67 941 days	58.2%	60.3%	44.0%	43.7%	48.6%	45.7%	42.7%
*1967-71 413 days	42.4	54.2	52.1	48.2	47.0	48.9	46.2
1971-75 1007 days	47.3	45.6	45.1	47.2	51.3	44.8	46.4
1975-79 1012 days	45.9	47.7	44.2	47.4	60.0	48.7	46.4
1979-82 769 days	44.7	51.8	46.6	49.6	53.9	44.0	46.0
1982-85 713 days	50.2	47.3	44.2	53.0	48.4	44.2	51.3
1963-85 4855 days	**48.7%**	**50.8%**	**45.4%**	**47.9%**	**52.2%**	**45.9%**	**46.3%**

*Excludes last seven months of 1968, when market operated on a four day week, and 1969, when markets were closing earlier due to a processing overload.

Based on number of times the Dow Jones industrial average increased over previous hour.

SHIFTS IN TRADING PATTERNS

Twenty-two years of hourly data compressed into one composite day, as in Figure 1, can mask changes in trading patterns. But, by dividing the data chronologically into six parts in Table 1, I see several shifts taking place. Strong morning markets in the 1963-67 period disappeared over the next eighteen years, as bear markets, which had normally lasted less than a year, began to increase in duration. Another change was that the third, fourth and closing hours grew stronger.

Though the Dow Jones industrial average doubled since 1963, only 26% of the hourly figures show gains, on average, over the previous hours. This anomaly was explained with Figure 1. Simply, the Dow could open five points higher than the previous day, give up half a point in each of the next six hours of the trading day, and end up with a two-point gain.

Separating hourly performance by individual days for different eras in Table 2 reveals many shifts in trading patterns. Whereas the fourth hour of trading ending at 2 P.M. tended to be the strongest for all days, strength shifted to the third hour on average during the 1982-85 period. Also note that Tuesday openings and Monday and Friday closing hours on the New York Stock Exchange were the strongest ever.

The weakest hours of the week for many years continue to be the morning hours on Mondays. More on Mondays in Chapter 2.

FIGURE 2

MARKET PERFORMANCE EACH HOUR OF THE WEEK

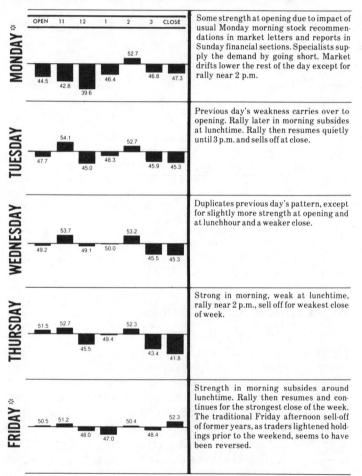

*Research indicates that where Tuesday is the first trading day of the week, it follows the Monday pattern. Therefore, all such Tuesdays were combined with the Mondays here. Thursdays which are the final trading day of a given week behave like Fridays, and were similarly grouped with Fridays.

HOUR BY HOUR, THROUGH THE WEEK

Tuesdays, Wednesdays, and Thursdays have similar hourly composite patterns. However, Mondays and Fridays are somewhat different. Figure 2 shows the percentage of times the Dow-Jones industrial average rose over the preceding hour for each day of the week between November 1963 and April 1985.*

TABLE 2

PERFORMANCE EACH HOUR, EACH DAY, IN DIFFERENT ERAS

	OPEN	11 AM	NOON	1 PM	2 PM	3 PM	CLOSE
MONDAY							
1963-67	60.5%	50.8%	35.9%	35.9%	43.6%	37.4%	36.9%
1967-71*	47.1	48.2	50.6	50.6	51.8	55.3	45.9
1971-75	42.3	39.4	32.7	41.8	49.0	45.7	51.4
1975-79	41.9	36.1	38.7	50.8	67.0	56.0	46.6
1979-82	36.4	39.7	47.7	48.3	51.7	45.0	47.7
1982-85	37.4	44.2	40.8	55.8	52.4	46.3	55.1
Average	**44.6**	**42.6**	**39.6**	**46.3**	**52.6**	**46.9**	**47.1**
TUESDAY							
1963-67	50.0	64.0	43.3	46.6	49.4	50.6	41.6
1967-71*	30.3	52.8	52.8	40.4	36.0	41.6	39.3
1971-75	46.3	45.8	47.9	54.7	56.3	46.3	44.2
1975-79	48.8	50.7	39.1	41.1	55.1	47.8	45.4
1979-82	42.6	58.7	45.8	49.0	52.3	40.0	49.0
1982-85	57.6	47.7	42.4	56.8	53.8	40.2	47.0
Average	**47.5**	**53.9**	**45.0**	**48.8**	**52.4**	**45.6**	**45.2**
WEDNESDAY							
1963-67	54.2	65.6	47.9	49.5	52.6	49.5	40.1
1967-71*	41.2	49.4	50.6	45.9	51.8	48.2·	43.5
1971-75	53.7	50.2	51.2	45.9	50.2	43.4	45.4
1975-79	45.0	53.1	47.4	46.9	58.9	46.4	45.0
1979-82	48.7	48.1	48.7	58.3	59.0	43.6	46.2
1982-85	49.3	52.1	48.0	55.5	46.6	43.2	52.1
Average	**49.5**	**53.7**	**48.8**	**50.2**	**53.5**	**45.6**	**45.2**
THURSDAY							
1963-67	61.3	59.1	42.5	47.5	53.0	43.6	39.2
1967-71*	43.0	57.0	54.4	49.4	43.0	39.2	41.8
1971-75	48.7	49.2	46.2	44.2	48.2	41.1	40.6
1975-79	47.5	50.5	46.5	52.5	60.4	45.5	43.1
1979-82	51.6	56.2	43.1	43.1	56.2	43.8	40.5
1982-85	53.9	46.1	44.7	51.8	46.1	43.3	44.7
Average	**51.6**	**52.7**	**45.5**	**49.5**	**52.3**	**43.1**	**41.6**
FRIDAY							
1963-67	64.6	62.1	50.2	42.1	44.6	46.7	55.4
1967-71*	45.9	57.6	45.9	49.4	47.1	54.1	55.3
1971-75	45.4	44.0	47.8	49.8	53.1	47.8	49.8
1975-79	46.3	47.3	48.8	46.3	59.1	48.3	52.2
1979-82	44.2	55.8	47.4	48.7	50.0	47.4	46.8
1982-85	53.7	46.3	44.9	45.6	43.5	47.6	57.1
Average	**50.5**	**51.6**	**47.8**	**46.7**	**50.3**	**48.3**	**52.5**

* Excludes last 7 months of 1968, when market operated on a 4-day week, and 1969, when markets were closing earlier due to a processing overload.

Based on number of times the Dow Jones Industrial Average increased over previous hour.

FIRST-HOUR VOLUME AVALANCHE
A TEMPORARY KISS OF DEATH

Consider the scenario: The market has been in a state of decline for a spell. Wall Street is down in the dumps, in the doldrums. One day the selling stops. Prices begin to edge higher . . . and higher . . . and higher.

Suddenly a buying panic erupts. Frantic professionals with huge short positions rush to cover their shorts to avoid losing their proverbial shirts. Institutional money managers with giant portfolios and embarrassingly large cash positions spring into action and gobble up huge blocks of anything in sight. Alert traders, adrenalin flowing, cover shorts and switch to long positions to catch the trend.

FIGURE 3

FIVE REVERSAL DAYS IN 1984

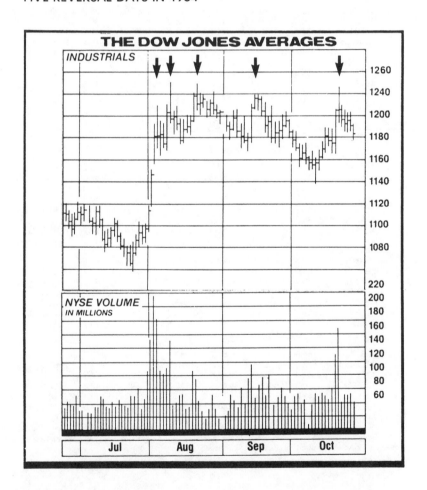

In a matter of days, or weeks, the Dow Jones industrial average has soared well over one hundred points. Many investors who missed the boat are sorely disappointed, even downright angry.

Buying panics, like those which began in January of 1975 and 1976, in April of 1978 and 1980, and in August of 1982 and 1984, have produced a unique trading pattern. I first discovered it in 1977.

As the market moves up, the "boat-missers" grow increasingly anxious. After a double-digit point gain in the Dow on a given day, many of them try to jump on board as the market opens the following morning. This causes an enormous bulge in volume during the first hour of trading (one and a half to two times the shares traded in the previous day's first hour) and, often, a further jump in prices. This volume avalanche (or "blow-off") in the first hour results most of the time in at least a temporary "kiss of death"—a ten- to twenty-point decline within twenty-four hours. More often, these blow-offs are short-term trend reversal points from which the market turns down.

Five reversal days are noted in Figure 3 with arrows, all preceded by gains the previous day of twenty-two to thirty-six points in the Dow. Volume in the first hour of the following day was significantly higher

TABLE 3

DOW JONES HOURLY AVERAGES

			30 Industrials		
	Oct 15	16	17	18	19
Open	1190.04	1203.40	1194.02	1193.24	1237.74
11:00	1193.57	1202.41	1196.22	1195.56	**1233.66**
12:00	1198.65	1203.95	1195.67	1192.69	1234.32
1:00	1199.76	1202.52	1192.58	1195.01	1233.11
2:00	1204.28	1197.22	1195.45	1197.44	1234.65
3:00	1199.54	1196.67	1202.74	1204.28	1222.06
Close	1202.96	1197.77	1195.89	**1225.38**	1225.93
High	1209.58	1209.36	1208.59	1226.70	1246.02
Low	1186.73	1192.25	1185.62	1185.73	1213.56
Change	+ 12.26	—5.19	—1.88	+ 29.49	+ 0.55
	Intra-day range:		High 1246.02		Low 1185.62

SHARES TRADED ON N.Y. EXCHANGE

	Oct 15	16	17	18	19
10-11	19,540	25,720	26,140	**34,110**	**69,110**
11-12	13,990	13.420	12,440	20,130	39,000
12- 1	13,470	12,600	14,100	16,720	22,100
1- 2	13,110	10,760	12,160	17,410	16,010
2- 3	14,680	10,100	17,330	21,090	19,750
3- 4	12,800	10,330	17,570	40,080	20,930
Total, thousands	87,590	82,930	99,740	149,540	186,900

than the first hour of the previous day. The Dow had additional gains in the first hour of twenty-one, twenty, four, nine, and eight points, respectively. As can be seen, these days were followed by short-term downswings.

Table 3 from *Barron's* Market Page, October 22, 1984, shows actual hourly prices on the Dow Jones industrials and the hourly volume during each day of the week. Notice on Friday, October 19, the strong opening following the previous day's twenty-nine point gain with the Dow tumbling from over 1240 (intraday high was 1246) to 1225. Since the New York Stock Exchange switched to a 9:30 A.M. opening on September 30, 1985, one-half hour earlier than had been its custom for years, Barron's now reports volume on a half-hourly basis.

Table 4 shows the many occasions since the August 1982 buying panic where the Dow had good gains the previous day that were followed by strong first-hour volume avalanches.

This phenomenon was first reported in the 1977 *Stock Trader's Almanac* following the buying panics that began in January 1975 and January 1976. The total volume in those days averaged fifteen million shares a day, and eight to ten million shares in the first hour alone was very heavy. I noted then:

> Learn to recognize these volume aberrations and remember to stand back for at least a day when you hear that first-hour volume is enormous with the market strong, following strength the previous day. It's just everybody trying to get through the same "narrow door" at the same time. You should be able to buy what you want somewhat cheaper later that day or tomorrow.
>
> Investors who hedge options or convertibles, etc., have a golden opportunity during these volume bulges. They can initiate the short side of a position first and do the long side at a lower price a day later. There are some risks, of course, but the percentages seem to favor use of this strategy.

FIGURE 4 | FIGURE 5

BUYING PANIC 1975 | BUYING PANIC 1976

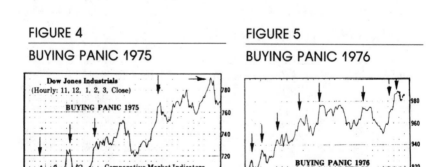

TABLE 4

FIRST HOUR VOLUME AVALANCHES SINCE AUGUST 1982

Previous Day			Next Day First Hour			Following Day	
DJI Gain	First Hour Shares (Mil.)	1982	Shares (Mil.)	Gain	DJI	Intra-Day Low	Change To Low
38.81	22	Aug. 18	37	18	849.03	824.49	−24.54
21.88	25	21	36	−8	883.66	867.87	−15.79
9.99	22	26	33	11	895.64	874.14	−21.50
14.35	16	Sept. 3	40	16	925.31	906.92	−18.39
18.49	18	22	36	8	942.14	915.38	−26.76
37.07	17	Oct. 7	43	15	959.44	961.64	+ 2.20*
20.88	32	11	36	21	1007.27	992.00	−15.27
26.12	20	19	32	6	1025.39	1005.98	−19.41
20.32	21	21	38	9	1043.05	1024.37	−18.68
43.41	29	Nov. 4	46	−1	1064.20	1040.65	−23.55
22.81	25	10	32	10	1070.92	1030.35	−40.57
36.43	20	Dec. 1	31	−5	1034.22	1027.04	− 6.18
24.29	16	7	30	0	1055.10	1041.30	−13.80
		1983					
26.03	25	Jan. 7	40	2	1072.66	1065.12	− 5.50
20.33	25	Feb. 11	30	5	1092.45	1080.64	−11.81
16.54	21	24	32	11	1107.49	115.13	+ 7.64*
18.09	25	Mar. 2	32	−1	1129.55	1128.39	− 1.16
12.10	20	31	30	6	1149.57	1115.13	−34.44
16.93	25	Apr. 21	32	3	1194.85	1184.21	−10.64
22.25	21	27	41	3	1212.27	1201.04	−11.23
11.12	21	29	30	−2	1217.88	1197.27	−20.61
18.48	28	May 25	41	0	1219.81	1215.17	− 4.64
10.02	25	Jun. 16	36	7	1244.99	1232.87	−12.12
30.74	33	Jul. 21	32	3	1230.87	1220.45	−10.42
14.23	24	Sep. 23	32	−3	1254.78	1247.56	− 7.22
13.51	26	Oct. 6	30	3	1253.56	1262.60	+ 9.04*
17.78	28	Nov. 22	30	6	1274.09	1265.04	− 9.05
17.38	24	30	32	−1	1286.18	1265.45	−20.73
		1984					
16.31	22	Jan. 5	48	8	1277.22	1268.74	− 8.48
13.71	24	Feb. 15	28	0	1163.74	1143.74	−20.00
26.17	24	Apr. 13	35	8	1165.31	1139.55	−25.76
10.15	17	17	26	5	1165.20	1151.07	−14.13
19.50	24	Jun. 4	30	8	1132.65	1117.13	−15.52
15.80	25	21	32	1	1132.84	1118.93	−13.91
36.00	72	Aug. 6	60	21	1223.17	1184.96	−38.21
27.94	25	10	64	20	1244.92	1204.39	−40.53
22.75	26	22	34	4	1243.60	1221.51	−22.09
27.94	23	Sept. 14	44	9	1237.85	1226.26	−11.59
29.49	34	Oct. 19	69	8	1233.66	1210.80	−22.86
34.78	48	Dec. 19	49	8	1219.63	1198.87	−20.76
		1985					
16.45	24	Jan. 15	51	3	1237.52	1220.74	−16.78
34.01	25	22	56	6	1267.01	1252.54	−14.47
14.79	28	30	57	4	1296.49	1272.64	−23.85
12.36	25	Feb. 5	41	−1	1288.98	1275.07	−13.91
21.31	32	14	42	−1	1296.82	1275.08	−21.74
10.49	26	May 10	45	8	1268.11	1268.77	+ 0.66
10.98	26	Jul. 11	36	4	1336.25	1326.39	− 9.86
12.43	31	17	49	7	1354.39	1345.32	− 9.07

*Start of 4-day 100-point move (New buying panic)

TABLE 5

FIRST HOUR VOLUME AVALANCHES 1975, 1976

| Previous Day | | Next Day First Hour | | | | Following Day | |
DJI Gain	First Hour Shares (Mil.)	1975	Shares (Mil.)	Gain	DJI	Intra-Day Low	Change To Low
11.19	4.8	Jan. 30	9.4	5.24	711.20	690.16	−21.04
9.78	6.4	Feb. 5	9.1	6.26	724.11	697.51	−26.60
7.43	4.6	Feb. 13	10.2	12.21	727.24	719.81	− 7.43
14.08	5.1	Mar. 4	9.0	11.41	764.24	745.54	−13.70
13.06	6.1	Mar. 18	8.4	6.26	792.79	761.19	−31.60
		1976					
11.26	5.7	Jan. 13	9.8	4.56	926.95	908.22	−18.73
16.69	6.0	Jan. 15	10.9	5.98	935.61	917.98	−17.63
14.09	6.4	Jan. 20	10.6	1.34	945.06	934.35	−10.71
10.47	6.8	Jan. 26	9.2	7.09	961.04	950.80	−10.25
17.40	6.5	Jan. 30	12.1	8.34	977.09	962.06	−15.03
11.57	6.2	Feb. 11	9.6	5.51	974.26	963.00	−11.26
9.52	6.7	Feb. 19	10.4	10.28	970.17	977.80	+ 7.63
15.67	10.4	Feb. 20	13.0	9.75	985.52	977.25	− 8.27

2
BEST DAYS OF THE WEEK

FRIDAYS RISE MORE TIMES THAN MONDAYS

A most unusual phenomenon in the stock market is the startling contrast between the first and last trading days of the week.

A tabulation of all the trading days in the thirty-three-year period of June 1952-June 1985 reveals that the first trading day of the week (including Tuesday when Monday is a holiday) has a rising market only 43.0% of the time. Conversely, the strongest day of the week is the last trading day of the week (including Thursday, when Friday is a holiday), when the market closes higher 58.0% of the time.

FIGURE 6

MARKET PERFORMANCE EACH DAY OF THE WEEK

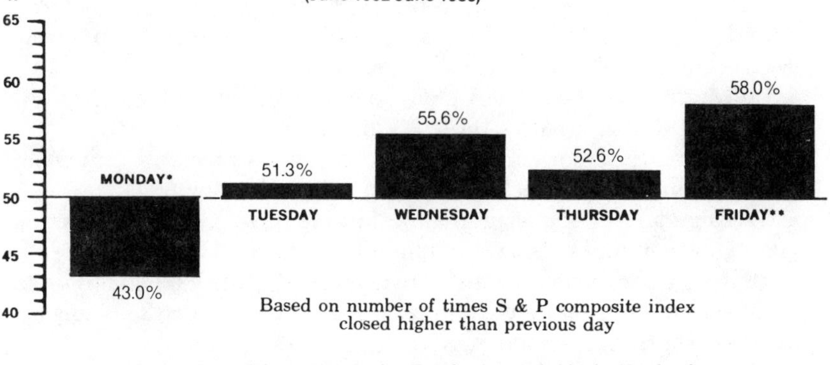

(June 1952-June 1985)

%

65

60 — 58.0%

55 — 55.6%

52.6%

51.3%

MONDAY*

50

TUESDAY   WEDNESDAY   THURSDAY   FRIDAY**

45

43.0%   Based on number of times S & P composite index
40   closed higher than previous day

*On Monday holidays, the following Tuesday is included in the Monday figure.
**On Friday holidays, the preceding Thursday is included in the Friday figure.

17

THE DOWN ON FRIDAY/DOWN ON MONDAY EFFECT

The profound effect of Friday's activity on Monday's markets was discovered by Frank Cross of Niederhoffer, Cross & Zeckhauser. When the market is down on Friday, chances are three to one that Monday will also decline. During the 1953-1985 period only 26.8% of the Mondays were able to rise after declining Fridays. A cluster of three or four up-Mondays following down-Fridays occurred around important market bottoms in 1966, 1968, 1970, 1973, 1974, and 1982. This is highly significant.

DAILY PERFORMANCE EACH YEAR SINCE 1952

To determine if market trend alters performance of different days of the week, I separated the twelve bear years of 1953, 57, 60, 62, 66, 69, 70, 73, 74, 77, 81, and 84 from the twenty-one bull market years. While middle days—Tuesday, Wednesday and Thursday—did not vary much on average between bull and bear years, Mondays and Fridays were sharply affected by changes in market climate. There was a swing of 12.6 percentage points in Monday's performance and 12.8 percentage points in Friday's.

A TRADER'S DAILY DIARY

In *How To Buy*,* Justin Mamis discusses the market peculiarities that occur on certain days of the week:

WHAT DAY OF THE WEEK TO BUY

Monday is the most difficult day of the week. This is especially true on Monday mornings. Often the market will trade higher for perhaps half an hour on an accumulation of orders and then drift. Usually Monday is a carry-over down day in a troubled market or, in a strong market, a difficult day for any further advance.

If Monday has been a down day, and the market has become oversold, look for a turnaround on Tuesday morning. Conversely, if you are looking for a correction and Monday has wobbled about without prices giving way, the decline is apt to begin on Tuesday.

Wednesdays are typically trend-following days. Good markets will carry through; weak ones will continue to falter.

Early-week declines that are in the nature of profit-taking dips often rebound in the last hour of trading on Thursdays. Be alert to taking action on Thursday afternoons.

Fridays, too, tend to be trend-following days. But because there is typically so much of a struggle on Mondays, Friday afternoons are not a time when it is imperative to buy.

*Farrar, Straus Giroux, 19 Union Square West, NY, NY 10003

TABLE 6

PERCENTAGE OF TIMES MARKET
CLOSED HIGHER THAN PREVIOUS DAY

(Based on S&P composite index, 1952-1984)

Year	Monday	Tuesday	Wednesday	Thursday	Friday
1952	50.0%	57.7%	56.7%	61.5%	65.5%
1953	32.7	47.9	54.9	60.8	56.6
1954	51.9	57.4	63.5	60.0	73.1
1955	48.1	45.7	67.3	60.8	80.8
1956	34.0	40.0	44.9	50.0	61.5
1957	25.0	58.0	64.7	46.8	46.2
1958	59.6	53.1	59.6	68.1	73.1
1959	40.4	51.0	58.3	51.0	69.2
1960	36.5	52.2	44.2	56.3	61.5
1961	53.8	54.3	62.0	54.0	64.2
1962	28.3	52.1	58.0	51.0	50.0
1963	46.2	63.3	51.0	57.4	69.2
1964	40.4	48.0	62.7	59.6	78.8
1965	46.2	52.1	55.8	51.0	69.2
1966	36.5	47.8	53.8	42.0	57.7
1967	40.4	52.2	58.8	64.0	63.5
1968*	39.1	65.0	60.9	45.0	56.5
1969	32.1	46.9	50.0	67.4	52.8
1970	38.5	44.0	63.5	46.8	51.9
1971	44.2	62.5	55.8	50.0	55.8
1972	38.5	60.4	55.8	51.0	67.3
1973	30.8	51.1	52.9	44.9	42.3
1974	34.6	56.3	52.0	38.8	34.6
1975	53.8	38.8	59.6	58.3	57.7
1976	55.8	56.5	55.8	40.8	56.6
1977	40.4	40.4	46.2	53.1	55.8
1978	51.9	43.5	59.6	54.0	48.1
1979	54.7	51.0	58.8	66.0	44.2
1980	57.6	56.2	69.8	33.3	59.6
1981	46.2	38.8	53.8	54.2	46.2
1982	44.2	39.6	44.2	46.0	48.1
1983	50.0	46.8	59.6	52.0	55.8
1984	39.6	62.5	30.8	44.9	44.2
Average	**43.1%**	**51.3%**	**55.9%**	**52.8%**	**58.1%**
21 Bull Years	**47.7%**	**52.1%**	**58.1%**	**54.0%**	**62.8%**
12 Bear Years	**35.1%**	**49.8%**	**52.1%**	**50.6%**	**50.0%**

* Excludes last six months of four-day market weeks.

DON'T SELL STOCKS
ON MONDAYS

I computed the Dow's performance for different days of the week for each year since 1953 and summarized the results in Table 7. The most shocking revelation is the Monday "horror show." While the market during thirty-two years was gaining 930 Dow points, Mondays alone were losing an astounding 1,565 points. Until 1975, Mondays were losers on balance every year except for the big bull years of 1954, and 1958, and 1968 which was affected by the fact that the market was closed on

Wednesday in the last seven months of that year. Surprisingly, half of 1976's gains were netted during Monday markets. While Fridays gained most points, it was an "extreme" day—great in bull years, poor in down years.

One of the most valuable parts of this book is the section in the Appendix containing the daily point change for each day of the year since January 1, 1953, the first full year with no Saturday morning trading on the New York Stock Exchange. (Trading on six days of the week was customary in prior years.) As far as I know, no one has ever published this data before. These views of entire years on single pages have been invaluable to me in my study of the stock market.

TABLE 7

ANNUAL DOW POINT CHANGES FOR DAYS OF THE WEEK SINCE 1953

Year	Monday	Tuesday	Wednesday	Thursday	Friday	Year's Closing D.J.I.	Year's Point Change
1953	−37.39	−6.70	19.63	7.25	6.21	280.90	−11.00
1954	9.81	9.14	24.31	36.05	44.18	404.39	123.49
1955	−56.09	34.31	45.83	1.18	58.78	488.40	84.01
1956	−30.15	−16.36	−15.30	9.86	63.02	499.47	11.07
1957	−111.28	−5.93	64.12	4.26	−14.95	435.69	−63.78
1958	14.36	26.73	29.10	24.25	53.52	583.65	147.96
1959	−35.69	20.25	4.11	19.98	87.06	679.36	95.71
1960	−104.89	−9.90	−5.62	10.36	46.58	615.89	−63.47
1961	−17.76	4.29	67.51	14.26	46.95	731.14	115.25
1962	−88.44	13.03	9.97	−4.46	−9.14	652.10	−79.04
1963	−43.61	81.85	16.23	26.07	30.31	762.95	110.85
1964	−3.70	−14.53	39.84	21.96	67.61	874.13	111.18
1965	−70.23	36.65	57.03	2.75	68.93	969.26	95.13
1966	−126.23	−54.74	56.13	−45.69	−13.04	785.69	−183.57
1967	−73.07	35.93	25.41	98.37	32.78	905.11	119.42
1968*	3.38	37.97	25.16	−59.00	31.13	943.75	38.64
1969	−152.05	−48.82	18.33	17.79	21.36	800.36	−143.39
1970	−99.00	−47.14	116.07	1.81	66.82	838.92	38.56
1971	−16.16	22.46	13.66	6.25	25.07	890.20	51.28
1972	−85.08	−3.55	65.24	16.14	137.07	1020.02	129.82
1973	−192.68	29.09	−5.94	41.56	−41.19	850.86	−169.16
1974	−131.00	29.11	−20.28	−12.60	−99.85	616.24	−234.62
1975	59.74	−129.96	56.75	129.66	119.98	852.41	236.17
1976	81.16	61.32	50.89	−26.80	−14.33	1004.65	152.24
1977	−66.38	−43.60	−79.70	−2.74	18.94	831.17	−173.48
1978	−31.81	−70.32	71.33	−65.71	70.35	805.01	−26.16
1979	−27.82	4.72	−18.84	73.97	1.70	838.74	33.73
1980	−89.40	138.02	137.67	−112.78	51.74	963.99	125.25
1981	−64.47	−30.72	−13.95	−13.66	33.81	875.00	−88.99
1982	21.69	70.22	28.27	14.75	36.61	1046.54	171.54
1983	39.34	−39.75	149.68	47.90	14.93	1258.64	212.10
1984	−40.48	44.70	−139.24	94.36	−6.41	1211.57	−47.07
Totals	−1565.38	177.77	893.40	377.35	1036.53		919.67

*Most Wednesdays closed last 7 mos.

have been invaluable to me in my study of the stock market.

Table 8 shows 1984 in its entirety with months separated by alternate shadings. Each week's close of the Dow Jones industrial average and its net change for the week are also shown. You'll find similar tables for each of the past thirty-two years in the Appendix. If you ever intend to trade index futures or any of the options based on the Standard & Poor's index, you'll be delighted by the wealth of data compressed in these tables.

I have always been astounded by the pounding stocks tend to take on Mondays, especially during some bear markets when the term "blue Monday" begins to appear in the financial pages. The first twenty-six weeks of 1962 was such a period. The Dow declined twenty-two times on the first day of the week, was up just a fraction of a point three times, and climbed a meager 1.26 points on one occasion.

Why is Monday such a downer? There are no satisfactory explanations but here are some factors to consider: First, the market has been closed for two days; second, many investors here, and in foreign countries, may make decisions on weekends, having more time to deliberate; third, many unexpected events take place on weekends; fourth, many traders who covered their short positions on Friday afternoon, so as to sleep better, reinstate them Monday mornings if the market doesn't appear to be heading up; and finally, after greed has had its fling and a bear market starts, fear takes over and more and more investors "throw in their towels" on Mondays as stocks continue sinking week after week.

My analysis of the 553 down weeks in the twenty-two years between 1963 and 1984 (Table 9) showed a total loss in the Dow Jones industrial average of 7485.01 points. In contrast, 591 upweeks gained 8044.48 points. The Dow began the period at 652.10 on January 1, 1963 and ended at 1211.57 on December 31, 1984 for a net gain of 559.47 points.

What I wanted to see was how badly the market performed on Mondays after a losing week. The result: Two out of three Mondays were down and gave up a total of 2570.59 Dow points, while the other Mondays which rose gained 1097.31 points.

The reason I say DON'T SELL STOCK ON MONDAY is to caution you against being frightened into abandoning your positions when the market has been hit hard on Monday. Traders especially should be ready to take advantage of the Monday *opportunity*. Why do I call it an opportunity? Because common sense tells us that the further anything falls, the higher it will bounce back. Corroboration for this was achieved by actually measuring the distance between the intraday lows and the close for all the days of the week. I found that Monday was by far the best *comeback* day. What makes it even more

TABLE 8

1984 DAILY DOW POINT CHANGES
(Dow Jones Industrial Average)

WEEK #	MONDAY	TUESDAY	WEDNESDAY	THURSDAY	FRIDAY	WEEKLY DOW CLOSE	NET POINT CHANGE
					1984 Close: 1258.64		
1	H	− 5.90	16.31	13.19	4.40	1286.64	28.00
2	− 0.42	− 7.74	− 1.16	1.99	− 9.21	1270.10	−16.54
3	− 2.51	3.87	− 2.09	− 3.35	− 6.91	1259.11	−10.99
4	−14.66	− 1.57	−10.99	− 2.20	0.31	1230.00	−29.11
5	− 8.48	− 0.94	− 8.27	1.57	−16.85	1197.03	−32.97
6	−22.72	6.18	−24.19	− 3.56	7.96	1160.70	−36.33
7	−10.57	13.71	− 5.13	− 3.77	− 6.07	1148.87	−11.83
8	H	− 9.53	− 5.13	0.42	30.47	1165.10	16.23
9	14.86	−22.82	− 2.51	4.81	12.04	1171.48	6.38
10	− 6.28	−12.67	− 8.90	3.46	− 7.33	1139.76	−31.72
11	15.60	9.42	1.26	1.36	16.96	1184.36	44.60
12	−12.98	4.39	− 4.92	−14.97	− 1.04	1154.84	−29.52
13	− 1.89	1.36	20.31	− 3.87	− 5.86	1164.89	10.05
14	−11.73	− 4.40	− 0.20	−18.01	1.67	1132.22	−32.67
15	1.68	4.40	− 7.33	26.17	− 7.01	1150.13	17.91
16	10.15	4.29	− 8.06	1.57	H	1158.08	7.95
17	− 8.58	13.40	0.63	11.72	− 6.18	1169.07	10.99
18	1.68	12.25	3.56	− 5.03	−16.22	1165.31	− 3.76
19	1.25	9.74	−10.78	1.67	−10.05	1157.14	− 8.17
20	− 6.07	− 0.21	2.30	−10.89	− 8.48	1133.79	−23.35
21	− 8.48	− 8.69	− 2.82	−10.37	3.67	1107.10	−26.69
22	H	− 5.86	1.35	2.26	19.50	1124.35	17.25
23	7.22	− 6.68	8.95	− 1.40	− 1.19	1131.25	6.90
24	−15.64	− 5.08	n/c	−12.92	−10.71	1086.90	−44.35
25	22.75	6.18	15.80	− 4.42	3.86	1131.07	44.17
26	− 0.55	− 7.73	− 6.07	9.83	5.85	1132.40	1.33
27	− 2.32	− 4.20	H	− 9.72	− 1.99	1122.57	− 9.83
28	11.48	− 7.17	−18.33	− 3.98	5.30	1109.87	−12.70
29	6.96	6.07	−11.26	− 8.72	− 1.55	1101.37	− 8.50
30	− 4.75	−10.05	10.38	10.60	7.07	1114.62	13.25
31	− 4.64	5.30	19.33	31.47	36.00	1202.08	87.46
32	0.88	1.66	− 8.51	27.94	− 5.96	1218.09	16.01
33	1.99	− 5.97	−15.13	10.16	2.76	1211.90	− 6.19
34	5.08	22.75	− 7.95	0.66	4.09	1236.53	24.63
35	− 8.61	4.19	− 5.19	− 3.64	1.10	1224.38	−12.15
36	H	−12.03	− 3.32	9.83	−11.48	1207.38	−17.00
37	− 4.86	− 4.53	2.32	27.94	9.27	1237.52	30.14
38	− 0.44	−10.82	−13.25	3.53	−14.80	1201.74	−35.78
39	3.32	2.10	4.96	4.64	−10.05	1206.71	4.97
40	− 7.73	− 7.62	− 8.50	4.53	− 4.86	1182.53	−24.18
41	− 4.64	− 2.76	2.10	5.85	7.62	1190.70	8.17
42	12.26	− 5.19	− 1.88	29.49	0.55	1225.93	35.23
43	− 8.73	− 4.19	3.42	− 5.41	− 6.07	1204.95	−20.98
44	− 3.54	15.90	− 9.93	9.71	− 0.44	1216.65	11.70
45	12.59	14.91	−10.93	− 4.53	− 9.72	1218.97	2.32
46	0.22	−12.59	0.33	− 0.77	−18.22	1187.94	−31.03
47	− 2.65	9.83	6.40	H	18.78	1220.30	32.36
48	− 7.95	7.84	−14.80	−11.93	− 4.52	1188.94	−31.36
49	− 6.52	2.65	−13.47	− 1.11	− 7.28	1163.21	−25.73
50	9.05	6.07	− 3.20	− 6.29	7.07	1175.91	12.70
51	0.88	34.78	− 3.53	− 4.75	− 4.31	1198.98	23.07
52	11.16	H	− 1.22	− 6.40	1.65	1204.17	5.19
53	7.40				(Year's Close)	1211.57	7.40*
TOTALS	**−40.48**	**44.70**	**−139.24**	**94.36**	**− 6.41**		**−47.07**

* Partial Week

significant is that the market often continues its bounce back into Tuesday. Get the picture? Test this phenomenon yourself over the past thirty-two years in the Daily Dow Point Changes tables in the Appendix. Just remember that the change in the Dow on any Monday does not tell you its low for the day. Also, the low given for the Dow is hypothetical. To pursue this further, use either the S&P 500 index future or the Major Market index (MMI). Both can be found on the commodity page. I prefer the MMI which is one-fifth of the Dow— when the Dow moves five points, the MMI will usually move one point.

Monday comebacks—between the Monday low and the Tuesday high—averaged the equivalent of twenty Dow points over an eighteen-week period in 1984. Tuesday, Wednesday, and Thursday comebacks averaged about sixteen points each. The worst ones were Fridays. Their average gain was only thirteen Dow points, nearly fifty percent less than Mondays.

TABLE 9

553 DOWN WEEKS, 7485.01 DOW POINTS LOST

	Dow Jones Industrials High-Low	# of Down Weeks	Total Points Lost	Avg. Loss	What the Market Did on Following Mondays			
					# Up	Points	# Down	Points
1963	767-646	18	134.17	7.45	6	+ 45.19	12	— 54.73
1964	891-766	20	102.75	5.14	7	+ 25.27	13	— 36.23
1965	969-840	18	149.86	8.32	5	+ 12.11	13	— 79.83
1966	995-744	28	432.40	15.44	6	+ 36.09	22	—180.32
1967	943-786	24	229.58	9.57	4	+ 8.46	20	—106.28
1968	985-825	28	258.79	9.24	10	+ 38.19	18	—110.60
1969	968-769	30	390.77	13.02	7	+ 29.12	23	—147.66
1970	842-631	26	333.30	12.81	6	+ 14.06	20	—133.16
1971	950-797	26	269.68	10.37	6	+ 17.69	20	—123.71
1972	1036-889	24	193.05	8.04	7	+ 30.80	17	—107.29
1973	1051-788	29	643.03	22.17	8	+ 63.05	21	—229.05
1974	891-577	31	652.36	21.04	12	+ 90.81	19	—181.74
1975	881-632	21	270.71	12.89	10	+ 59.60	11	— 93.00
1976	1014-858	24	258.38	10.77	12	+ 87.45	12	— 70.09
1977	999-800	34	398.61	11.72	19	+ 73.38	15	— 66.87
1978	907-742	23	378.45	16.45	9	+ 45.83	14	— 99.37
1979	897-796	23	280.26	12.19	10	+ 59.92	13	— 78.28
1980	1000-759	22	347.27	15.10	7	+ 44.71	15	—153.69
1981	1024-824	27	404.89	15.00	10	+ 94.06	17	—142.07
1982	1070-776	25	389.36	15.57	10	+ 60.41	15	—140.69
1983	1287-1027	26	393.91	15.15	15	+ 100.51	11	—106.17
1984	1286-1086	26	573.43	22.06	9	+ 60.60	17	—129.76
	Totals	**553**	**7485.01**		**195** 35.3%	**+1097.31**	**358** 64.7%	**—2570.59**

HOW TO FORECAST WHAT THE MARKET MIGHT DO TOMORROW

To predict the market's probable direction successfully is most gratifying. Having the knack can not only improve your performance, but it can also help to reduce the emotional shocks and strains of "watching the market."

An interesting challenge is to forecast what the market might do tomorrow based on what it did the previous day. The day-to-day indicators presented here were excerpted from *Granville's New Strategy of Daily Stock Market Timing for Maximum Profit,* by Joseph E. Granville (Prentice Hall).

The list of points to be checked off are available in your morning newspaper. They primarily deal with: divergence between the Dow and other broader market averages and advancing and declining issues; the quality of market leadership; most active list; volume; the overbought/oversold condition; one-day reversals; the three-day rule; churning; reaction to news; General Motors as bellwether; new daily highs and lows; and how the market closes.

The author states that the market is its own best indicator and "tips its hand as to what it is going to do the next day 95% of the time."

Even if you are not a trader and don't give a hoot what the market will do tomorrow, you are bound to be a better long-term investor when you can call the market with greater confidence and accuracy.

THE MARKET WILL CONTINUE TO ADVANCE TOMORROW OR TURN UP (IF IT'S DECLINING) IF:

1. Dow Jones industrial average (DJIA) **declines** but advancing issues **outnumber** declining issues.
2. DJIA **advances** and advancing issues **outnumber** declining issues.
3. Dow Jones transportation average (DJTA) **advances more,** percentagewise, than DJIA.
4. The quality of market leadership **deteriorates** on a **downswing** in the DJIA (most active stock list features more and more lower caliber stocks).
5. The quality of market leadership **improves** on an **upswing** in the DJIA.
6. DJIA **declines** but a majority of the fifteen **most active stocks advance.**
7. DJIA **advances** and so do a **majority** of the fifteen most active stocks.
8. The **decline** in the DJIA is **not "real"**—it is a distortion caused by sharp declines in one or two stocks.

9. The **decline** in the DJIA is not **matched** percentagewise by a decline in the Standard & Poor 500 or NYSE Index.
10. The S&P 500 and NYSE Index **advances more** than the DJIA.
11. When **dullness** prevails following a decline.
12. The DJIA **declines** five or six or more days in a row.
13. DJIA hits a **new decline low** but closes well above the lows for the day.
14. DJIA declines **sharply** three days in a row.
15. DJIA **declines** for several days, then is followed by a **day of little net change** but with **heavy volume.**
16. Market **fails** to move down on **bearish news.**
17. A positive trend for IBM **bodes well** for the market.
18. In absence of negative overnight news, a **strong closing** in the market spills over with **further strength** the next day.
19. "**Technical**" **rebounds** are more likely to **follow sharp declines** rather than periods of slow and gradual declines.
20. The trend of new **daily highs** is on the **increase.**
21. The trend of new **daily lows** is on the **decrease.**

THE MARKET WILL CONTINUE TO DECLINE TOMORROW OR TURN DOWN (IF IT'S ADVANCING) IF:

1. Dow Jones industrial average (DJIA) **advances** but declining issues **outnumber** advancing issues.
2. DJIA **declines** and declining issues **outnumber** advancing issues.
3. Dow Jones transportation average (DJTA) **declines more,** percentagewise, than DJIA.
4. The quality of market leadership **deteriorates** on an **upswing** in the DJIA (most active stock list features more and more lower caliber stocks).
5. The quality of market leadership **improves** on a **downswing** in the DJIA.
6. DJIA **advances** but a majority of the fifteen **most active stocks decline.**
7. DJIA **declines** and so do a **majority** of the fifteen most active stocks.
8. The **advance** in the DJIA is **not** "**real**"—it is a distortion caused by sharp advances in one or two stocks.
9. The **advance** in the DJIA is not **matched** percentagewise by an advance in the Standard & Poor 500 or NYSE Index.
10. The S&P 500 and NYSE Index **declines more** than the DJIA.
11. When **dullness** prevails following an advance.
12. The DJIA **advances** five or six or more days in a row.

13. DJIA hits a **new rally top** but is followed by a failure to hold the gains for the day.
14. DJIA advances **sharply** three days in a row.
15. DJIA **advances** for several days, then is followed by a **day of little net change** but with **heavy volume.**
16. Market **fails** to move down on **bullish news.**
17. A negative trend for IBM **bodes poorly** for the market.
18. In absence of positive overnight news, a **weak closing** in the market spills over with **further weakness** the next day.
19. **"Technical" declines** are more likely to **follow sharp advances** rather than periods of slow and gradual declines.
20. The trend of new **daily lows** is on the **increase.**
21. The trend of new **daily highs** is on the **decrease.**

MORE SIMPLE SIGNALS TO FORECAST TOMORROW'S MARKET

Thousands of professional traders attempt to forecast whether the market will open strong or weak tomorrow based upon its actions to-day. Many have tried to systematize the many factors involved to produce almost automatic signals. Another individual besides Joseph E. Granville who has pondered many of these signals is R. Earl Andrews, who publishes an investment newsletter (*Andrews' Market Cycle Investing,* 10164 Parkwood Drive, Cupertino, CA 95014). With his permission, I am reproducing a selection of them in Table 9.

TABLE 9

SIGNALS OF MARKET ACTION

Market Daily Event	Market's Next Move is
Market opens higher, then closes off	Down
Market opens lower, then closes up	Up
Weak close in market	Weak spillover
Strong close in market	Rally spillover
– declines exceed advances, DJI closes up	Down
– advances exceed declines, DJI closes off	Down continues
– advances exceed declines, DJI unchanged	Up
– declines exceed advances, DJI off/unchanged	Down
– advances exceed declines, DJI closes up	Up continues
– declines exceed advances, DJI closes up	Up
DJI rises, weak sell-off, closes up	UP
DJI falls, tick off lightly, closes up	Up
DJI rises, DJ Transportation declines	Decline coming
DJI falls, DJ Transportation rallies/weak	Decline coming
DJI rises from few stocks, DJT weak	Sharp break 2 days
DJI falls or stalls, DJT up in 2 stocks	Decline coming
DJI falls or weak, DJT rallies	Decline coming
DJI falls, DJT falls	Trend still down
DJI rises, DJT rises	Trend still up
DJI falls, DJT rises, closes off	Down
DJI rises, then falls in day, closes up	Up
DJI rises with gaps, then closes off	Down
DJI falls with gaps, then closes up	Up in few days
DJI rises modestly, light volume for 2 days	Down
DJI falls sharply, light volume for 2 days	Up
DJI rises modestly, low price stocks are leaders	Sharp break coming
DJI falls modestly, low price stocks decline	Strong rally coming
DJI rises modestly, DJT strong	Strong rally coming
DJI falls, and high price quality stocks decline	Down trend continues
DJI rises strongly, high price quality stocks follow	Up trend continues
Most actives fall, DJI falls	Down
Most actives rise, DJI rises	Up
Most actives fall, DJI rises	Down 1 or 2 days
Most actives rise, DJI falls	Up 1 or 2 days
DJI falls from stocks like DD, GM, EK	Rally in 1 or 2 days, BUY POINT
DJI rally in stocks like DD, GM, EK	Decline in 1 or 2 days, SELL POINT
DJI rally, S&P 500 fails to follow	Decline coming
DJI falls, S&P 500 fails to decline	Rally coming
DJI rallies, S&P 500 equally strong	Rally continues
DJI falls, S&P 500 follows equally	Sharp decline continues

Copyright 1981 by R. Earl Andrews

3
BEST DAYS
OF THE MONTH

THE MONTHLY FIVE-DAY BULGE

The market rises more often (60.8%) on the second trading day of the month than on any other. And a period of five consecutive trading days, the last, first, second, third, and fourth, distinctly outperforms the rest of the days of the month. In a 398-month study (May 1952-June 1985) the market was up 57.6% of the time on these five bullish days, as compared to an average of 50.2% for the remaining sixteen trading days of a typical month. (See Figure 7.)

This occurs because we all, individually and institutionally, tend to operate on a monthly fiscal basis. Consequently, the big cash inflows at banks, funds and insurance companies around the end or beginning of the month often cause upward pressure due to simultaneous purchase decisions.

Much of the market strength in these thirty-three years has centered around the last plus the first four trading days of the month. While the market has risen on average 52.0% of the time, the **prime five days** have risen 57.6%

Sophisticated short-term traders, floor specialists, and portfolio managers could benefit immensely by studying this month-end/beginning upward bias and perhaps devising some seat-of-the-pants trading strategy. It would be difficult though for long-term investors to take advantage of this phenomenon.

I have no pat formula for instant riches here. However, I have observed the market so many times at month's end pausing during a sharp downturn, spurting after a resting or quiet phase, or accelerating its previously gradual rate of climb during a bull market.

FIGURE 7

MARKET PERFORMANCE EACH DAY OF THE MONTH
(May 1952-June 1985)

Based on number of times S&P composite closed higher than previous day

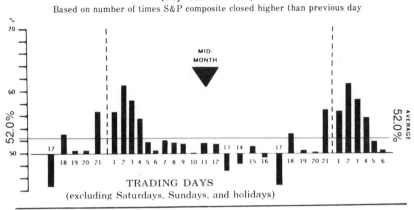

TRADING DAYS
(excluding Saturdays, Sundays, and holidays)

LAST + FIRST FOUR DAYS vs. REST OF MONTH 1976-84

If you could arrange over the years to be invested only during the last plus the first four days of the month, you would far outperform anyone who would be invested only during the remaining sixteen days (on average) of the month. The recent nine-year period in Table 10 shows 285.31 points gained on 540 prime days compared to just 76.83 points gained during the remaining 1728 days.

MARKET GAINS MORE ON FIVE DAYS OF MONTH THAN ON ALL REMAINING DAYS COMBINED

Let's examine this winning investment strategy over the years—to have been invested only on the last trading day of the month and on the first, second, third and fourth days of the following month (the "best five days") and then switching into money market funds for the remaining days of the month, alternating back and forth each month.

From the beginning of 1967 (Dow 785.69) to the end of 1984 (Dow 1211.57), the Dow Jones industrial average gained 425.88 points. However, it is incredible that the "best five days" of the 216 months of the eighteen-year period produced a gain of 804.23 points in contrast to a loss of 378.35 points on the rest of the trading days (16 on average) of these months. Remember that the last trading day of the month goes into the following month for these calculations.

TABLE 10

NET CHANGE IN DOW POINTS SHOWING MONTHLY BIAS

	Best 5 Days	Rest of Month	Best 5 Days	Rest of Month	Best 5 Days	Rest of Month
	1976		**1977**		**1978**	
Jan.	46.28	70.06	−19.20	−22.36	−37.30	−21.05
Feb.	− 3.94	14.02	− 9.64	−14.46	− 3.82	−20.27
Mar.	− 8.19	21.49	20.03	−32.25	− 5.63	16.90
Apr.	9.52	0.48	− 6.48	12.59	4.33	62.97
May	−12.60	−23.96	16.12	−44.61	− 2.51	9.79
June	− 1.67	36.75	− 4.24	10.26	32.31	−44.87
July	− 9.49	−11.87	− 3.82	−19.52	− 9.18	43.83
Aug.	7.39	−17.76	− 1.82	−29.28	32.14	− 7.71
Sept.	27.67	− 5.40	17.50	−36.30	12.99	−32.40
Oct.	−31.50	− 7.06	1.99	−19.40	15.16	−64.62
Nov.	− 9.56	6.98	−12.74	17.33	3.03	−24.77
Dec.	11.72	37.32	−20.36	24.48	31.79	−16.84
Totals	25.63	121.05	−14.18	−153.52	73.31	−99.04
Average	2.14	10.09	− 1.18	−12.79	6.11	− 8.25
	1979		**1980**		**1981**	
Jan.	25.67	21.05	− 6.91	49.91	16.90	−32.00
Feb.	−28.93	−15.85	− 0.08	−27.39	− 0.51	20.05
Mar.	19.58	40.19	−26.37	−50.42	− 9.96	27.54
Apr.	10.83	−20.96	− 9.31	42.75	− 9.63	10.08
May	− 9.10	−25.38	4.95	30.21	−24.41	20.91
June	13.34	7.54	12.45	23.13	− 5.01	− 2.15
July	3.12	− 7.42	16.38	37.97	−22.73	− 9.04
Aug.	9.81	35.15	2.05	− 7.85	0.57	−60.69
Sept.	− 9.55	13.31	10.58	−19.03	−19.79	−13.79
Oct.	2.64	−66.29	43.77	−47.95	6.28	−23.31
Nov.	−17.33	25.26	14.67	57.26	6.56	26.83
Dec.	3.33	3.84	−19.20	− 8.45	3.71	−19.59
Totals	23.41	10.44	42.98	80.14	−58.02	−55.16
Average	1.95	0.87	3.58	6.67	− 4.84	− 4.60
	1982		**1983**		**1984**	
Jan.	−11.32	2.47	23.55	− 6.17	26.48	−63.24
Feb.	−17.22	−21.21	13.16	43.03	−47.21	−17.17
Mar.	−18.27	16.94	20.02	2.33	− 4.61	18.22
Apr.	14.84	5.61	−25.64	101.87	−40.20	38.52
May	18.26	−38.24	0.20	− 3.58	− 3.76	−62.72
June	−19.98	7.23	− 3.10	0.80	31.25	− 5.89
July	−12.55	12.55	− 3.40	5.91	− 3.98	− 7.95
Aug.	−16.36	97.45	−33.26	12.95	92.98	20.32
Sept.	20.98	− 8.01	50.10	− 6.00	−15.90	9.38
Oct.	37.99	46.73	28.66	−45.32	−29.37	29.92
Nov.	59.23	−47.37	− 5.19	68.91	26.84	−50.69
Dec.	52.80	− 9.11	−17.81	− 9.23	3.97	33.68
Totals	108.40	65.04	47.29	165.50	36.49	−57.62
Average	9.03	5.42	3.94	13.79	3.04	− 4.80

	Best Five Days		Rest of Month (16 Days)	
108 MONTH TOTALS	Net D.J. Points	285.31	Net D.J. Points	76.83
	Average Period	2.64	Average Period	0.71
	Average Day	0.53	Average Day	0.04

The most Dow points during the "best five days" were gained in January (200), followed by September (195), June (139), March (131), August (102), October (96), May (62), November (43), and December (34). February was the worst month losing 106 Dow points. July and April were also losers with 47 points each. July was a loser eleven times in eighteen years, February, ten times.

An important factor to be aware of in this seasonality pattern (shown shaded in the table) is that February and July have been losers for this investment strategy in ten of the last twelve years. Odds favor avoiding them.

TABLE 11

NET DOW POINT CHANGES FOR PRIME FIVE DAYS (1967-1984)

	JAN	FEB	MAR	APR	MAY	JUN	JUL	AUG	SEP	OCT	NOV	DEC
1967	22.39	7.01	5.56	— 8.74	7.13	— 2.27	7.11	22.24	14.45	2.25	—30.73	9.13
1968	3.41	1.68	— 7.51	37.40	6.19	14.92	13.84	— 6.44	26.92	22.89	— 0.43	1.92
1969	—19.39	4.54	10.51	—12.10	27.96	— 6.21	13.45	22.30	— 8.64	— 8.64	4.69	—13.99
1970	7.13	1.91	23.10	6.53	—19.00	22.38	—13.55	—11.91	5.34	21.57	18.00	34.71
1971	— 3.49	9.65	9.38	9.34	—10.76	16.37	13.58	—11.97	15.04	16.72	5.55	25.99
1972	19.42	0.30	25.89	26.42	— 8.66	—19.72	11.81	25.06	4.59	—13.85	38.38	9.33
1973	39.81	—13.02	31.08	—35.68	31.68	—10.69	—24.53	—20.99	16.10	2.63	—55.46	—20.99
1974	28.83	—37.70	16.43	4.54	9.46	41.77	—11.89	8.21	21.04	—37.39	— 3.91	—32.27
1975	37.94	17.75	30.66	—23.00	31.68	27.15	—12.04	—17.99	6.50	14.43	1.50	—29.44
1976	46.28	— 3.94	— 8.19	9.52	—12.60	— 1.67	— 9.49	7.39	27.76	—31.50	9.56	11.72
1977	—19.20	— 9.64	—20.03	— 6.48	16.12	— 4.24	— 3.82	1.82	17.50	1.99	—12.74	—20.36
1978	—37.30	— 3.82	— 5.63	4.33	— 2.51	32.31	— 9.18	32.14	12.99	15.16	3.03	31.79
1979	25.67	—28.93	19.58	10.83	— 9.10	13.34	3.12	9.81	— 9.55	2.64	—17.33	3.33
1980	— 6.91	— 0.08	—26.37	— 9.31	4.95	12.45	16.38	2.05	10.58	43.77	14.67	—19.20
1981	16.90	— 0.51	— 9.96	— 9.63	—24.41	— 5.01	—22.73	0.57	—19.79	6.28	6.56	3.71
1982	—11.32	—17.22	—18.27	14.84	18.26	—19.98	—12.55	—16.36	20.98	37.99	59.23	52.80
1983	23.55	13.16	20.02	—25.64	0.20	— 3.10	— 3.40	—33.26	50.10	28.66	— 5.19	—17.81
1984	26.48	—47.21	— 4.61	—40.20	3.76	31.25	— 3.98	92.98	—15.90	—29.37	26.84	3.97
Total	200.20	—106.07	131.70	—47.03	62.83	139.05	—47.87	102.01	195.74	96.23	43.10	34.34
Up	12	8	11	9	10	9	7	10	14	12	10	11
Down	6	10	7	9	8	9	11	8	4	6	8	7

THE BEST WEEK OF THE MONTH

The week which includes the first trading day of the month far outperformed all other weeks during the 1967-1971 period. These first weeks
of the month—there were sixty of them in the five years—gained a total
of 240.35 Dow Jones points, while the 201 other weeks suffered a combined loss of 135.89 points. From the table below, we can see that third
weeks did not perform too badly, while most of the damage tended to
cluster around second, fourth, and fifth weeks. Also, the results of the
last and first four days of the month (see Figure 7) are even more spectacular than those of first weeks. Therefore, I never updated this table
as it would have only proven what was already known—until the advent
of index futures trading.

TABLE 12

WEEKLY POINT CHANGES IN
DOW JONES INDUSTRIALS (1967-1971)

Each Year Separately

	First Weeks	Second Weeks	Third Weeks	Fourth & Fifth Weeks
1967	35.22	48.67	69.54	—34.07
1968	52.66	24.89	—29.30	— 0.85
1969	— 3.52	—98.75	—28.83	—23.75
1970	62.19	—63.67	45.88	— 3.13
1971	93.80	16.96	2.78	—62.26
TOTALS	**240.35**	**—71.90**	**60.07**	**—124.06**

Each Month Separately

	First Weeks	Second Weeks	Third Weeks	Fourth & Fifth Weeks
January	28.20	— 4.63	3.48	—39.22
February	30.50	— 8.36	—50.00	18.91
March	21.58	—21.87	45.43	32.76
April	4.67	68.41	12.06	— 5.85
May	36.82	—34.60	—53.42	—49.79
June	5.01	—36.11	—12.35	—79.34
July	45.67	20.65	34.33	—92.38
August	— 2.67	—16.32	70.51	48.63
September	25.07	— 3.99	33.16	—19.28
October	14.52	—12.81	1.16	—38.42
November	—22.18	—34.09	—20.42	49.56
December	53.16	11.82	— 3.87	50.36
TOTALS	**240.35**	**—71.90**	**60.07**	**—124.06**

HOW INDEX FUTURES ARE CHANGING TRADING PATTERNS, ARBITRAGE CAUSES MANY VIOLENT SWINGS

It's late in the afternoon on Friday, March 15, 1985, with one hour left before they ring the bell on the floor of the New York Stock Exchange. Today is the third Friday of the month and, as usual, expiration day for index futures contracts. Suddenly, a selling squall in blue chips develops and the Dow Jones industrials starts dropping rapidly. In one hour the Dow plunges twelve points.

On another expiration day, Friday, June 21, 1985, the Dow is already up nearly ten points at 1309 one hour before closing. This time a buying stampede begins among the blue chips and the Dow shoots up fifteen more points in the final hour alone.

Such violent swings in short time spans scare individual investors and might even frighten them out of the stock market. This seemingly irrational behavior has been traced to a small band of professionals —arbitrageurs—operating out of large, well-capitalized, Wall Street brokerage houses. When index futures were introduced in 1982, the arbitrage possibilities became apparent to those sharp-eyed pros who seized the opportunity.

It's too complex to explain all the maneuvers without examining trading records, which only the Securities & Exchange Commission or the NYSE can access. However, let's take a look at a simple hypothetical example: The Major Market Index (MMI) was constructed to mimic the Dow Jones industrial average. It contains just twenty high-priced blue chips, most of which are in the DJI. If you thought these twenty stocks (the "market") would be going higher, you could buy the index future (MMI) instead of having to make decisions on individual stocks. Likewise, you could sell the MMI if you thought "stocks" would be heading lower.

One major factor to consider when trading index futures is whether they are being offered at a premium, a discount, or flat. Another consideration is the expiration date. If the market "appears" to be moving higher, traders will all want to buy the MMI causing the contract expiring one month from now to sell, let's say, at a 10% premium. By the third Friday of that month the contract will expire and the premium will naturally disappear.

As an arbitrageur with a member firm there are little or no trading commissions to pay. Given this advantage, you simultaneously buy a group of stocks equivalent to the twenty components of the MMI and sell a number of MMI contracts—at the 10% premium, of course— equivalent in value to the package of stocks you bought. Now you're hedged on both sides—arbitraged. If the market zooms up, you're a gainer on stocks, a loser on the index; if down, the reverse. Soon, the weeks pass and the premium starts to erode. At some point, depending on your nerve and acumen, you close out both positions. If you netted 3% on $5 million dollars, you made $150,000 in just a few weeks.

Nice work! But there's another dimension to the story. Because so many players waited till the last minute and dumped a ton of stock in the last hour on Friday, March 15, 1985, or bought a ton in the final hour on June 21, 1985, both on index futures expiration days, the tape action shocked the public. Hopefully, the Securities & Exchange Commission and the various exchanges will bring about changes in the trading practices that will be less devastating to the public.

WEEK AFTER EXPIRATION NOW BETTER THAN START OF THE MONTH

By compressing a year's daily changes of the Dow onto one page as I always do (see Appendix), I was able to see at a glance a phenomenon that startled me. I noted all the big jumps in 1985 between the January 15 market turnaround and October 31. There were seven big days. Suddenly, it became clear! *All seven surges occurred within two days of the third Friday of the month,* expiration day for index futures contracts (Table 13).

TABLE 13

BIGGEST ONE-DAY GAINS IN DOW IN 1985
(JANUARY 15 — OCTOBER 31)

Month	Date	Day of Week	Dow Points Gained	Trading Days Before or After Expiration Day
January	21	Monday	34.01	+ 1
February	13	Wednesday	21.31	— 2
March	19	Tuesday	21.42	+ 2
May	20	Monday	19.54	+ 1
June	21	Friday	24.75	0
September	23	Monday	18.37	+ 1
October	16	Wednesday	17.69	— 2

This was highly significant! I then checked back to see how long this had been going on. Beside a twenty-point gain on January 10 related to a change of trend, there were five big point days after the August 1984, seven-day, 108-point rally. Four of them occurred within four days of the expiration day for certain index future contracts. The fifth one, however, was not close. Checking back further to early 1984, 1983, 1982, I found only random one-day jumps that did not seem to be related to any expiration of index futures. So, something had to be responsible for this sudden change in August 1984 and I realized it was the launching at that time of the new Major Market Index futures contracts. There were already three others—the Standard & Poor's 500, the NYSE composite, and the Value Line —which had been trading since spring of 1982.

But at this juncture, there was a new twist. While the others had had only four expiration days a year—March, June, September, and December—the new MMI would have contracts expiring every month.

Further examination of expiration weeks, and the following weeks after, brought another revelation: The best market weeks have been those after the expirations.

Mouth-watering results in anybody's book. With weeks immediately following expirations showing gains of over ten points a week on

TABLE 14

GAINS IN WEEK AFTER EXPIRATION FRIDAYS

	Number of Weeks After Expirations	Dow Total Change	All Other Weeks	Dow Total Change
1982 (Last 7 months)	7	91.16	24	135.84
1983	12	188.78	40	23.32
1984	12	45.49	40	—92.56
1985 (First 10 Months)	10	112.52	33	50.21
Totals	**41**	**437.95**	**137**	**116.81**
		Average Week **10.68**		**0.85**
		Average Day **2.13**		**0.17**

average, you couldn't ask for a better edge! Especially, considering that all other weeks since June 1982 show gains of less than one point each. Put another way: The Dow has gained 554.76 points during these three years and five months with 79% of the gains in the 41 weeks immediately following expirations, and 21% in all the other 137 weeks. No contest!

Will this exploitable pattern remain? Well, first of all, publishing the data lets too many people in on it and that usually kills it. Secondly, the huge sums of money that have been made have attracted greater numbers of players, increasing the competition. This will undoubtedly tend to shrink premiums and discounts on index futures, options on futures, and options on stocks, providing fewer possibilities for arbitrage. A third consideration is that the authorities are trying to influence the big houses to conduct their arbitrage activities in a more graceful and responsible manner.

Some observations:

1. In nine of the fifteen past months, down expiration weeks preceded up weeks, or up expiration weeks preceded down weeks. If there was a mass selling off of stock positions in one week, it seemed to trigger massive buying the following week, and vice versa.

2. In the March, June, September, and December months of the Standard & Poor's 500 index futures expirations since June 1982, eleven of fourteen expirations had reversals from down week to up week or up week to down week.

3. However, all of the eight S&P expiration weeks which were down were followed by up weeks, and with big numbers at that. The eight prior weeks lost 172.48 Dow points and the eight following weeks gained 184.39. An average 21.56-point loss for the Dow in one week was followed by an average 23.05-point gain the next.

4. If the market is sharply higher in the previous three weeks, expect a sell-off during the expiration week, especially on expiration day. Conversely, if the market has been falling, a strong one-day jump during expiration week is a possibility.

IS THE MARKET JINXED ON FRIDAY THE THIRTEENTH?

Cornelius Vanderbilt hired mediums and held seances to raise the spirits of departed financiers in order to obtain stock tips from them. J.P. Morgan consulted with an astrologer named Evangeline Adams early in this century, as did two presidents of the New York Stock Exchange, Jacob Stout and Seymore Cromwell. Jesse Livermore was believed to be clairvoyant after he shorted a block of Union Pacific one day before the San Francisco earthquake in 1906.

In *Witchcraft on Wall Street* (Bernard Geis Associates, 1971), Max Gunther documented many accounts of successful investments and forecasts made by an assortment of "witches," astrologers, and clairvoyants.

To cover all bases, I examined market activity on every Friday the Thirteenth since 1940. What the Dow Jones industrials gained or lost on each occasion is listed and summarized in Table 15.

TABLE 15

GAINS OR LOSSES ON FRIDAY THE 13TH (1940-1969) IN THE DOW JONES INDUSTRIAL AVERAGE

Year	Month	Value	Year	Month	Value	Year	Month	Value
1940	Sep	—0.13	1950	Jan	—1.12	1960	May	8.16
	Dec	0.21		Oct	—0.43	1961	Jan	5.15
1941	Jun	—0.67	1951	Apr	3.09		Oct	—2.19
1942	Feb	0.21		Jul	1.73	1962	Apr	2.23
	Mar	0.50	1952	Jun	0.65		Jul	—0.08
	Nov	—0.20	1953	Feb	1.54	1963	Sep	—0.13
1943	Aug	0.95		Mar	1.04		Dec	2.74
1944	Oct	—0.09		Nov	1.30	1964	Mar	2.00
1945	Apr	1.27	1954	Aug	0.80		Nov	—0.49
	Jul	—0.18	1955	May	1.37	1965	Aug	6.89
1946	Sep	1.69	1956	Jan	n/c	1966	May	—9.46
	Dec	—0.01		Apr	0.84	1967	Sep	5.18
1947	Jun	1.71		Jul	3.66		Oct	4.97
1948	Feb	0.64	1957	Sep	0.46	1968	Sep	1.56
	Aug	n/c		Dec	2.00		Dec	4.16
1949	May	0.12	1958	Jun	3.35	1969	Jan	2.26
			1959	Feb	6.08			
				Mar	0.94			
				Nov	—2.55			

As many traders today are superstitious and have been known to wear the same tie, shirt, or suit day after day during a winning streak, I expected to see significantly more losses than gains. In fact, the reverse was true during the first thirty years of the period. We were in bull markets 75% of the time. Of fifty-one occasions, only fourteen losses occurred.

Strangely, the next five, the Nixon years, 1970 to 1974, saw nine straight losses on Friday the Thirteenth. However, they had a bearish bias. For the first time in over thirty years, a bear market extended into a second year in 1970. Again in 1973 and 1974, a bear market lasted almost two whole years.

TABLE 16

FRIDAY THE THIRTEENTH 1970-1984

1970	Feb	−2.31	1975	Jun	5.16
	Mar	−4.36	1976	Feb	−8.42
	Nov	−8.21		Aug	3.07
1971	Aug	−38.99	1977	May	2.80
1972	Oct	−7.00	1978	Jan	−2.42
1973	Apr	−4.67		Oct	0.35
	Jul	−5.95	1979	Jul	−3.33
1974	Sep	−14.55	1980	Jun	3.76
	Dec	−3.60	1981	Mar	−4.05
				Nov	−4.66
			1982	Aug	11.13
			1983	May	4.35
			1984	Jan	−9.21
				Apr	−7.01
				Jul	5.30

In the recent ten-year period which was half bull and half bear, there were seven losses and eight gains on Friday the Thirteenth. Make of it what you will!

TABLE 17

FRIDAY THE THIRTEENTH SUMMARY

# Years	Period	# Up	N/C	# Down	Friday 13ths
10	1940 — 1949	9	1	6	16
10	1950 — 1959	15	1	3	19
10	1960 — 1969	11		5	16
5	1970 — 1974	0		9	9
10	1975 — 1984	8		7	15
45	**TOTALS**	**43**	**2**	**30**	**75**

4
BEST MONTHS
OF THE YEAR

NOVEMBER, DECEMBER, AND
JANUARY COMPRISE BEST THREE-
MONTH SPAN

The most important observation to be made from a chart showing the average monthly percent change in market prices since 1950 is that institutions (mutual funds, pension funds, banks, etc.) determine the trading patterns in today's market.

The "investment calendar" reflects the annual, semiannual, and quarterly operations of institutions during January, April, and July. October, besides being a "tight money" month, the beginning of the new car year, and the last campaign month before elections, is also the time when most bear markets seem to end, as in 1946, 1957, 1960, 1966, and 1974.

Unusual year-end strength comes from corporate and private pension funds. Most of them receive new investment funds once a year in a lump sum, producing a lopsided effect in the year-end market.

Between 1934 and 1949, when the market stayed within the one-hundred to two-hundred range in the Dow Jones industrial average, January, June, July, and October stood out as the strongest months of the year. It is obvious that a decided shift in investment seasons has occured in recent years.

The most volatile months in both directions have been January, far out front, followed by August, November, and July. December has been the least dangerous month. April and March are also relatively safe.

FIGURE 8

MARKET PERFORMANCE EACH MONTH OF THE YEAR

35½ Years (January 1950-June 1985)

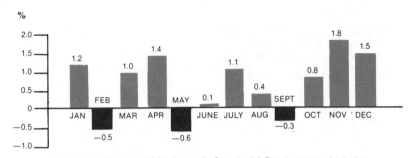

Average month-to-month % change in Standard & Poor's composite index
(Based on monthly closing prices)

TABLE 18

MONTHLY % CHANGES
(JANUARY 1950-JUNE 1985)

	S & P 500					DOW JONES INDUSTRIALS			
MONTH	TOTAL % CHANGE	AVG. % CHANGE	# UP	# DN	MONTH	TOTAL POINTS CHANGE	AVG. POINTS CHANGE	# UP	# DN
Jan	43.3%	1.2%	21	15	Jan	259.15	7.20	23	13
Feb	—16.4	—0.5	17	19	Feb	—157.77	— 4.38	18	18
Mar	36.4	1.0	23	13	Mar	197.96	5.50	22	14
Apr	51.9	1.4	25	11	Apr	464.06	12.89	24	12
May	—22.6	—0.6	16	20	May	—324.38	— 9.01	15	21
Jun	2.3	0.1	18	18	Jun	— 54.47	— 1.51	17	19
Jul	38.9	1.1	21	14	Jul	96.79	2.76	20	15
Aug	13.4	0.4	19	16	Aug	126.72	3.62	20	15
Sep	—10.7	—0.3	16	19	Sep	—155.10	— 4.43	13	22
Oct	28.6	0.8	20	15	Oct	55.95	1.60	19	16
Nov	61.9	1.8	23	12	Nov	289.33	8.27	23	12
Dec	51.1	1.5	25	10	Dec	314.18	8.98	24	11
% Rank					**Points Rank**				
Nov	61.9%	1.8%	23	12	Apr	464.06	12.89	24	12
Dec	51.1	1.5	25	10	Dec	314.18	8.98	24	11
Apr	51.9	1.4	25	11	Nov	289.33	8.27	23	12
Jan	43.3	1.2	21	15	Jan	259.15	7.20	23	13
Jul	38.9	1.1	21	14	Mar	197.96	5.50	22	14
Mar	36.4	1.0	23	13	Aug	126.72	3.62	20	15
Oct	28.6	0.8	20	15	Jul	96.79	2.76	20	15
Aug	13.4	0.4	19	16	Oct	55.45	1.60	19	16
Jun	2.3	0.1	18	18	Jun	— 54.47	— 1.51	17	19
Sep	—10.7	—0.3	16	19	Feb	—157.77	— 4.30	18	18
Feb	—16.4	—0.5	17	19	Sep	—155.10	— 4.43	13	22
May	—22.6	—0.6	16	20	May	—324.38	— 9.01	15	21

See Appendix for all monthly closing prices and percent changes for Standard & Poor's
500 composite index and point changes for the Dow Jones industrial index.

BEST MONTHS IN PAST 35½ YEARS

Seasonality for different months of the year is usually based on the number of times the month has closed higher in either the Dow industrials or the S&P 500. A much more dramatic picture is presented when percent changes are cumulated.

The hottest month in recent years has been April with 464.06 Dow points gained since 1950. Over 117 of these points were netted in the last four years due likely to the newly enacted legislation making IRA accounts more attractive. This has triggered a massive inflow of funds before the April 15 deadline.

Worst month as usual is May, down 324.38 Dow points and 22.6% in the S&P 500. Biggest surprise has been January. From the Number One position based on average monthly prices, January fell to Fourth based on closing S&P prices. November shot up from Fourth to First with an average monthly change of 1.8%.

5
THE BULL/BEAR CYCLE

TRANSITION FROM BULL TO BEAR IN THE TYPICAL MARKET CYCLE

The tide wells in from the sea and ebbs away again. Money flows into the stock market in a like manner during a bull market and recedes as the bear's paw shows itself. Many technical analysts construct a composite index of indicators which have succesfully pinpointed previous market tops (and bottoms). In *The Dow Jones-Irwin Guide To Stock Market Cycles,* author Michael Hayes examines a number of indicators that measure the Federal Reserve Board's control of the "spigot," the swelling of speculative fever, market momentum, divergence, etc. Each of these indicators were traced through five market cycles.

Figure 9 shows the typical market cycle in the Dow Jones industrial average and the progression of signals that normally indicate the transition from a bull to a bear market. Evidence to support a major bear market seemed to be lacking in the fall of 1985.

HOW TO TELL THE END OF A BEAR MARKET

Bear markets usually begin inauspiciously in climates of optimism and amid reports of high earnings, record auto sales, labor shortages, and projections of eternal prosperity. Conversely, they end in atmospheres of gloom, panic, despair and apathy. In either case, history can often help investors rise above the general emotional climate towards a more dispassionate evaluation of what is taking place.

Here are some of the characteristics of recent bear market endings:

FIGURE 9

WHEN INDICATORS TRIGGER SELL SIGNALS

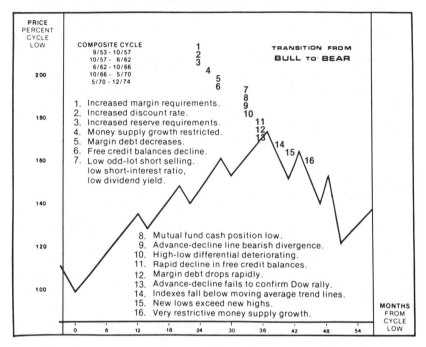

1. The emotional climate is highly pessimistic. Newspapers are referring frequently to previous bear markets and to the crash of 1929. Talk of depression, the collapse of the economy, failures of brokerage houses fills the air.

2. Declines in the market are severe; charts appear almost vertical on the downside. Volume on down days begins to expand. This reflects the public panic and desire to sell at any cost.

3. A cluster of three or four up-Mondays follow down-Fridays. This shows nervous covering of short positions and some anticipation by professionals.

4. Mutual funds have accumulated large cash positions, in the area of 9-12%.

5. Specialists and knowledgeable floor traders are selling short in smaller proportions than the general public. Specialist short sales represent only 30% or less of all the short sales taking place.

6. Interest rates are high but appear to resist further expansion. The bond market shows signs of firmness.

7. The London stock market begins to develop strength.

8. Advisory services, usually bullish, show a distinctly bearish bias.

9. The Fed moves to ease the credit situation and to prop up the stock market. Money supply is loosened. The discount rate is lowered and stock margin requirements are eased.

10. You, yourself, probably are apathetic regarding the stock market and find yourself primarily interested in other vehicles for investment.

The necessary data to follow any of these indicators is available in *Barron's, The Wall Street Journal,* or any newspaper with extensive financial coverage. Watch carefully! When you see stocks no longer declining on bad news, when the number of issues making new lows refuses to expand, and when utility stocks begin to show better strength than the Dow—prepare for better days!

BULL MARKET'S FIRST TWELVE MONTHS PROVIDE GREATEST PORTION OF GAIN

The investor who tends to be attracted to stocks after the market has had a long upward climb just as easily becomes repelled by stocks when prices drop sharply. This is understandable, but unfortunate! For during the doom-and-gloom climate of a bear market, while small investors are dropping out of the market, sophisticated investors are preparing for the subsequent swift and spectacular rise that always seems to follow.

The table below shows the major market tops and bottoms since World War II. The average extent of decline has been 26.0% and its length about twelve months. The 1973-1974 decline at its lowest depth was 33%, its length nearly twenty months. A decline to the 675-700 area would equal the size of the 1969-1970 drop.

TABLE 19

LENGTH & SIZE OF BEAR MARKET DECLINES; SUBSEQUENT GAINS

Oct 23, 1948	190.64	Jun 14, 1949	160.62	8	−15.7%	42.7%	83.7%
Jan 5, 1953	295.06	Sep 15, 1953	254.36	8	−13.8	43.9	105.7
Jul 16, 1957	523.11	Oct 22, 1957	416.15	3	−20.4	32.1	65.4
Jan 4, 1960	688.21	Oct 25, 1960	564.23	10	−18.0	30.0	31.4
Nov15, 1961	741.30	Jun 25, 1962	524.55	7	−29.2	39.7	90.9
Feb 9, 1966	1001.11	Oct 10, 1966	735.74	8	−26.5	29.3	35.2
Dec 2, 1968	994.65	May 26, 1970	627.46	18	−36.9	52.7	70.2
Jan 11, 1973	1067.20	Oct 4, 1974	573.22	21	−46.3	42.4	79.0
Sep 22, 1976	1026.26	Mar 1, 1978	736.75	17	−28.2	11.1	39.9
Apr 27, 1981	1030.98	Aug 11, 1982	772.17	16	−25.1	53.6	76.9*
					Average	**37.8%**	**67.8%**

*Through July 1985

An analysis of the table's last two columns is most revealing! While the average bull market has lasted nearly three years and has risen 67.8% on average, the first year's average gain (37.8%) has been far greater than the gain in the remainder of the bull period. At first glance it appears that after the 37.8% first year's gain, there still remains a 30.0% appreciation (37.8 plus 30.0 equals 67.8). This is incorrect! A rise from Dow 1000 to 1386 and from 1000 to 1689, for instance, would result in gains of 38.6 and 68.9%. However, the rise from 1386 to 1689 is only a gain of 21.9%! Further, the latter gain, assuming a typical three-year bull cycle, is spread out over two years. The potential investment return in the first year, thus, is nearly 40%. However, for the investor who enters the market a year later, the potential return is roughly 10% a year. With a four-to-one ratio, the obvious moral is: *The early bird catches the worm!*

INITIAL STAGES
OF A BULL MARKET

Bull markets, of course, offer a variety of avenues for profit to investors, particularly during initial stages. The early phases of bull markets are usually marked by broad participation in the advance; blue chips, glamour stocks, secondaries and tertiaries—all share in the move. Bond prices advance also, as interest rates decline. Mutual funds perform quite well, particularly the more speculative funds.

Although the overall advance is usually broad, experience has shown that intermediate rallies are usually led by blue chips and high-priced glamour issues. Stocks in the $25-$40 range have their day slightly later, followed by investor concentration in very low-priced issues. Intermediate advances are generally close to completion when the most active lists are dominated by low-priced shares.

Here, by category, are some bull market characteristics:

1. Blue chips will usually join any market advance. During early phases, these securities will be outperformed by speculative glamour stocks, particularly since they have lesser volatility than the glamours. However, blue chips will continue their ultimate rise longer and are less susceptible to intermediate decline.

2. Glamour issues and high grade growth stocks will perform very well. Highly volatile, they offer exciting profit potential during early bull moves. However, corrective declines can be severe. These are favorites of professional traders.

3. Secondary stocks will slightly lag the glamours in market action, but almost always join market advances as their group develops strength. Stocks in the $20-$40 range are public favorites.

4. Low-priced stocks lag the others a bit, and are more unreliable in their market action. However, research has shown that low-priced stocks are more capable of doubling than high-priced issues and, in general, show a greater percentage of price appreciation than higher-priced securities. Low-priced issues participate at some point in most bull moves but, as a group, did top out early during the 1970-1973 bull market.

5. Bonds, convertible and regular, will also participate in the general mark-up. Deeply discounted convertible bonds will move slowly at first in proportion to their underlying common shares, but retain high degrees of safety while providing strong yields. Margin requirements and commission reductions reduce the volatility handicap that these convertibles suffer. However, for fast action during new bull markets, common shares are preferred.

6. High volatility mutual funds will be stellar performers during the initial phases of bull markets.

OPPORTUNITY ALWAYS KNOCKS TWICE WHEN BULL MARKETS BEGIN

Few investors are either fortunate or astute enough to catch the actual low points of bear markets. However, the stock market is fortunately quite forgiving, and a secondary buying opportunity generally develops within three months of the actual low. This provides a second chance for investors who are caught unawares at first or who wish to await further proof that the bull market is really at hand.

Table 20 illustrates the course of the stock market following the major bear markets since World War II.

TABLE 20

GETTING A SECOND CHANCE
AFTER FIRST BULL MARKET RALLIES

Bear Market Ended	D. J. Low Point	First Rally To	% Gain	Retracement To	% Loss	% of First Rally Retraced	Time Elapsed From Low To Low
6-14-49	160.62	184.09	14.6%	177.63	−3.5%	27.5%	15 weeks
9-15-53	254.36	285.20	12.1	275.91	−3.3	30.1	13 weeks
10-22-57	416.15	452.49	8.7	423.86	−6.3	78.8	9 weeks
10-25-60	564.23	614.09	8.8	589.82	−4.0	48.7	6 weeks
6-25-62	524.55	622.02	18.6	549.65	−11.6	74.2	18 weeks
10-10-66	735.74	827.33	12.4	776.16	−6.2	55.9	12 weeks
5-26-70	627.46	728.23	16.1	665.32	−8.6	62.4	6 weeks
10-4-74	573.22	692.82	20.9	570.01	−17.7	102.7	9 weeks
3-1-78	736.75	917.24	24.5	779.11	−15.1	76.5	8 weeks
8-11-82	772.17	951.16	23.2	891.28	− 6.3	33.5	8 weeks
Averages			**16.0%**		**− 8.3%**	**59.0%**	**10 weeks**

On average, the "typical" stock market during these periods:

1. Gained 16% in the initial rally following the actual low reading of the preceding bear market.

2. Lost 8.3% of the market's price level after the rally. This loss represented 59.0% of the gains made from the bear market low to the high point of the initial rally.

3. The whole process, on average, lasted 10 weeks or just under three months.

The tactics implied are quite clear. Should you miss the initial surge, be patient! The market will almost always come back to provide another opportunity. Notice that the "second chance" occurred even after the strong initial surges of recent years. However, because institutions have come to dominate the market over the past two decades, first rallies have become ferocious— no one wishes to miss the boat. Very little was given back in the last retracement and it was over in a wink (eight days).

HOW TO TELL THE END OF A BULL MARKET

Optimism is wonderful, but all good things—bull markets included— must come to an end. The signs will be there for all to see. Woe to the investor who fails to heed to the following:

PSYCHOLOGICAL WARNING SIGNS

The public is rampantly bullish; euphoric tape watchers crowd the brokerage boardrooms; oneupmanship is evident at cocktail parties and country clubs; top-performing money managers are sought after for interviews, and the same success stories are repeated in financial columns and magazines; hot tips abound from the proverbial "bartenders, bootblacks and barbers"—furthermore, the touted stocks even go up; a preponderance of advisory services are bullish—several of their advertisements feature the complete super results of their stock recommendations; the booming market frequently makes the front pages of your daily newspaper (run for the hills if *Time* or *Newsweek* has a major market article with an illustration of a charging bull on the cover); many investors doing extremely well display cockiness, unaware that "financial genius is a rising stock market."

GOVERNMENT WARNING SIGNS

The Federal Reserve Board has switched from an expansionary monetary policy to one of restraint and has slowed down the rate of expansion in the nation's money supply; a series of restrictive measures have been imposed during the bull move by the FRB raising the discount rate, the reserve requirements of member banks, or the margin rate (how much money you must put up to buy stocks on margin).

FUNDAMENTAL WARNING SIGNS

The auto industry is having a banner year (sales have hit an all-time record); corporate earnings reports are spectacular (What will they do for an encore?); there is a substantial shrinkage in plant capacity, a sharp increase in the length of the average workweek and in overtime hours, a 1% or 2% drop in the unemployment rate over the past twelve months, a climb of approximately 50% in short-term interest rates (ninety-day Treasury Bills) during the recent twelve- to eighteen-month period.

TECHNICAL WARNING SIGNS

Stocks simply stop rising on good news; while popular market averages (D.J.I., S&P) are still advancing, the majority of stocks (as measured by the advance-decline line) are turning down; there is a surge in new issues and/or secondary offerings, a loss of momentum in the market's advance; the number of issues making new highs on the NYSE are unable to exceed previous peaks; distribution on a large scale by sophisticated money managers becomes evident in chart patterns showing broadening top formations; margin debt, after a hefty increase for a year, begins to flatten out or turn down; there is a significant widening in the spread between corporate bond yields (rising) and common stock dividend yields (falling).

TIMING AN INDUSTRY'S OPTIMISM/PESSIMISM CYCLE

Knowing *when* to buy is much more important than knowing *what* to buy. Understanding this is often half the battle for long-term investors. But this investment ideal is unattainable for those investors who are unable to disassociate themselves from their sheeplike—and sometimes lemming-like—tendencies. Consequently, their purchases come at the wrong time, when everyone and his brother seem to be buying the current "hot" stock. This may be all right for the shrewd investors/traders who know when to get out, but not for those who will be left holding the bag.

Stock prices, business conditions in general, and conditions in particular industries follow definite patterns of optimism and pessimism. This is illustrated in Table 21, which appeared in Claude N. Rosenberg's book, *The Common Sense Way to Stock Market Profits* (World Publishing Co.) and also appears in his later work, *Psycho-Cybernetics and the Stock Market* (Playboy Press).

The classic pattern is evident. It has been repeated over and over again throughout economic history. First some new (or old) product experiences strong demand. Investors are slow to react. Then other businessmen catch on and try to get a piece of the action while investors become enthusiastic. Inevitably, this leads to overcapacity, reduced profits, and disenchantment with the stock(s). What happened in the personal computer field just recently is a perfect example. A new cycle will eventually begin and go through similar stages. Often, many of the former participants will replay their identical roles.

Sophisticated investors and institutions will tend to buy during stages one and four, while the unsophisticated will tend to appear on the scene during the latter part of stages two and six. Obviously, it's more profitable to be among the former group—and if you study the contents of this book, you will automatically qualify.

TABLE 21

AVOIDING THE NEW PRODUCT CYCLE TRAP

Conditions In Industry	Attitudes of Investors	
1. Product(s) experiencing strong demand; probably few important companies participating.	1. Limited understanding of potentials by investors.	**Buy Point** ←
2. Recognition of this leads to expansion and numerous new entries into industry.	2. Market reacts; enthusiasm grows.	
3. Combination of new entries and expansion leads to overcapacity, price cutting, and sharply reduced profits.	3. Steady disenchantment with industry prospects.	
4. "Freezeout" period. No new entries; demand catches up with supply.	4. Stocks not in vogue; out of favor.	**Buy Point** ←
5. Supply-demand favorable. Profits reappearing.	5. Some buyers "catching on."	
6. Prices advance; profits soar. This leads to new round of expansion and new entries.	6. Enthusiasm again.	

SQUARE ROOT RULE FAVORS LOW-PRICED STOCKS

Experience has shown that, during bull markets, investments in low-priced stocks have paid off far more handsomely than equal amounts of money invested in higher-priced stocks. The following table, which appeared in an article, "Low Priced Versus High Priced Stocks," by Harry D. Comer, *The Analysts Journal,* Vol. I, No. 2, April, 1945, shows the percentage gains that were realized during bull markets, 1897-1929, by stocks in various price ranges. Similar relative performance could be expected nowadays.

The relationship between the expected move of the one stock against the other can be determined by the "Square Root Rule." Bull swings tend to add equal increments to the square roots of stock prices. Bear markets tend to subtract equal increments from the square roots of stock prices. Another table from Mr. Comer's article demonstrates this

TABLE 22

PERCENTAGE GAINS IN
ALL BULL MARKETS (1897-1929)

Price Groups at Lows	Average Percentage Gain
$ 0 - 5	241%
5-10	146
10-15	127
15-20	106
20-30	94
30-40	79
40-55	73
55-70	49
70-100	43
over 100	36

TABLE 23

THE SQUARE ROOT RULE IN OPERATION

Starting Price	Square Root	Amount Added to Square Root of Starting Price	Move Up To*	Percent Rise
$ 4	(2)	2	$ 16 (4x4)	300%
9	(3)	2	25 (5x5)	178
16	(4)	2	36 (6x6)	125
25	(5)	2	49 (7x7)	96
36	(6)	2	64 (8x8)	78
49	(7)	2	81 (9x9)	65
64	(8)	2	100 (10x10)	56
81	(9)	2	121 (11x11)	49
100	(10)	2	144 (12x12)	44
121	(11)	2	169 (13x13)	40

* Each figure in this column is arrived at by adding 2 to the square root of the corresponding figure in the first column and then squaring the sum. For instance, the square root of 9 (in first column) equals 3; adding 2 we have 5, which, squared, produces 25.

principle.

A bull market which carries an average $16 stock to $36 would carry an average $4 stock to $16. A bull market which added some other number to the square root of one stock would add the same increment to the square root of another. For example, suppose a $4 stock advanced to $25. Three has been added to the square root. (The square root of 4 is 2; 2 + 3 = 5; 5^2 = 25.) A stock starting at $9 would theoretically end the same bull market at $36. (The square root of 9 is 3; 3 plus increment 3 = 6; 6^2 = 36.)

To sum up: During bull markets, the greatest profits are achieved by holding low-priced stocks. During bear markets, low-priced stocks will show the highest percentage loss. The amount one stock will advance compared to another can be determined by the Square Root Rule.

IS YOUR STOCK A GOOD LONG-TERM HOLDING? SIX STAGES OF THE "PROGRESS PATTERN"

A good number of growth industries and companies, like living things, go through a series of life cycles of progressions. Some are long-lived; others last a relatively short time. These progressions often terminate in conjunction with the fading momentum of the "breakthrough" or change which started the progression in the first place.

The typical price configurations traced out over the years by stocks or industries in this category have been astutely analyzed by Vari Investment Management, Inc. (7911 Herschel at Wall Street, La Jolla, California 92037) and divided into a six-stage **"progress pattern."** By evaluating which stage of growth some of your long-term holdings are in, you may be able to estimate their future potential as investments.

A TYPICAL "PROGRESS PATTERN"

1. Acceleration Phase (Rising Prices)

A) **Inception Stage:** The basic change is initiated, or a new product is developed.

B) **Advancement Stage:** Stock begins to rise as potential impact on earnings by "new development" is anticipated, attracting "sponsorship" (institutions and large investors "getting in on the ground floor").

C) **Maturation Stage:** Mass acceptance by consumer and investing public. Ownership of the stock becomes popular and its price advance is often of major magnitude.

2. Deceleration Phase (Declining Prices)

D) **First Termination Stage:** Public pushes price of stock to an unrealistic value. Much "distribution" by "insiders" and "sponsors" has already taken place. Prices falter and begin to decline.

E) **Rally Failure:** Attempt is made to reinfuse new life into the "product," or a new merchandising effort is made. The stock rallies in hope but fails to surpass the previous highs.

F) **Final Termination Stage:** Growth falters. Only sellers remain. Prices decline sharply.

As a classic example of this, compare the chart of Polaroid (Figure 11) with the progress pattern alongside. The issue's pattern reflects the growth of Polaroid during the 1960s, through the difficulties with its SX-70, which brought the company's problems into sharp focus.

FIGURE 10

THE PROGRESS PATTERN

THE PROGRESS PATTERN

FIGURE 11

POLAROID CORPORATION

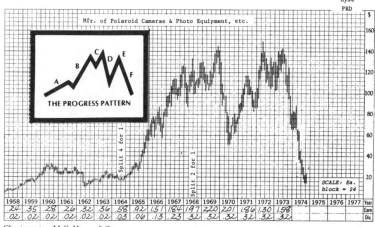

Chart courtesy M.C. Horsey & Co.

A WAY TO RECOGNIZE THE BULL MARKET IN SMALL COMPANIES

Look at a long-term chart of the Dow Jones industrial average and you can't help notice that between 1964 and 1982 the thirty blue chips had spent part of each of the eighteen years in the 800s. As the venerable Dow is synonymous with "the market" to most people, it's no wonder the public perceived that stocks went nowhere for many years (especially since the Dow in mid-1982 was lower than it was at the start of 1976).

Not so! The chart below from Wilshire Associates in Santa Monica, California is made up of 5,122 common stocks on the New York and American stock exchanges and the Over-the-Counter market. The lower "weighted" portion, which gives greater importance to giants such as IBM, General Motors, and American Telephone, was only 43% higher since January 1, 1976. The "unweighted" portion, which treats percent changes of all companies equally, was 300% higher in the same period.

This means that an invisible boom occurred under our noses in small companies, masked by misleading major averages such as the Dow, Standard & Poor's, and NYSE.

Another way to understand the effect of weighting is this: The DJI represents 19% of the weighted Wilshire but only 0.6% of the unweighted one. For the S&P 500, the difference is 69.2% versus 9.8%. However, OTC stocks, with only 7.5% of the weighted index, account for virtually half of the unweighted version.

What's the market doing? Which market?

FIGURE 12

THE WEIGHTED AND UNWEIGHTED WILSHIRE INDEX

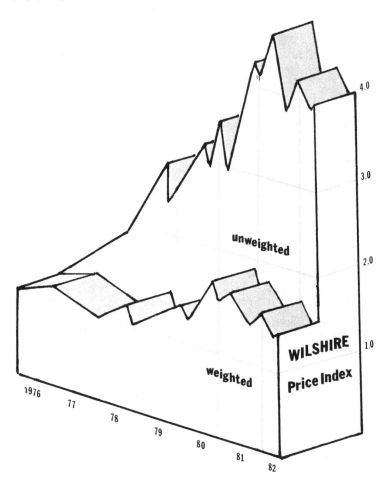

THE DISCOVERY CYCLE: GETTING IN AHEAD OF THE CROWD

Wouldn't you just love to "get in on the ground floor" of a new IBM, Xerox, or Polaroid? Who wouldn't? The major problem is that future great success stories in business are rarely recognized at early stages except in hindsight. Also, many investors tend to shun these young, unseasoned, embryonic companies in favor of "solid" blue chips such as Eastman Kodak, General Motors, Sears Roebuck, Union Carbide, Avon Corporation, BankAmerica and U.S. Steel.

FIGURE 13

WHERE DIFFERENT BUYING WAVES APPEAR
DURING A GROWTH CYCLE

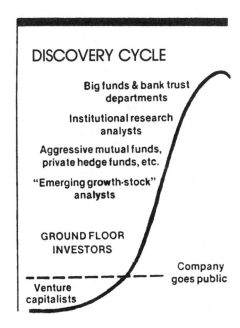

Is the ground-floor or blue-chip approach better? Considering that the first four blue chips above are at about the same share price as ten years ago and that Avon, BankAmerica and U.S. Steel are at half the price, it's hard to ignore the ground-floor approach.

Granted we may be entering a new, blue-chip, bull market era which could see the big "blues" double and triple in this decade, such an investment climate would most likely be accompanied by ten- and twentyfold increases in the price of promising high technology stocks and new ground-floor concept companies.

"Getting in on the ground floor" means: (1) buying into companies on the threshold of a major growth cycle, and (2) buying shares at a price that hasn't yet taken that potential into account.

Ground floor opportunities include companies that have been public for awhile but that, after being parked on the runway a few years, are just now ready for takeoff. It can include established companies with a dramatic new product coming off the drawing board, large companies undergoing a turnaround, or "Lazarus stocks"—companies emerging from the fires of bankruptcy.

In every successful growth stock, buying appears in waves according to different investors' willingness to take risks. Each new wave is less eager to take risks, and each drives the price higher, creating gains for the previous wave of buyers. We call this the "Discovery Cycle." After a company experiences a rapid sales expansion, the first Wall Street group to recognize it is usually a small band of analysts devoted to emerging growth stocks. Word about the stock spreads and buying interest expands (see Figure 13).

When the stock's growth trend is even better established, analysts who cater to the biggest and most conservative institutions then get interested. The last wave of buying comes from large mutual funds, pension funds, bank trust departments, and insurance companies. That's when a stock has truly "made it." The trouble is, there's no new group of buyers to push the stock's price/earnings multiple up further. The institutions have no new group to sell to and often end up holding the bag.

WIDELY-USED MARKET CYCLES

Quite a few professionals and sophisticated investors practice the art of technical analysis. Certain tools help them estimate in which direction a market or stock may be headed. Chart patterns provide one major source of information for technicians. Figure 14 is a simple daily bar chart of the Dow Jones industrial average during Spring 1974. Lines drawn through and connecting the tops and bottoms of minor swings show how well a descending channel was formed clearly defining the downmove. Traders would be expected to take advantage of this pattern by buying when prices reached the bottom of the channel and by selling when prices touched the top.

A small band of technicians go one step further and count days. They would have found that low points and high points were both spaced approximately three to four weeks apart. The channel showed them where, and the cycle, when. A powerful combination indeed!

Market cyclists often use longer term cycles to plan on more significant moves. Important ones include:

1.) **Seventeen-year cycle**—Significant low points appeared in 1898, 1915, 1932, 1949, 1966, and 1982.

2.) **Four-year cycle**—Presidential elections have influenced the economy and the stock market for over 150 years. Bottoms have occurred with monotonous regularity in 1962, 1966, 1970, 1974, 1978 , 1982, and many are betting on a recurrence in 1986, but there are no guarantees in the stock market.

3.) **Seventeen-month cycle**— After a string of lows in May 1970, November 1971, July 1973, and December 1974, approximately seventeen months apart, there was a cycle failure. A resumption of the cycle saw lows in November 1976, April 1978, October 1979, February 1981, August 1982, February 1984, and June 1985.

Trading patterns do change in time. There used to be a six-month cycle which was likely tied into the six-month capital gains tax. Gerald Appel, editor of *Systems & Forecasts* in Great Neck, New York, is a leading cycle theorist. In the past three years he has been demonstrating a fourteen-week cycle which at times stretches to one of seventeen weeks.

FIGURE 14

DOW JONES INDUSTRIALS (SPRING 1974)

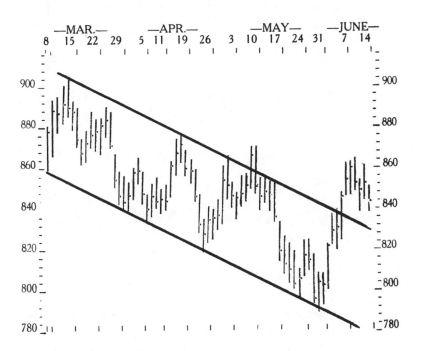

FIGURE 15

GREAT NORTHERN NEKOOSA CORP.

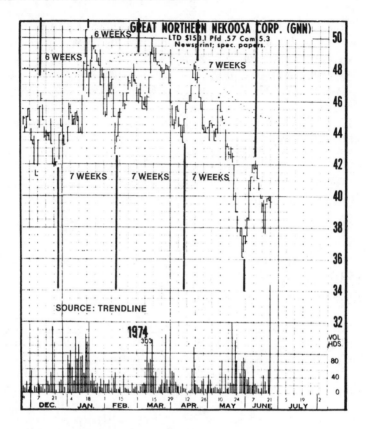

THE CYCLES OF INDIVIDUAL STOCKS

Do individual stocks demonstrate cyclical movements as well? They certainly do, most often in harmony with the overall market. The chart of Great Northern Nekoosa in 1974 illustrates that story, showing a beautiful cycle of six to seven weeks between tops and six to seven weeks between lows.

TRADING TIPS FOR CYCLE WATCHERS

1) If the market is due for a cyclical low, but the correction is almost imperceptible, the next move up should be very strong.
2) If the market is due for a rally but the cyclical rally is weak, the

next downthrust may be very powerful (these rules are not ironclad).

3) Buy, as a time cyclical low is approaching, on the first upturn, particularly if the stock is uptrended. The eight-week cycle is a valuable trading cycle.

4) Sell a downtrended stock as the next cyclical peak fails due.

5) Study a number of charts to familiarize yourself with the appearance of cyclical patterns.

6) Avoid purchases near the end of cyclical upturns; it usually pays to wait for the cyclical reaction.

7) This technique applies to commodities as well as to the securities markets.

8) A period when several cycles coalesce will combine the effect of all of them. For example, back in 1971, the decline that ended in November was very sharp because a number of down cycles—the seventeen-month, six-month, twelve-, eight-, and four-week, all coalesced right at that point.

THE STOKEN MARKET TIMING SYSTEM TURNS $1,000 INTO $56,195,150 in 65 YEARS

After I gave the Best-Investment-Book-Of-The Year award to *Strategic Investment Timing* * by Dick A. Stoken in the 1985 Stock Trader's Almanac, I kept reading the book over and over again, I was that impressed with it. Any hypothetical investor who followed Stoken's amazingly simple system over the years would have become a multi-millionaire many times over. Starting in 1921 with just $1,000 and staying long in bull markets and going short in bear markets, as per Stoken's 23 signals, would have resulted in an appreciation to $56,195,150.

Though the gain on $1,000 may seem astronomical, it's just the combination of Stoken's system and the awesome power of compound interest, at an 18.4 percent annual rate. Of course, 65 years is a long time, but you could have achieved the same result in 51 years if you had started with $10,000, or in 37 years, with $100,000.

The system itself requires very little, not even a computer or a calculator. Just watch four items in the financial section of your newspaper: the level of interest rates, the Dow Jones industrial average, the annual rate of inflation, and today's date in relation to the next presidential election. The gist of Stoken's signals is summarized on the next page along with a chart of the Dow since 1945 showing where the buys and sells would have occurred.

*Published by Macmillan

FIGURE 16

STOKEN SIGNALS SINCE 1945

BUY STOCKS

When

1. THE INVESTMENT
CLIMATE BECOMES
FAVORABLE

and

THE STOCK MARKET IS
IN A BUY ZONE

Or

2. FIVE MONTHS AFTER
A LEVEL OF EXTREME
PESSIMISM IS REACHED

* When either short-term (90-day T Bills) or long-term (AAA Corporate Bonds) interest rates fall to a 15-month low

* Or the favorable phase of the political cycle begins (Oct. 1, two years before a presidential election)

* One week after the Dow closes at a two-year low (five-year low in a deflationary environment)

* When the Dow closes at a five-year low

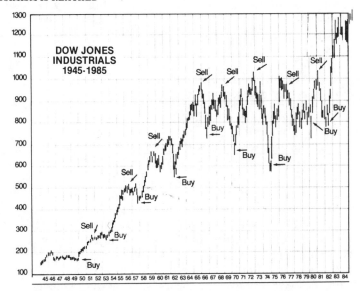

DOW JONES INDUSTRIALS 1945-1985

SELL STOCKS

When

1. THE STOCK MARKET IS IN A
CAUTION ZONE

and

THE INVESTMENT CLIMATE
TURNS HOSTILE

Or

2. SEVEN MONTHS AFTER THE
INVESTMENT CLIMATE TURNS
HOSTILE

Or

3. AN INFLATIONARY SPIRAL
BEGINS

* Nine months after the Dow closes at a two-year high (five year high in a deflationary environment)

* If both short- and long-term rates are at seven-year highs (15 month highs in a deflationary environment)

* When inflation climbs to a five-percent annual rate and is the highest rate in a year (Stock market must be in caution zone if we are in a deflationary environment)

TABLE 24

JUST 23 SIGNALS (12 BUYS, 11 SELLS)
SINCE 1921 WITHIN 4 PERCENT OF
TOPS AND BOTTOMS ON AVERAGE

	Buy Signal	Dow	Sell Signal	Dow	Long Gain	Short Gain	$1,000 Becomes
1	7/5/21	67	9/7/29	377	463%	88%	$ 10,584
2	7/9/32	41	4/17/37	180	339	46	67,840
3	4/21/42	97	7/15/46	200	106	20	167,700
4	6/13/49	161	1/2/52	269	67	3	288,460
5	9/22/53	261	9/4/56	507	94	14	637,958
6	12/31/57	435	1/4/60	679	56	19	1,184,305
7	6/21/62	550	1/18/66	994	81	24	2,658,055
8	10/3/66	757	12/20/68	966	28	29	4,388,980
9	6/30/70	683	12/15/72	1027	50	41	9,282,693
10	10/1/74	604	3/15/77	965	60	15	17,080,154
11	5/13/80	816	4/20/81	1015	24	20	25,415,268
12	8/3/82	816			121*		56,195,150

*Through March 20, 1986, Dow 1804.

THE FEDERAL RESERVE BOARD
WRITES THE MARKET LETTER FOR WALL STREET

If the Stoken system relies heavily on interest rates, is there any doubt who calls the shots on Wall Street? The Federal Reserve Board has to be at or near the top of anyone's list.

While I recognize that the trend in stock prices reflects many diverse economic, fundamental, technical, and political developments, the impact of FRB policy changes has recorded a remarkably consistent and impressive record for reversing stock market trends.

Monetary policy, administered through the FRB, has been a tool used by administrations over the years for stimulating or cooling off our economy. As such, FRB policy has been very influential in determining the direction of the stock market.

The arrows in Figure 17 reflect both the direction and impact of three of the most potent forces used by the FRB to implement policy.

1. **Discount Rate:** This is the interest rate charged member banks to borrow from the Federal Reserve. Increases in the discount rate have the effect of forcing other interest rates up, discouraging borrowing. Decreases force them down, thus making it attractive for businesses to borrow.

2. **Reserve Requirements:** This specifies how much money member banks must hold in reserve as a percentage of deposits. Increases in these requirements reduce lendable funds banks have available for borrowers; decreases make more funds available.

3. **Margin Requirement:** This rate regulates the amount of money investors can borrow from their brokers to purchase stocks. Increases in this rate reduce investors' purchasing power; conversely, a reduction in this rate will increase that power.

As the Fed (a nickname for the FRB) only used the discount rate in the last decade as a monetary tool and ignored the other two, there's no point in bringing the chart up to date. Instead, just remember two simple rules:

1. **Three Steps and a Stumble**—Invented by Edson Gould. When the discount rate is raised three times in succession in a rising market, it's time to get out of the market as it's due for a whack.

2. **Two Tumbles and a Jump**—Norman Fosback, editor of *Market Logic* in Fort Lauderdale, came up with this one. When the market is weak and the economy is in trouble, if the Fed lowers the discount rate twice, look for the market to take off. Summer 1982 was a case in point. Conditions could not have been worse. But Chairman Volker and associates lowered the discount rate three times in four weeks and triggered the market explosion that eventually took the Dow Jones industrial average up over 500 points.

FIGURE 17

RESTRICTIVE AND EXPANSIVE GESTURES OF FRB (1947-1975)

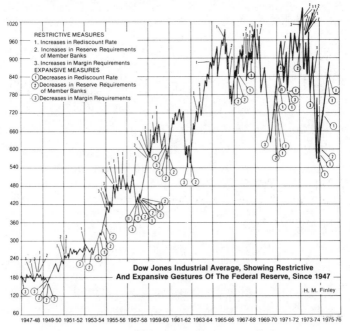

6
THE POLITICAL
STOCK MARKET CYCLE

HOW PRESIDENTIAL ELECTIONS
IMPACTED STOCK PRICES
FOR 150 YEARS

Each president of the United States must face political realities every four years if he wants to stay in the White House, or at least keep his party in power. It is no mere coincidence that the last two years (election year and pre-election year) of the thirty-eight administrations since 1832 produced a total net market gain of 515%, dwarfing the 8% gain of the first two years of these administrations.

A powerful bull market began in August 1982 resulting in the first decent midterm year since the Eisenhower era. With only one bad pre-election year (1931) in seventy-five years, 1983 continued the tradition of mostly double-digit winners. In a reversal of form, 1984 was flat, and an unbroken century-long string of winners in years ending in "five" seemed to be continuing in 1985. New high ground should be reached by most market averages in 1986 and 1987.

HOW THE GOVERNMENT
MANIPULATES THE ECONOMY TO
STAY IN POWER

Investors are well aware that stock prices tend to rise in a pre-presidential election year and fall in the year immediately following the election.

The "making of presidents," I have long observed, is invariably accompanied by an unsubtle manipulation of the economy. (We may

TABLE 25

ANNUAL STOCK MARKET ACTION SINCE 1832

Net change from year to year based on average December prices in S&P composite index.

PRESIDENT ELECTED	4-year cycle beginning	Election Year	Post-Election Year	Mid-term	Pre-Election Year
Jackson (D)	1832	15%	− 3%	10%	2%
Van Buren (D)	1836	− 8	− 8	1	−13
W.H. Harrison (W)**	1840*	5	−14	−13	36
Polk (D)	1844*	8	6	−15	1
Taylor (W)**	1848*	− 4	0	19	− 3
Pierce (D)	1852*	20	−13	−30	1
Buchanan (D)	1856	4	−30	− 7	− 7
Lincoln (R)	1860*	− 4	− 4	43	30
Lincoln (R)**	1864	0	−14	− 3	− 6
Grant (R)	1868	2	− 7	− 4	7
Grant (R)	1872	7	−13	3	− 4
Hayes (R)	1876	−18	−10	6	43
Garfield (R)**	1880	19	3	− 3	− 9
Cleveland (D)	1884*	−19	20	9	− 7
B. Harrison (R)	1888*	− 2	3	−14	18
Cleveland (D)	1892*	1	−20	− 3	1
McKinley (R)	1896*	− 2	13	19	7
McKinley (R)**	1900	14	16	1	−19
1832-1903 totals		38%	−75%	19%	78%
T. Roosevelt (R)	1904	25	16	3	−33
Taft (R)	1908	37	14	−12	1
Wilson (D)	1912*	3	−14	− 9	32
Wilson (D)	1916	3	−31	16	13
Harding (R)**	1920*	−24	7	20	− 3
Coolidge (R)	1924	19	23	5	26
Hoover (R)	1928	36	−15	−29	−47
F. Roosevelt (D)	1932*	−18	48	− 2	39
F. Roosevelt (D)	1936	28	−34	13	0
F. Roosevelt (D)	1940	−12	−15	6	21
F. Roosevelt (D)**	1944	14	33	−10	− 2
Truman (D)	1948	− 2	11	20	15
Eisenhower (R)	1952*	7	− 3	39	23
Eisenhower (R)	1956	4	−13	33	11
Kennedy (D)**	1960*	− 4	27	−13	18
Johnson (D)	1964	13	9	−11	17
Nixon (R)	1968*	12	−14	− 1	10
Nixon (R)***	1972	12	−19	−32	32
Carter (D)	1976*	18	−10	2	11
Reagan (R)	1980*	26	− 7	13	18
Reagan (R)	1984	0			
1904-1984 totals		197%	13%	51%	202%
1832-1984 totals		235%	−62%	70%	280%

*Party in power ousted **Death in office ***Resigned **D**—Democrat, **W**—Whig, **R**—Republican

cleverly deduce that incumbent administrations wish to retain power!) Subsequently, the "piper must be paid," inducing what I have coined the "Post-Presidential Year Syndrome." These are years when most big, bad bear markets began—1929, 1937, 1957, 1969, 1973, 1977, 1981.

Some cold, hard facts to support these hypotheses have appeared in a book by Edward R. Tufte, *Political Control of the Economy,* Princeton University Press, Princeton, N.J. The author investigated the timing of stimulative fiscal measures designed to increase per capita disposable income—and which would have provided a sense of well-being to the voting public. Such measures included: increases in federal budget deficits, government spending, and social security benefits; interest rate reductions on government loans; and speed-ups of project funding. Some of the findings of the investigation were:

Federal Spending—An average increase that was 29% higher in election than in non-election years during 1962-1973.

Social Security—There were nine increases during the 1952-1974 period. Half of the six election-year increases became effective in the month of September, perfectly timed to remain fresh in voters' minds as they trotted to the polls eight weeks later. Three increases in non-election years took effect in January. The average increase in payments was 100% higher in presidential than in midterm election years.

Real Disposable Income—Accelerated in eight of the nine election years between 1947 and 1973 (excluding the Eisenhower years), while only one of the nine odd-numbered years (1973) showed a marked acceleration.

Unemployment—Tends to follow a four-year cycle reaching a low point at the time of the presidential election.

Coincidence? Doubtful. Most likely, herein lies the explanation of our political (four-year) stock market cycle.

And we were supposed to be the very model of a modern "free economy?"

The Reagan administration is no different than the others. We paid the piper in 1981 and 1982, and then prospects brightened. You may have also noticed that the biggest deficit ever came right on schedule.

MARKET BETTER UNDER DEMOCRATS, DOLLAR BETTER UNDER REPUBLICANS

Members of the Wall Street establishment have been known to shudder at the thought of a Democrat occupying the White House. One might surmise that the reason for the bias is that stock prices rise more under the Republicans than under the Democrats. However, an examination of market performance since 1900 shows that investors have done far better during Democratic administrations.

A $10,000 investment compounded during Democratic eras would have grown to $83,005 in 40 years. The same investment during 44 Republican years would have appreciated to only $33,025. Deducting the original investment leaves a net appreciation for the Democrats over triple that of the Republicans.

Now, let's flip over to the other side of the (declining) coin, inflation, which puts the Republicans in a more favorable light.

TABLE 26

THE STOCK MARKET UNDER REPUBLICANS AND DEMOCRATS

(Based on Dow Jones Industrial Average on Election Day)

Republican Eras		% Change	Democratic Eras		% Change
1901-12	12 years	48.3%	1913-20	8 years	29.2%
1921-32	12 years	−24.5	1933-52	20 years	318.4
1953-60	8 years	121.2	1961-68	8 years	58.3
1969-76	8 years	2.1	1977-80	4 years	−3.0
1981-84	4 years	30.6			
Totals:	**44 years**	**177.7%**	**Totals:**	**40 years**	**402.9%**
Average Annual Change:		**4.0%**	**Average Annual Change:**		**10.1%**

Adjusting the stock market performance above for loss of purchasing power, would reduce the Democrats' $83,005 to $12,119 and the Republicans $33,025 to $17,569. Of course, Democrats will squawk and quickly point out that the Republicans' 46.7% gain in purchasing power (mostly during the Depression of the early thirties) was not too meaningful to those of the 25% who were unemployed.

For the record, there have been thirteen recessions and eleven bear markets under the Republicans and seven recessions and nine bear markets under the Democrats. While the Dems can boast of "their" stock market gains, Republicans can counter that all four wars of the century began while the Democrats were in power. And so on, ad infinitum.

TABLE 27

DECLINE OF THE DOLLAR UNDER REPUBLICANS AND DEMOCRATS

(Based on Average Annual Consumer Price Index)

Republican Eras		Loss in Purchasing Power	Democratic Eras		Loss in Purchasing Power
1901-12	12 years	−13.8%	1913-20	8 years	−51.7%
1921-32	12 years	+46.7	1933-52	20 years	−48.6
1953-60	8 years	−10.4	1961-68	8 years	−14.9
1969-76	8 years	−38.9	1976-80	4 years	−30.9
1981-84	4 years	−23.1			

The Republican dollar declined to 53.2¢ in 40 years.   **The Democratic dollar declined to 14.6¢ in 40 years.**

FORECASTING THE FUTURE
FROM PATTERNS OF THE PAST

By arranging the last thirty-six years chronologically in bull and bear groups in Table 28, we see that all pre-presidential election years (1951, '55, '59, '63, '67, '71, '75, '79, '83) were bull market years.

Interestingly, the twenty-year period 1949-1968 had fourteen bull years and six bear years. However, the climate changed dramatically after 1968, and we experienced seven bull and eight bear years. Bear markets in the earlier period (there were six of them) were over within ten months. The four in the later period lasted over a year and extended into part of a second year.

Other observations of aid to prognosticators are: 1) Only one presidential election year of eight was in the bear camp (Eisenhower did little to prevent the 1960 recession); 2) In contrast, seven of nine post-elections years suffered bear markets (a recession during the previous year helped 1961 escape the post-election year syndrome, and a similar fate was likely avoided in 1965 by our guns-and-butter policy in Vietnam); 3) Six bear markets in a row ended during midterm election years in 1962, '66, '70, '74, '78, and 1982.

A flat 1984 helped 1985 escape the post-election year syndrome.

TABLE 28

BULL AND BEAR MARKET YEARS DURING PRESIDENTIAL CYCLES

BEAR PHASE				BULL PHASE				
% Change	Bottom Year	% Change		% Change		% Change		% Change
	1949	10.3%	1950	21.8%	1951	16.5%	1952	11.8%
	1953	−6.6	1954	45.0	1955	26.4	1956	2.6
	1957	−14.3	1958	38.1	1959	8.5		
	1960	−3.0	1961	23.1				
	1962	−11.8	1963	18.9	1964	13.0	1965	9.1
	1966	−13.1	1967	20.1	1968	7.7		
1969 −11.4%	1970	0.1	1971	10.8	1972	15.6		
1973 −17.4	1974	−29.7	1975	31.5	1976	19.1		
1977 −11.5	1978	1.1	1979	12.3	1980	25.8		
1981 −9.7	1982	14.8	1983	??	1984	1.4		

*Election years are boxed, post-election years have grey screen, midterm years have shaded screen, pre-presidential election years are boldfaced.

%change based on year—end close of S & P Composite index.

HANDICAPPING THE 1988 PRESIDENTIAL RACE

To help you gain perspective for the 1988 election, a number of forecasting tools and charts are presented in the next few pages. The data immediately following, which were compiled for the last election, should be of interest:

Each party returning to power since 1896 usually retains the White House for an additional four years in the following election (except for the Democrats in 1980).

In the past half century, each party returning to power usually scored a greater electoral victory the second time around—in addition to taking a larger plurality of the popular vote.

Roosevelt was invincible in 1936, winning by 523 electoral votes. In 1932, he garnered 472.

Eisenhower retook the White House for the Republicans in 1952 with 442 votes. This was increased to 457 votes in 1956.

The last two political eras began with cliffhangers. Kennedy eked out a 120,000 plurality in 1960 with 303 electoral votes. The Democrats under Johnson increased the latter figure sharply to 486 votes in 1964. Similarly, Nixon took Humphrey by only a 520,000 plurality in 1968 with 301 electoral votes. The greatest landslide since 1936 ensued four years later when Nixon carried everything but one state (Massachusetts) and the District of Columbia for a total of 521 of the 538 electoral votes.

Carter recaptured the presidency for the Democrats with only 297 electoral votes in 1976, but failed to hold onto the White House for four more years. This had not happened since 1896.

Reagan's victory in 1984 was of epic proportions. He won every state but Minnesota. His 525 electoral votes were the highest number in history but Roosevelt's 523 in 1936 were slightly higher percentage-wise as there were fewer electoral votes then.

Should George Bush win the nomination and the presidency in 1988, it will be the first time in 150 years that a current vice president was elected to the White House. Nixon made it, but eight years had elapsed since he left the vice presidency. Humphrey and Mondale were both unsuccessful in their attempts.

THE WINNER OF THE 1988 ELECTION MAY BE FORETOLD BY THE DOW'S DIRECTION

One of the best political polls can be found on Wall Street.

If the Dow Jones industrial average is higher on the Monday before

FIGURE 18

PRESIDENTIAL ELECTION YEAR MARKETS

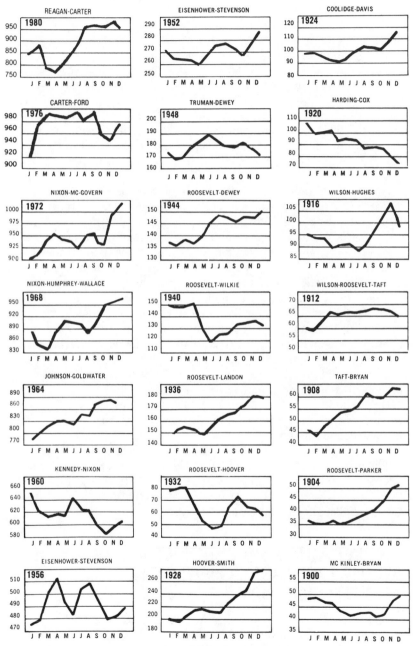

Based on Dow Jones industrial stock average mean of the month

Election Day than it was at the start of 1988, then a Republican president will most likely be in the White House in January 1989. If, on the other hand, the average is lower than it was New Year's Day 1988, the Democratic party will most likely take over the presidency.

Since 1900, the stock market, as represented by the thirty Dow Jones industrial stocks, has foretold a presidential victory for the party in power by gaining ground between January 1 and Election Day. Six exceptions did occur. In 1912, although the market had scored a gain, Teddy Roosevelt (running on the Progressive ticket in a three-way race) split the Republican party and caused it to lose the presidency. In 1940, though the market was depressed by the fall of France, the Democrats and Franklin D. Roosevelt were still able to win the election. In 1968 this indicator failed, but it never really had a chance to show its stuff due to a third party in the race and President Johnson's withdrawal as a candidate.

Anyone could have confidently predicted a resounding Republican defeat in 1976 had Nixon not been forced to resign. Favoring the Democrats was the disenchantment by the electorate with both major parties since World War II, resulting in a change of power every eight years. Also hanging over Republican heads was the pattern that has evolved during this century when incumbent parties have been ousted. Three Democratic eras ended following "unpopular" wars: 1920 (World War I); 1952 (Korea); and 1968 (Vietnam). Excluding 1912, when the Republican party split in two and threw the presidency away, the two other Republican eras ended following adverse economic conditions: 1932 (depression); 1960 (recession). Despite no recession and a rising Dow in 1976, the Republicans narrowly lost.

The party in power was ousted in 1980 though the market rose. A third party candidate was in the race.

Despite lower prices in the first seven months of 1984, the Dow recovered by Election Day and just missed (by ten points) getting back to where it was on January 1.

As there will be no incumbent candidate in 1988, the stock market will be better able to predict the victor. There were six other incumbentless races in this century: 1908, 1920, 1928, 1952, 1960, and 1968. The Dow correctly indicated the election result in each race but the last— George Wallace made 1968 a three-way race.

MARKET ACTS AS A BAROMETER BETWEEN THE LAST CONVENTION AND ELECTION DAY

Another election-year phenomenon, one with an outstanding track record is the Post-Convention-to-Election-Day Forecaster. Here again, the direction of the Dow between the close of the last presidential convention and Election Day reflects voter sentiment (Table 29).

Of the fourteen presidential elections since 1900 where the incumbent parties were victorious, twelve were foretold by rising stock prices. The two exceptions were minor (1948—0.5%, and 1956—2.3%). Gains for the period averaged 8.0%. Conversely, dissatisfaction with an incumbent party is most times reflected by a decline between the last convention and Election Day. Here, five out of eight election years produced declines.

THE MARKET PREFERS REPUBLICANS

Since 1900, the market has shown an obvious preference for Republican presidents by rising the following day on eight of the eleven occasions a Republican has won (average change +0.94%) and on only three of the ten occasions a Democrat has won (average change —0.77%). The week and month following Republican victories saw gains of 2.12% and 3.27%; losses of 0.62% and 2.06% followed Democratic victories. I didn't include the 1984 results as the market was open on Election Day for the first time and the outcome was a foregone conclusion.

Paradoxically, 44 years of Republican eras were accompanied by a total market rise of 177.7% (based on prices prior to Election Days); meanwhile, forty years under the Democrats produced a total gain of 402.9%.

TABLE 29

POST-CONVENTION-TO-ELECTION MARKETS

Year Incumbent Party Won	% Change	Year Incumbent Party Lost	% Change
1900	8.3%	1912	— 1.8
1904	22.6	1920	— 9.1
1908	9.6	1932	48.6
1916	15.9	1952	— 2.8
1924	6.7	1960	— 2.8
1928	22.4	1968	— 3.1
1936	11.5	1978	— 5.6
1940	9.9	1980	— 0.8
1944	0.8	**Average**	**4.8%**
1948	— 0.5		
1956	— 2.3		
1964	4.8		
1972	1.5		
1984	1.0		
Average	**8.0%**		

% change based on Dow Jones industrial average.

INCUMBENT VICTORIES
VS. INCUMBENT DEFEATS

As we have learned earlier, the Dow Jones industrial average (with just six exceptions) has foretold the outcome of presidential elections in this century. When the venerable average gains ground between New Year's Day and Election Day, the incumbent party will usually win the election. A loss in the average during the period will usually result in the "ins" being ousted.

The chart below (designed by the late Ralph A. Rotnem of Smith Barney, Harris Upham) tells the story. The Dow tends to move up and gain 15.4% on average, based on the fourteen elections when the incumbent party retained the presidency. An average loss of 1.5% ensued when the incumbents lost (eight times).

FIGURE 19

STOCK PRICE TREND IN ELECTION YEARS, 1900-1984

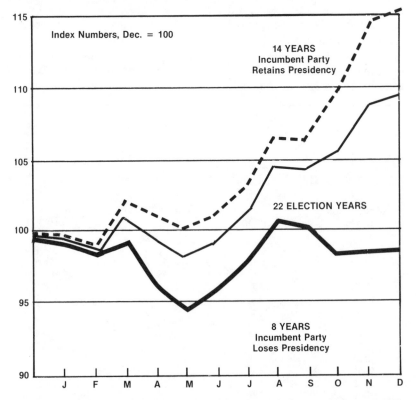

There have been three notable strong market months: March, up eighteen times, down four times; August, up sixteen times, down six times; and often November, especially when Republicans are victorious.

FIGURE 20

POST-PRESIDENTIAL ELECTION YEAR MARKETS

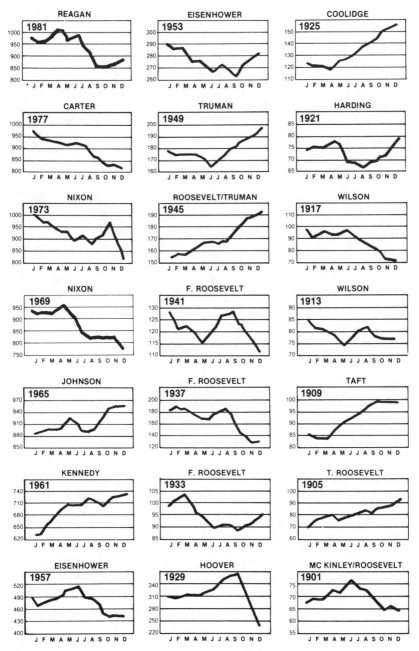

Based on Dow Jones Industrial Average mean of the month

POST-ELECTION YEARS: PAYING THE PIPER

Politics being what it is, incumbent administrations during election years try to make the economy look good to impress the electorate and tend to put off unpopular decisions until the votes are counted. This produces an American phenomenom—the Post-Election Year Syndrome. The year begins with an inaugural ball after which the piper must be paid, and we Americans have paid and paid and paid dearly in the past seventy years.

It is rare indeed when a victorious candidate succeeds in fulfilling his winning (!) campaign promise of "peace and prosperity." In the past eighteen post-election years, three major wars began: World War I (1917), World War II (1941), and Vietnam (1965); four drastic bear markets started in 1929, 1937, 1969, and 1973; and less severe bear markets occurred or were in progress in 1913, 1917, 1921, 1941, 1949, 1953, 1957, 1977, and 1981. Only in 1925 were Americans blessed with peace and prosperity. Perhaps 1985 may now be included.

Any difference between a Republican change in administration and a Democratic one? Postwar bear markets followed the three Republican takeovers in 1921 (World War I), 1953 (Korea), and 1969 (Vietnam). A sixteen-month bear market began in 1981 and ended in August 1982 with

TABLE 30

POST-ELECTION YEAR RECORD SINCE 1913

1913: Wilson, D.	Minor bear market.
1917: Wilson, D.	World War I and a bear market.
1921: Harding, R.	Postwar depression and bear market.
1925: Coolidge, R.	Peace and prosperity. Hallelujah!
1929: Hoover, R.	Worst market crash in history..
1933: Roosevelt, D.	Devaluation, bank failures, depression still on but market strong.
1937: Roosevelt, D.	Another crash, 20% unemployment rate.
1941: Roosevelt, D.	World War II and a continuing bear.
1945: Roosevelt, D.	Postwar industrial contraction, strong market precedes 1946 crash.
1949: Truman, D.	Minor bear market.
1953: Eisenhower, R.	Minor postwar (Korea) bear market.
1957: Eisenhower, R.	Major bear market.
1961: Kennedy, D.	Bay of Pigs fiasco, strong market precedes 1962 crash.
1965: Johnson, D.	Dow theory bear market signal given but cancelled out by Vietnam escalation. Bear came anyway in 1966.
1969: Nixon, R.	Start of worst bear market since 1937.
1973: Nixon, Ford, R.	Start of worst bear market since 1929.
1977: Carter, D.	Bear market in blue chip stocks.
1981: Reagan, R.	Bear strikes again.
1985: Reagan, R.	No bear in sight.

FIGURE 21

THE DOW JONES DURING POST-ELECTION YEARS

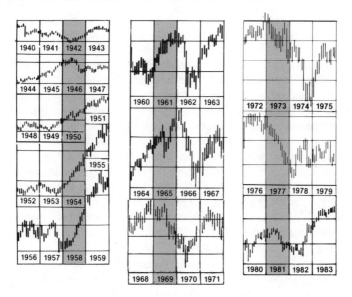

the Dow off 24.1%. Democrats fared better when they recaptured the White House. Though a bear market occurred under Woodrow Wilson in 1913, Franklin Roosevelt, in 1933, inherited a situation in which the market had nowhere to go but up. John Kennedy also benefited from an Eisenhower recession. Pipers were paid after both Carter and Reagan were inaugurated.

TABLE 31

LANDSLIDES OF OVER 400 ELECTORAL VOTES
SINCE 1900 AND EXTENT OF
SUBSEQUENT BEAR MARKETS

WINNING CANDIDATE	Election Year	Electoral Votes	DOW-JONES INDUSTRIALS Subsequent High	DOW-JONES INDUSTRIALS Subsequent Low	Extent of Decline
Woodrow Wilson (D)	1912	435	91.94 (11/12)	72.11 (6/13)	−21.6%
Warren G. Harding (R)	1920	404	85.48 (11/20)	63.90 (8/20)	−25.2
Herbert Hoover (R)	1928	444	381.17 (9/29)	41.22 (7/32)	−89.2
Franklin D. Roosevelt (D)	1932	472	68.04 (11/32)	50.16 (2/33)	−26.3
''	1936	523	194.40 (3/37)	98.95 (3/38)	−49.1
''	1940	449	138.12 (11/40)	92.92 (4/42)	−32.7
''	1944	432	No Decline		−
Dwight D. Eisenhower (R)	1952	442	293.79 (9/53)	255.49 (9/53)	−13.0
''	1956	457	520.77 (7/57)	419.79 (10/57)	−19.4
Lyndon B. Johnson (D)	1964	486	995.15 (2/66)	744.32 (10/66)	−25.2
Richard M. Nixon (R)	1972	520	1051.70 (1/73)	577.60 (12/74)	−45.1
Ronald Reagan (R)	1980	489	1024.05 (4/81)	776.92 (8/82)	−24.1
''	1984	525	??	??	
				Average	−30.9%

TAKE A VACATION FROM THE STOCK MARKET WHEN PRESIDENT WINS BY LANDSLIDE

The greater a presidential victory in an election, the worse off the country is bound to be. What an irony!

After what happened to us in 1972 and 1973, I researched the correlation between stock prices and presidential landslides of over 400 electoral votes. The results are shown in Table 31. Declines of 30.9% on average followed all but one of the twelve landslide victories. The smallest was 13.0% in 1953 following Eisenhower's election to his first term in office; the largest, 89.2%, was during the Great Depression.

Even more distressing is to examine the four occasions when the victor captured over 60% of the popular vote: Harding brought us the Teapot Dome Scandal; Roosevelt, in his second term, grabbed for more power and attempted to pack the Supreme Court; Johnson gave us Vietnam, which triggered the greatest inflationary spiral in four centuries; and Nixon brought us Watergate, which weakened the country and emboldened OPEC to strike right after the "Saturday Night Massacre."

One consolation is that only four bear markets began in November, during the same month in which the landslide victories occurred (and they were prior to 1940). Two declines began in the January following the election, four were kicked off slightly later in March, April, July, and September, and one began fifteen months later in February (1966).

TABLE 32

ELECTION YEAR LOSERS IN THIS CENTURY*

Year	% Change Election Year	% Change Post-Election Year
1920	—32.9%	+12.7%
1932	—23.1	+66.7
1948	— 2.1	+12.9
1960	— 9.3	+18.7
1984	— 3.7	

* Excludes was years (1916, 1940)

% changes based on year end close Dow Jones Industrial Average

TABLE 33

BULL MARKETS THAT FOLLOWED DOWN ELECTION YEARS

Bull Era	% Gain
1921-1929	+504%
1933-1937	+288
1949-1956	+222
1962-1966	+ 86

By winning the largest number of electoral votes in history, 525, and 59.1% of the popular vote, Reagan scored an overwhelming victory. This would normally be alarming as many previous White House occupants went to political extremes believing they had a mandate, and the country eventually suffered the consequences. However, there is a big difference to consider here. President Reagan was enormously popular, but his victory, while a personal triumph, was not accompanied by great gains in Congress. For example, Harding had 300 party members elected to the House of Representatives on Election Day, Roosevelt in 1936 had 333, and Johnson had 295. In contrast, Reagan could only muster 180 House seats. Even Nixon in 1972 had more, 192.

Another important factor which should allay landslide phobia is that the Dow Jones industrial average was off 3.7% in 1984. That was bullish. Why? Because presidents who want to stay in power or hand over the White House to a successor from their own party are usually capable of temporarily inflating the economy and stock prices during election years. These years are usually upbeat and euphoric until after the election, when, as the saying goes, "the piper must be paid." There were no excesses in the stock market in 1984, so we didn't need the customary correction in 1985.

All the election-year losers in this century—1920, 1932, 1948, and 1960 (excluding war years)—were followed by post-election years which ended in the plus column (Table 32). And best of all, these years were followed by big, bull eras (Table 33).

MIDTERM ELECTION YEARS: WHERE BOTTOM PICKERS FIND PARADISE

American presidents have danced the Quadrennial Quadrille over the past two centuries. After the midterm congressional election and the invariable seat loss by his party, the president during the next two years jiggles fiscal policies to get federal spending, disposable income and social security benefits up and interest rates and inflation down. By Election Day, he will have danced his way into the wallets and hearts of the electorate and, hopefully, will have choreographed four more years in the White House for his party.

After the Inaugural Ball is over, however, we pay the piper. Practically all bear markets began and ended in the two years after presidential elections. Bottoms often occurred in an air of crisis: the Cuban missile crisis in 1962, tight money in 1966, Cambodia in 1970, Watergate and Nixon's resignation in 1974, and threat of international monetary collapse in 1982. But remember, the word for "crisis" in Chinese is composed of two characters: the first, the symbol for danger; the second, opportunity. Of the 13 quadrennial cycles in the past 52 years, only three bottoms were reached in the post-presidential year. All others came in midterm years, including the last six in a row.

FIGURE 22

MIDTERM ELECTION YEAR MARKETS

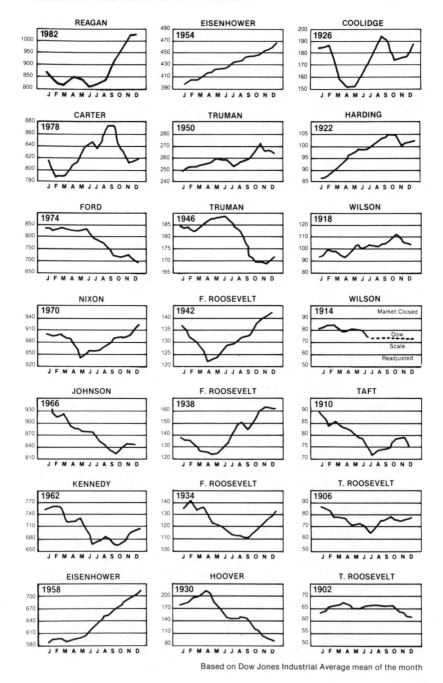

Based on Dow Jones Industrial Average mean of the month

TABLE 34

MIDTERM ELECTION YEAR RECORD SINCE 1914

1914: Wilson, D.	Bottom in July. War outbreak closed markets.
1918: Wilson, D.	Bottom 12 days prior to start of year.
1922: Harding, R.	Bottom 4½ months prior to start of year.
1926: Coolidge, R.	Only Coolidge drop (7 weeks, —17%) ends March 30.
1930: Hoover, R.	Crash of '29 continues through 1930. **No bottom.**
1934: Roosevelt, D.	First Roosevelt bear, Feb. to July 26 bottom (—23%).
1938: Roosevelt, D.	Big 1937 break ends in March, D.J.I. off 49%.
1942: Roosevelt, D.	World War II bottom in April.
1946: Truman, D.	Market tops in May, bottoms in October.
1950: Truman, D.	June 1949 bottom, but June 1950 Korean War outbreak causes 14% drop.
1954: Eisenhower, R.	September 1953 bottom, then straight up.
1958: Eisehnower, R.	October 1957 bottom, then straight up.
1962: Kennedy, D.	Bottoms in June and October.
1966: Johnson, D.	Bottom in October.
1970: Nixon, R.	Bottom in May.
1974: Nixon, Ford, R.	December Dow bottom but S&P 500 hit low in October.
1978: Carter, D.	March bottom despite October Massacre later.
1982: Reagan, R.	Bottom in August.

With an 18%, 200-point drop between January and July 1984, it's entirely possible we may go through this cycle without much of a correction in 1986.

FIGURE 23

THE DOW DURING MIDTERM YEARS

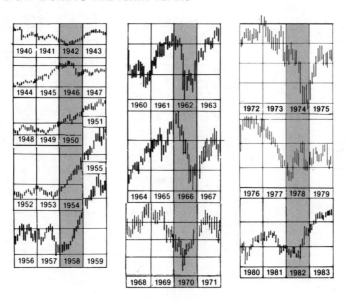

PROSPERITY MORE THAN PEACE DETERMINES OUTCOME OF CONGRESSIONAL RACES

Though the stock market in presidential election years is usually able to predict if the party in power will retain or lose the White House, the outcome of congressional races in midterm years is another matter entirely. Typically, the president's party will lose a number of House seats in these elections (1934 was a lone exception). It is considered a victory for the President when his party loses a small number of seats and a repudiation of sorts when a large number of seats are lost.

Table 35 would seem to indicate that there is no relationship between the stock market's behavior in the ten months prior to the election and the magnitude of Congressional seat losses. (Midterm years are arranged by size of seat loss by the president's party.) During Eisenhower's term, the midterm elections in 1954 and 1958 were both preceded by roaring bull markets; however, the Republicans lost few seats in one, and a huge number in the other. The Democrats gained seats in 1934 when the market was dull, but were clobbered while the market was rising sharply in 1938.

If the market does not offer a clue to the outcome of Congressional

---

TABLE 35

LAST SEVENTEEN MIDTERM ELECTIONS RANKED BY % LOSS OF SEATS BY PRESIDENT'S PARTY

	% Seats Gained/Lost Pres.'s Party	Year	President	Dow Jones Industrials New Year to Election Day	Election Day to Year End
1.	2.9%	1934	D: Roosevelt	− 3.8%	8.3%
2.	− 1.9	1962	D: Kennedy	−16.5	6.8
3.	− 4.0	1926	R: Coolidge	− 3.9	4.4
4.	− 5.1	1978	D: Carter	− 3.7	0.6
5.	− 6.3	1970	R: Nixon	− 5.3	10.7
6.	− 8.1	1954	R: Eisenhower	26.0	14.2
7.	−11.0	1950	D: Truman	11.2	− 5.8
8.	−12.0	1918	D: Wilson	15.2	− 4.1
9.	−14.1	1982	R: Reagan	14.9	4.1
10.	−15.9	1966	D: Johnson	−17.2	− 2.1
11.	−18.7	1942	D: Roosevelt	3.4	4.1
12.	−19.9	1930	R: Hoover	−25.4	−11.2
13.	−21.1	1938	D: Roosevelt	28.2	− 0.1
14.	−22.3	1946	D: Truman	− 9.6	1.6
15.	−23.5	1958	R: Eisenhower	25.1	7.1
16.	−24.4	1974	R: Ford	−22.8	− 6.2
17.	−25.2	1922	R: Harding	21.4	0.3

races, does anything? Yes! In the seventeen midterms, no war or recession began in the two years prior to the elections in 1934, 1962, 1926, and 1978, and Congressional victories resulted. In 1970 and 1954, moderate House losses followed mild recessions. The next group includes four Democrats who suffered sizable losses in their party's Congressional seats. What **they** all had in common was that a major war broke out between their reelections and the following midterm elections. The six worst repudiations of a president are at the bottom of the list. Their midterm Congressional elections were preceded by severe economic setbacks. **Obviously, prosperity is of greater importance to the electorate than peace!**

It is worth noting that presidents elected by a landslide vote (Harding 1920, Roosevelt 1936, Eisenhower 1956, Johnson 1964) fared quite badly two years later. What bitter victories! Nixon's landslide victory in 1972 was followed by a loss in 1974 of almost one fourth of the Republicans' House seats. Watergate and the economy were surely contributing factors.

There does seem to be more bullishness after midterm elections when the president's party loses a minimal number of seats.

TABLE 36

PERFECT RECORD SINCE 1962 FOR BI-ANNUAL SWITCHERS

Date:	S&P 500 Price	Annual Dividend	Annual Price Apprec.	Annual Total Return	Treasury Bills Risk-Free Return	2 Year S&P 500 Apprec.	2 Year S&P 500 Total Return	2 Year Risk-Free Return
11/30/62	62.26							
11/30/63	72.23	2.28	16.0%	19.7%	3.2%			
11/30/64	84.42	2.50	16.9%	20.3%	3.5%	35.6%	44.0%*	6.8%
11/30/65	91.61	2.72	8.5%	11.7%	3.9%			
11/30/66	80.45	2.87	−12.2%	− 9.0%	4.8%	− 4.7%	1.6%	8.9%*
11/30/67	94.00	2.92	16.8%	20.5%	4.2%			
11/30/68	108.37	3.07	15.3%	18.6%	5.2%	34.7%	42.9%*	9.6%
11/30/69	93.81	3.16	−13.4%	−10.5%	6.6%			
11/30/70	87.20	3.14	− 7.0%	− 3.7%	6.5%	−19.5%	−13.8%	13.5%*
11/30/71	93.99	3.07	7.8%	11.3%	4.4%			
11/30/72	116.67	3.15	24.1%	27.5%	3.8%	33.8%	41.9%*	8.4%
11/30/73	95.96	3.38	−17.8%	−14.9%	6.9%			
11/30/74	69.97	3.60	−27.1%	−23.3%	8.0%	−40.0%	−34.7%	15.5%*
11/30/75	91.24	3.68	30.4%	35.7%	5.8%			
11/30/76	102.10	4.05	11.9%	16.3%	5.1%	45.9%	57.8%*	11.2%
11/30/77	94.83	4.67	− 7.1%	− 2.5%	5.1%			
11/30/78	94.70	5.07	− 0.1%	5.2%	7.2%	− 7.2%	2.6%	12.7%*
11/30/79	106.16	5.65	12.1%	18.1%	9.8%			
11/30/80	140.52	6.16	32.4%	38.2%	11.9%	48.4%	63.2%*	22.9%
11/30/81	126.35	6.63	−10.1%	− 5.4%	13.9%			
11/30/82	138.54	6.87	9.6%	15.0%	10.5%	− 1.4%	8.8%	25.9%*
11/30/83	166.40	7.09	20.1%	25.2%	10.5%			
11/30/84	163.58	7.53	− 1.7%	2.8%	9.7%	18.0%	28.7%*	21.2%*
			22-Year Total Return		162.7%		517.8%	325.7%

* 2 Years Stocks/2 Years Treasuries 1860.4%*

BUY STOCKS TWO YEARS PRIOR TO ELECTION, SWITCH TO TREASURIES IN FOLLOWING TWO YEARS: A PROVEN SUPER STRATEGY SINCE 1962

The quadrennial political/stock market cycle has proven to be an invaluable investment strategy since I began researching it in 1967. It is no mere coincidence that the last two years of the thirty-eight administrations since 1832 produced a total net market gain of 515%, dwarfing the 8% gain of the first two years of all these administrations.

David MacNeill of Boston developed an investment strategy in 1973 utilizing the political cycle phenomena. Investing in stocks for the two years prior to election and switching to treasury bills for the next two years, back and forth, produced excellent results as reproduced in Table 36. The bi-annual switching strategy produced a twenty-two-year total return of 1860.4%, 3½ times the buy-hold return of 517.8% for the period. A continuing bull market in 1986 could derail this strategy.

INTEREST RATES ONE YEAR PRIOR TO ELECTION HAVE PREDICTED ALL WINNERS SINCE 1920

Television newscasters often predict election results by polling voters leaving voting booths. This practice has incurred the wrath of many citizens who feel that people who haven't voted yet may be influenced and thus decide not to vote.

Announcing victors hours before the final votes are cast might violate the spirit of democracy, but what if a simple statistic could tell election results a year in advance?

Knowing AAA Corporate bond yields would have enabled you to foretell the outcome of each presidential election since 1920—one year in advance. Dick A. Stoken * discovered that when the level of long-term interest rates was relatively high one year prior to the election, the party in power was ousted one year later. This phenomenon was at work in the elections of Harding (1920), Roosevelt (1932), Eisenhower (1952), Kennedy (1960), Nixon (1968), Carter (1976) and Reagan (1980).

When long-term rates fall to a fifteen-month low, a period of "low" interest rates begins which remains until rates climb again to a seven-year high. The other nine presidents in the table were all fortunate to have run during a period of low interest rates, enabling their parties to hold onto the White House for an additional four years.

Interest rates of 15.85% in October 1981 fell to 12.42% in November 1983, one year prior to the 1984 election. Gallup and Harris...move over!

* Strategic Investment Timing, Macmillan

FIGURE 24

PRE-ELECTION YEAR MARKETS

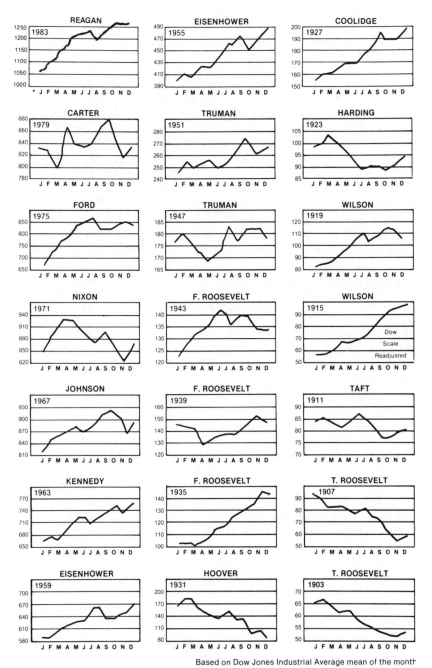

Based on Dow Jones Industrial Average mean of the month

TABLE 37

PRESIDENTIAL ELECTIONS AND INTEREST RATES ONE YEAR PRIOR

Election of	Interest Rates November 15 1 Year Earlier	Incumbent Party	Popular Vote %	Challenging Party	Popular Vote %	Plurality
1920	High	Cox (D)	34.1	*Harding* (R)	60.4	26.3%
1924	Low	*Coolidge* (R)	54.0	Davis (D)[a]	28.2	25.8%
1928	Low	*Hoover* (R)	58.1	Smith (D)	40.8	17.3%
1932	High	Hoover (R)	39.7	*Roosevelt* (D)	57.4	17.7%
1936	Low	*Roosevelt* (D)	60.8	Landon (D)	36.5	24.3%
1940	Low	*Roosevelt* (D)	54.7	Wilkie (R)	44.8	9.9%
1944	Low	*Roosevelt* (D)	53.4	Dewey (R)	45.9	7.5%
1948	Low	*Truman* (D)	49.6	Dewey (R)[b]	45.1	4.5%
1952	High	Stevenson (D)	44.4	*Eisenhower* (R)	55.1	10.7%
1956	Low	*Eisenhower* (R)	57.4	Stevenson (D)	42.0	15.4%
1960	High	Nixon (R)	49.5	*Kennedy* (D)	49.7	0.2%
1964	Low	*Johnson* (D)	61.1	Goldwater (R)	38.5	22.6%
1968	High	Humphrey (D)	42.7	*Nixon* (R)[c]	43.4	0.7%
1972	Low	*Nixon* (R)	60.7	McGovern (D)	37.5	23.2%
1976	High	Ford (R)	48.3	*Carter* (D)	50.4	2.1%
1980	High	Carter (D)	41.9	*Reagan* (R)	51.8	9.9%
1984	Low	*Reagan* (R)	59.1	Mondale (D)	40.9	18.2%

Winners in italics, a) LaFollette (Progressive) 16%, b) Thurmond and Henry Wallace combined 5%, c) Geo. Wallace 13%

7
THE TEN-YEAR PATTERN

DECENNIAL CYCLE: A MARKET PHENOMENON

By arranging each year's market gain or loss so that all the first years of each decade fall into the same column, etc., certain interesting patterns emerge—strong fifth and eighth years, weak seventh and zero years, etc.

This fascinating phenomenon was presented by Edgar Lawrence Smith in *Common Stocks and Business Cycles* (William-Frederick Press, 4th rev. ed., 1970).

When Smith first cut graphs of market prices into ten-year segments and placed them above one another, he observed that each decade tended to have three bull market cycles. It might also be pointed out that the longest and strongest bull markets seem to favor the middle years of a decade. Anthony Gaubis co-pioneered the decennial pattern with Smith.

Since the 1920s, low points of decades have been reached much earlier than in the previous fifty years.

What's the reason for such a consistent pattern? We're not sure, but every year ending with "5" in every decade for a century has been a bull market year. In 1975, the bulls charged out of the depths of the savage 1973-1974 bear market. In 1965, 1955, 1945, and 1935, the bull markets already in progress continued and produced handsome gains in those periods. The Roaring Twenties produced a nine-year bull market ending in 1929, and the advent of World War I in 1914 was the cause of a bear market which yielded to recovery the following year (1915).

Eight decades of monthly stock prices were combined into one composite decade at the bottom of Figure 25 by Edson Gould. Above that graph, the Fifties seem to be mimicking the composite pattern. How fascinating it was to then see the Sixties unfolding in the top graph in similar fashion, though a one-year time lag is evident. Edson retired some years ago so I never saw an update of this chart. However, take a look at what the market did in subsequent years in Table 38 and you'll see that the Seventies almost resembled the composite pattern—weakness in the third and fourth years and then again in the seventh and eighth years. So far in the Eighties, we have seen the market turn up sharply in 1982, decline mildly between June 1983 and July 1984, and then start to climb again. Will the market weaken in 1986 or 1987 and then resume its march to Dow 2000, 2500, 3000, or higher? Or will it forge a different pattern, depending on how we solve the problems with the deficit, the dollar and the balance of payments?

Over the last century, every fifth year of the decade has seen a gain averaging 31.3% in the Dow Jones industrials.

TABLE 38

THE TEN-YEAR STOCK MARKET CYCLE
Annual % change in Standard & Poor's Composite Index Past 100 Years

| | | | | Year of Decade | | | | | |
DECADES	1st	2nd	3rd	4th	5th	6th	7th	8th	9th	10th
1881-1890	—	—	—	—	20	9	— 7	— 2	3	—14
1891-1900	18	1	—20	— 3	1	— 2	13	19	7	14
1901-1910	16	1	—19	25	16	3	—33	37	14	—12
1911-1920	1	3	—14	— 9	32	3	—31	16	13	—24
1921-1930	7	20	— 3	19	23	5	26	36	—15	—29
1931-1940	—47	—18	48	— 2	39	28	—34	13	0	—12
1941-1950	—15	6	21	14	33	—10	— 2	— 2	11	20
1951-1960	15	7	— 3	39	23	4	—13	33	11	— 4
1961-1970	27	—13	18	13	9	—11	17	12	—14	— 1
1971-1980	10	12	—19	—32	32	18	—10	2	11	26
1981-1990	— 7	13	18	0	26	—	—	—	—	—
Up Years	7	8	4	6	11	7	3	8	8	3
Down Years	3	2	6	4	0	3	7	2	2	7
Total % Change	25%	32%	27%	64%	254%	47%	—74%	164%	41%	—36%

Based on average December prices.

FIGURE 25

10-YEAR PATTERNS OF INDUSTRIAL STOCK PRICES

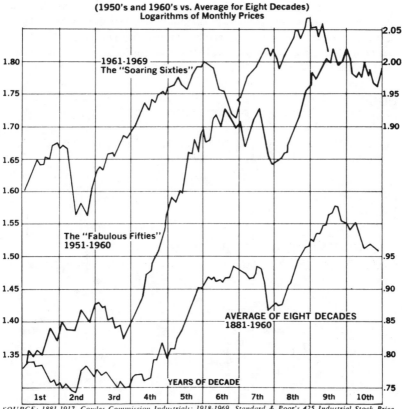

(1950's and 1960's vs. Average for Eight Decades)
Logarithms of Monthly Prices

1961-1969
The "Soaring Sixties"

The "Fabulous Fifties"
1951-1960

AVERAGE OF EIGHT DECADES
1881-1960

YEARS OF DECADE

| 1st | 2nd | 3rd | 4th | 5th | 6th | 7th | 8th | 9th | 10th |

SOURCE: 1881-1917, Cowles Commission Industrials; 1918-1969, Standard & Poor's 425 Industrial Stock Price Index (1941-43 = 10)

TABLE 39

FIFTH YEAR OF LAST 12 DECADES

Year	%Gain
1885	+ 27.7%
1895	+ 2.3
1905	+ 38.2
1915	+ 81.7
1925	+ 30.0
1935	+ 38.5
1945	+ 26.6
1955	+ 20.8
1965	+ 10.9
1975	+ 38.3
1985	+ 27.7
Average	**+ 31.3%**

% change based on year end close Dow Jones industrial average.

THE FIRST YEAR OF DECADES THROUGH THE TENTH

Except for the depressed Thirties and war-torn Forties, "first" years have been gainers on balance, though volatile. Post-election "one" years tended to do better than normal. While the Dow industrials declined in 1901, the other averages thrived—S&P composite up 16%. 1981 was off 9.2%.

FIGURE 26

"ONE" YEARS

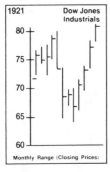

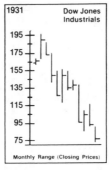

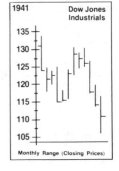

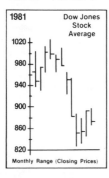

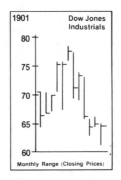

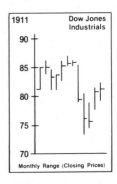

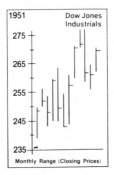

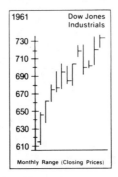

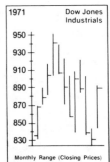

THE SECOND YEAR OF DECADES

Except for 1932 and 1962, "second" years have tended to be gainers, though of modest proportions. Republican presidential victories of 1952 and 1972 triggered dynamic market moves in contrast to the Democratic takeovers of 1892, 1912, and 1932. The Dow ended 1982 up 19.6% despite a bear market through August.

FIGURE 27

"TWO" YEARS

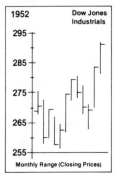
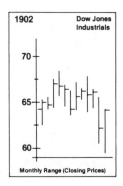
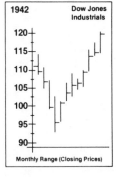
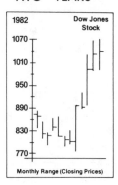
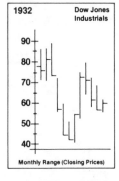
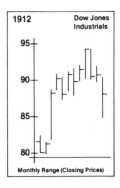
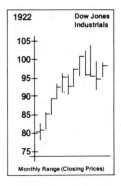
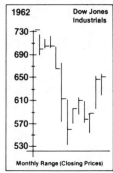
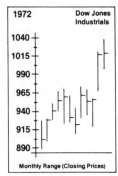

THE THIRD YEAR OF DECADES

The "third" years from 1893 to 1923 were down, down, down. The market rose out of the ashes in 1933 and doubled. Since then we have had three that preceded and two that followed election years. We usually have bull markets in the former and bear markets in the latter. A bull market in 1983 gained 20.3%.

FIGURE 28

"THREE" YEARS

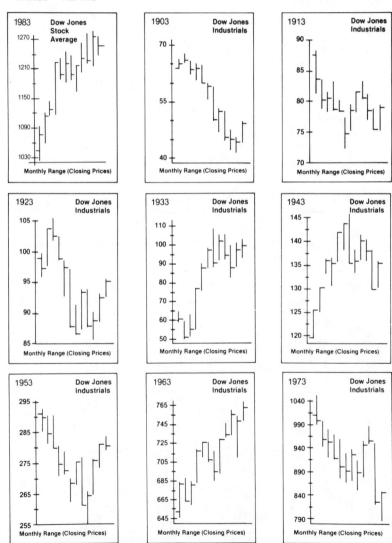

THE FOURTH YEAR OF DECADES

Five of the last ten decades had "four" years that occurred in midterm congressional election years. Except for 1954, they were terrible market years. The other five were good and had one thing in common—popular incumbents won reelection. Only the last five months of 1984 were bullish.

FIGURE 29

"FOUR" YEARS

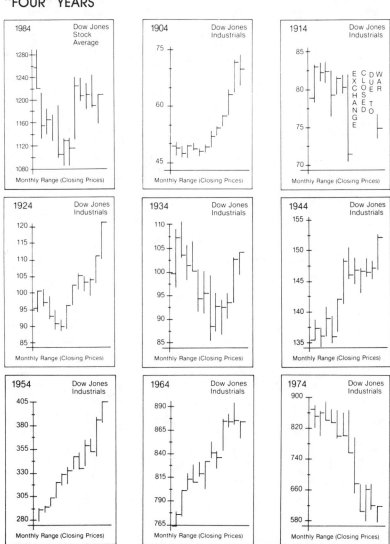

Monthly Range (Closing Prices)

THE FIFTH YEAR OF DECADES

There has not been one losing "five" year in ten decades. On the other hand, bear markets began early in all the last four post-presidential election years and continued into the midterm years. The winning streak continued as the Dow gained 27.7% in 1985.

FIGURE 30

"FIVE" YEARS

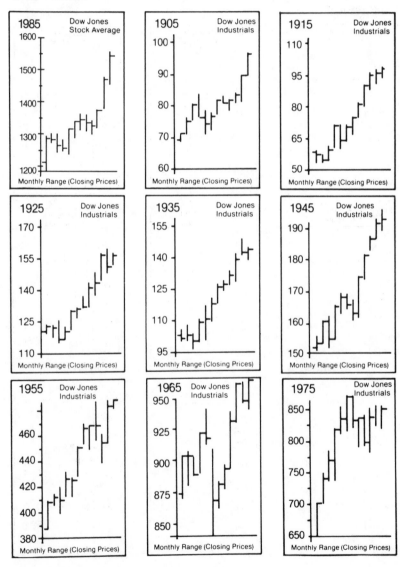

THE SIXTH YEAR OF DECADES

Decennial pattern watchers would have been cautious in 1986 as most "sixth" years of decades have seen few big percentage gains by the Dow except for 1936 and 1976, both presidential election years. However, midterm years in recent decades have provided super buying opportunities for that's where important bottoms occurred.

FIGURE 31

"SIX" YEARS

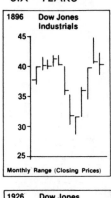

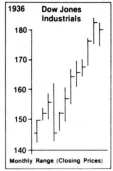

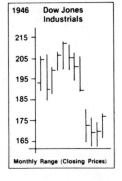

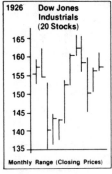

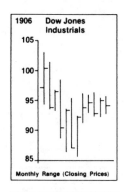

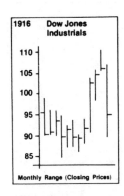

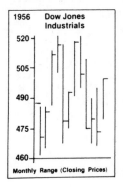

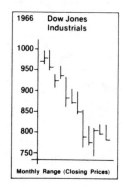

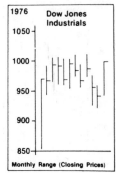

THE SEVENTH YEAR OF DECADES

Of the eight "seven" years in this century, only 1927 and 1967 were sizeable winners and both were pre-presidential election years. The six others were rather terrible (1977 was off 17.3%). Prospects for pre-election 1987 are better.

FIGURE 32

"SEVEN" YEARS

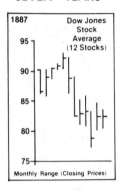

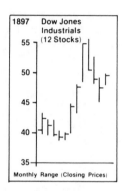

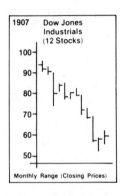

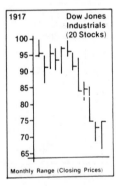

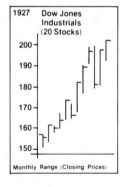

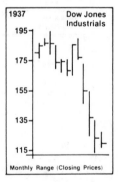

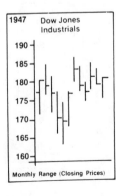

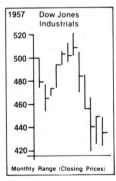

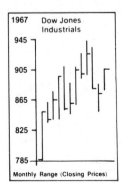

THE EIGHTH YEAR OF DECADES

"Eight" years are great years, like the "five" years. Only 1888 and 1948 were slightly negative. 1978's "October Massacre" caused Dow to be off 3.1% while the S&P 500 was up 1.1% for the year. The race for the White House in 1988 may strongly influence the market.

FIGURE 33

"EIGHT" YEARS

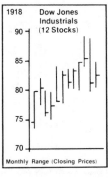

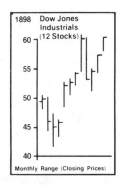

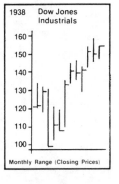

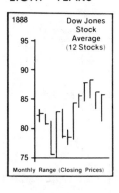

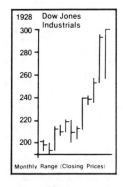

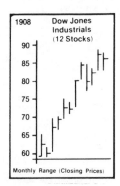

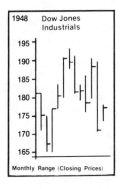

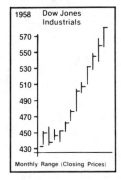

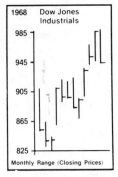

THE NINTH YEAR OF DECADES

Excluding 1929 and 1969, the "nine" years have been moderate gainers on balance. Pre-election years have fared best. The 20% drop within December 1899 was caused by British reverses in the Boer War and the capture of Winston Churchill. Despite another "October Massacre" and the Iran situation, Dow ended 1979 up 4.2%.

FIGURE 34

"NINE" YEARS

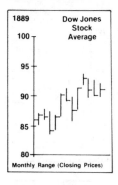
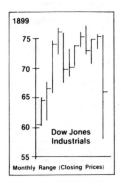
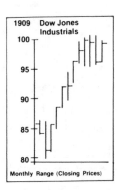
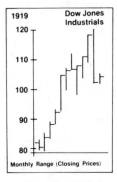
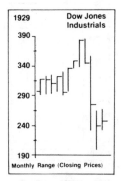
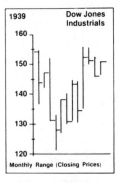
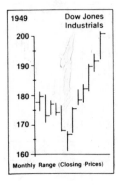
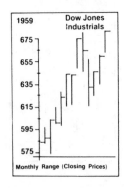
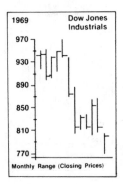

THE TENTH YEAR OF DECADES

Zero years have been dreadful years or have at least been hit hard before turning up in 1900 (September), 1950 (July), 1970 (May), and 1980 (March). Iran holding U.S. hostages affected all of 1980 and Carter's stature. Nevertheless, the Dow was up 14.9%.

FIGURE 35

"ZERO" YEARS

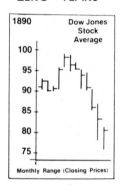

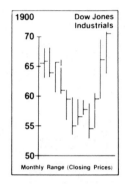

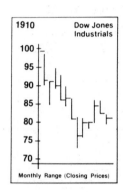

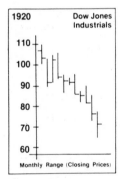

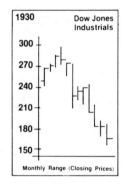

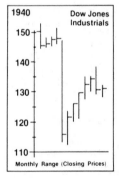

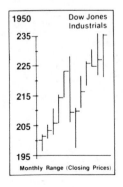

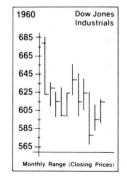

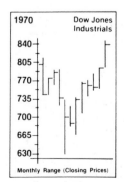

8
THE JANUARY BAROMETER

WHAT THE MARKET DOES IN JANUARY OFTEN SETS THE TONE FOR THE WHOLE YEAR

"As Maine goes, so goes the nation," they used to say in American political circles during presidential election years. We may have something similar in the stock market—*As January goes, so goes the rest of the year.*

It's just incredible how the January Barometer has consistently predicted the annual course of the stock market since 1950. I know of no other indicator that comes within a country mile of matching J.B.'s forecasting record. Based on whether the Standard & Poor's composite index is up or down in January, the market for most of the year has in essence followed suit thirty-one out of thirty-six years. What indicator sports an 86% batting average for even short spans of time?

Table 40 shows January performances chronologically and by rank. Note the top nineteen Januarys had gains of over 1% and launched the best market years of the period. Of the other sixteen Januarys, most were losers or had minuscule gains. The eleven bear market years since 1950 were all preceded by inferior Januarys. Just one great year followed a January loss and only three errors—1966, 1968 and 1982—were significant.

TABLE 40

AS JANUARY GOES, SO GOES THE YEAR

	Market Performance in January					January Performance by Rank	
Year	Previous Year's Close	January Close	January Change	Rank	Year	January Change	Year's Change
1950	16.76*	17.05*	1.7%	1.	1975	12.3%	31.5%
1951	20.41	21.66	6.1	2.	1976	11.8	19.1
1952	23.77	24.14	1.6	3.	1967	7.8	20.1
1953	26.57	26.38	−0.7	4.	1985	7.4	26.3
1954	24.81	26.08	5.1	5.	1961	6.3	23.1
1955	35.98	36.63	1.8	6.	1951	6.1	16.5
1956	45.48	43.82	−3.7	7.	1980	5.8	25.8
1957	46.67	44.72	−4.2	8.	1954	5.1	45.0
1958	39.99	41.70	4.3	9.	1963	4.9	18.9
1959	55.21	55.42	0.4	10.	1958	4.3	38.1
1960	59.89	55.61	−7.1	11.	1971	4.0	10.8
1961	58.11	61.78	6.3	12.	1979	4.0	12.3
1962	71.55	68.84	−3.8	13.	1983	3.3	17.3
1963	63.10	66.20	4.9	14.	1965	3.3	9.1
1964	75.02	77.04	2.7	15.	1964	2.7	13.0
1965	84.75	87.56	3.3	16.	1955	1.8	26.4
1966	92.43	92.88	0.5	17.	1972	1.8	15.6
1967	80.33	86.61	7.8	18.	1950	1.7	21.8
1968	96.47	92.24	−4.4	19.	1952	1.6	11.8
1969	103.86	103.01	−0.8	20.	1966	0.5	−13.1
1970	92.06	85.02	−7.6	21.	1959	0.4	8.5
1971	92.15	95.88	4.0	22.	1953	−0.7	− 6.6
1972	102.09	103.94	1.8	23.	1969	−0.8	−11.4
1973	118.05	116.03	−1.7	24.	1984	−0.9	1.4
1974	97.55	96.57	−1.0	25.	1974	−1.0	−29.7
1975	68.56	76.98	12.3	26.	1973	−1.7	−17.4
1976	90.19	100.86	11.8	27.	1982	−1.8	14.8
1977	107.46	102.03	−5.1	28.	1956	−3.6	2.6
1978	95.10	89.25	−6.2	29.	1962	−3.8	−11.8
1979	96.11	99.93	4.0	30.	1957	−4.2	−14.3
1980	107.94	114.16	5.8	31.	1968	−4.4	7.7
1981	135.76	129.55	−4.6	32.	1981	−4.6	− 9.7
1982	122.55	120.40	−1.8	33.	1977	−5.1	−11.5
1983	140.64	145.30	3.3	34.	1978	−6.2	1.1
1984	164.93	163.41	−0.9	35.	1960	−7.1	− 3.0
1985	167.24	179.63	7.4	36.	1970	−7.6	0.1

*S & P Composite Index

1933 "LAME DUCK" AMENDMENT REASON JANUARY BAROMETER WORKS

Until 1973, I never understood why the market in January was its own best indicator for the whole year. By researching back to the beginning of the century, I was able to discover why. Table 41 shows that in the 1901-1933 period the market direction in January was similar to that of the whole year (including January) nineteen times and different fourteen times. (Omitting

FIGURE 36

JANUARY BAROMETER IN GRAPHIC FORM

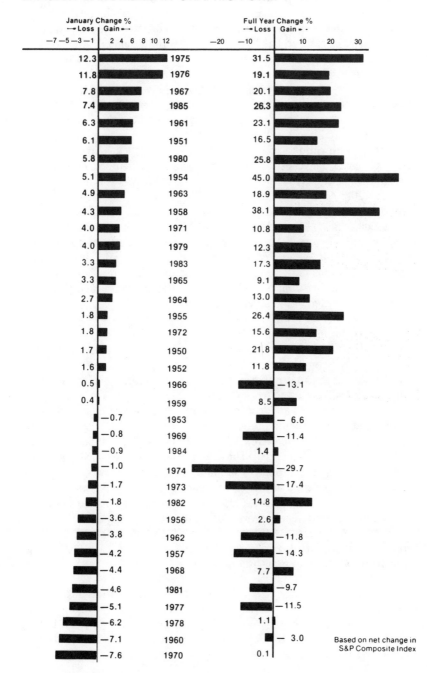

January Change %	Year	Full Year Change %
12.3	1975	31.5
11.8	1976	19.1
7.8	1967	20.1
7.4	1985	26.3
6.3	1961	23.1
6.1	1951	16.5
5.8	1980	25.8
5.1	1954	45.0
4.9	1963	18.9
4.3	1958	38.1
4.0	1971	10.8
4.0	1979	12.3
3.3	1983	17.3
3.3	1965	9.1
2.7	1964	13.0
1.8	1955	26.4
1.8	1972	15.6
1.7	1950	21.8
1.6	1952	11.8
0.5	1966	−13.1
0.4	1959	8.5
−0.7	1953	− 6.6
−0.8	1969	−11.4
−0.9	1984	1.4
−1.0	1974	−29.7
−1.7	1973	−17.4
−1.8	1982	14.8
−3.6	1956	2.6
−3.8	1962	−11.8
−4.2	1957	−14.3
−4.4	1968	7.7
−4.6	1981	−9.7
−5.1	1977	−11.5
−6.2	1978	1.1
−7.1	1960	− 3.0
−7.6	1970	0.1

Based on net change in
S&P Composite Index

January, there were sixteen similar and seventeen dissimilar years.)

However, a dramatic change occurred in 1934. Since then, the market in January has correctly indicated its annual trend in forty out of fifty years for an 80% batting average. (Excluding January produces thirty-five similar years out of fifty.) When I found what I believed to be the explanation I blurted out, "Eureka!" The answer was the Twentieth Amendment to the Constitution.

Prior to 1934, Congress convened the first Monday of each December. Senators and representatives, newly elected in November, did not take office until December the following year, **thirteen months later.** Defeated congressmen were still able to stay in Congress for all of the following session. They were known as "lame ducks."

With the ratification of the Twentieth or "Lame Duck" Amendment in 1933, Congress convenes January 3 and includes as members those newly elected the previous November. (Inauguration Day was also moved up to January 20.) As a result, several vital events which greatly affect our economy and the future course of the stock market have been squeezed into January: the "genuine" members of Congress convene and indicate their mood and direction; the President gives his State of the Union message, presents the annual fiscal budget, and sets national goals and priorities. It seems quite likely that if these most important events were switched to another month or occurred at different times each year, the January Barometer would surely lose its effectiveness.

If you wonder why three of the first four signals starting with 1934 were wrong, bear in mind that the Democrats had the most lopsided congressional margins in its history between 1933 and 1938, so there were no surprises expected come January.

It's interesting to note that in the forty-eight years since the January Barometer really began to work (thanks to the Lame Duck Amendment), we have not witnessed an error in an odd year. (Newly-elected congresses always convene for the first time in January of odd years.) The major errors have occurred in even years. Those in 1946, 1956, and 1966 were at the tail end of strong bull markets. The negative signal of 1968 was in question the moment President Johnson simultaneously stated he would not be a candidate for reelection and ordered a halt to the Vietnam bombing. The negative signals of 1970, 1978, and 1982 were in bear markets that extended into second years before ending. In the two decades prior, bear markets were always over within six to ten months. An election year mini-bear loss of 10% lasted for the first seven months of 1984—the one in 1960 lasted two months longer.

TABLE 41

MARKET DIRECTION FOR JANUARY AND WHOLE YEAR (1901-1985)

PRIOR TO 20TH AMENDMENT

January %Change*	Year's %Change*	Same	Opposite
−5.5%	− 8.7%	1901	
0.6	− 0.4		1902
1.4	−23.6		1903
−0.4	41.7		1904
2.5	38.2	1905	
4.7	− 1.9		1906
−2.8	−37.7	1907	
6.7	46.6	1908	
−2.4	15.0		1909
−7.2	−17.9	1910	
4.4	0.4	1911	
−1.8	7.6		1912
−4.7	−10.3	1913	
5.2	− 5.1		1914
7.5	86.5	1915	
−8.6	− 4.2	1916	
0.4	−21.7		1917
7.3	10.5	1918	
−2.0	30.5		1919
−3.2	−32.9	1920	
5.8	12.7	1921	
0.2	21.7	1922	
−1.3	− 3.3	1923	
5.4	26.2	1924	
2.2	30.0	1925	
0.5	0.3	1926	
−0.5	28.8		1927
−1.9	49.0		1928
5.7	−13.5		1929
6.2	−28.4		1930
4.8	−47.0		1931
−2.8	−15.1	1932	
0.7	46.5	1933	

*Dow Industrials 1901-1928; S&P 500 1929 to present

AFTER 20TH AMENDMENT

January %Change*	Year's %Change*	Same	Opposite
10.6%	− 6.0%		1934
−4.2	41.2		1935
6.6	28.0	1936	
3.8	−38.6		1937
1.3	25.2	1938	
−6.9	− 5.4	1939	
−3.6	−15.3	1940	
−4.8	−17.9	1941	
1.4	12.4	1942	
7.2	19.4	1943	
1.5	13.8	1944	
1.4	30.7	1945	
7.0	−11.9		1946
2.4	0.0	1947	
−4.0	− 0.7	1948	
0.1	10.3	1949	
1.7	21.8	1950	
6.1	16.5	1951	
1.6	11.8	1952	
−0.7	− 6.6	1953	
5.1	45.0	1954	
1.8	26.4	1955	
−3.6	2.6		1956
−4.2	−14.3	1957	
4.3	38.1	1958	
0.4	8.5	1959	
−7.1	− 3.0	1960	
6.3	23.1	1961	
−3.8	−11.8	1962	
4.9	18.9	1963	
2.7	13.0	1964	
3.3	9.1	1965	
0.5	−13.1		1966
7.8	20.1	1967	
−4.4	7.7		1968
−0.8	−11.4	1969	
−7.6	0.1		1970
4.0	10.8	1971	
1.8	15.6	1972	
−1.7	−17.4	1973	
−1.0	−29.7	1974	
12.3	31.5	1975	
11.8	19.1	1976	
−5.1	−11.5	1977	
−6.2	1.1		1978
4.0	12.3	1979	
5.8	25.8	1980	
−4.6	− 9.7	1981	
−1.8	14.8		1982
3.3	17.3	1983	
−0.9	1.4		1984
7.4	26.3	1985	

JANUARY'S "EARLY WARNING" SYSTEM: ONLY FIVE MAJOR ERRORS IN THIRTY-SIX YEARS

January followers can often get a glimpse of what lies ahead by watching the market's action during the first five trading days of the month. These five days serve as an excellent "early warning" system with a batting average almost equal to the January Barometer's 86%.

Early January gains since 1950 were matched by whole-year gains with two exceptions: 1973 and 1966. On twelve occasions, January got off to a bad start, and eight of these years ended on the downside. The four that didn't follow suit were 1955, 1956, 1978, and 1982. And both

TABLE 42

THE FIRST-FIVE-DAYS-IN-JANUARY INDICATOR

	Chronologic Data				Ranked By Performance		
Year	Previous Year's Close	5th Day in January	Change 1st 5 Days	Rank	Year	Change 1st 5 Days	Change For Year
1950	16.76*	17.09*	2.0%	1.	1976	4.9%	19.1%
1951	20.41	20.88	2.3	2.	1983	3.2	17.3
1952	23.77	23.91	0.6	3.	1967	3.1	20.1
1953	26.57	26.33	—0.9	4.	1979	2.8	12.3
1954	24.81	24.93	0.5	5.	1963	2.6	18.9
1955	35.98	35.33	—1.8	6.	1958	2.5	38.1
1956	45.48	44.51	—2.1	7.	1984	2.4	1.4
1957	46.67	46.25	—0.9	8.	1951	2.3	16.5
1958	39.99	40.99	2.5	9.	1975	2.2	31.5
1959	55.21	55.40	0.3	10.	1950	2.0	21.8
1960	59.89	59.50	—0.7	11.	1973	1.5	—17.4
1961	58.11	58.81	1.2	12.	1972	1.4	15.6
1962	71.55	69.12	—3.4	13.	1964	1.3	13.0
1963	63.10	64.74	2.6	14.	1961	1.2	23.1
1964	75.02	76.00	1.3	15.	1980	0.9	25.8
1965	84.75	85.37	0.7	16.	1966	0.8	—13.1
1966	92.43	93.14	0.8	17.	1965	0.7	9.1
1967	80.33	82.81	3.1	18.	1970	0.7	0.1
1968	96.47	96.62	0.2	19.	1952	0.6	11.8
1969	103.86	100.80	—2.9	20.	1954	0.5	45.0
1970	92.06	92.68	0.7	21.	1959	0.3	8.5
1971	92.15	92.19	0.0	22.	1968	0.2	7.7
1972	102.09	103.47	1.4	23.	1971	0.0	10.8
1973	118.05	119.85	1.5	24.	1960	—0.7	— 3.0
1974	97.55	96.12	—1.5	25.	1953	—0.9	— 6.6
1975	68.56	70.04	2.2	26.	1957	—0.9	—14.3
1976	90.19	94.58	4.9	27.	1974	—1.5	—29.7
1977	107.46	105.01	—2.3	28.	1955	—1.8	26.4
1978	95.10	90.69	—4.6	29.	1985	—1.9	26.3
1979	96.11	98.80	2.8	30.	1981	—2.0	— 9.7
1980	107.94	108.95	0.9	31.	1956	—2.1	2.6
1981	135.76	133.06	—2.0	32.	1977	—2.3	—11.5
1982	122.55	119.55	—2.4	33.	1982	—2.4	14.8
1983	140.64	145.18	3.2	34.	1969	—2.9	—11.4
1984	164.93	168.90	2.4	35.	1962	—3.4	—11.8
1985	167.24	163.99	—1.9	36.	1978	—4.6	1.1

*S & P Composite Index

TABLE 43

EVALUATION OF FIRST FIVE DAYS VS. ALL OF JANUARY

Year	Change 1st 5 Days*	January Change*	Change For Year*	Interpretation
1976	4.9%	11.8%	19.1%	BULLISH: Rise in first five trading
1983	3.2	3.3	17.3	days held onto, or followed by ad-
1967	3.1	7.8	20.1	ditional gain, during the rest of the
1979	2.8	4.0	12.3	month. Practically all of the best
1963	2.6	4.9	18.9	years since 1950 fall into this
1958	2.5	4.3	38.1	category. (Arbitrarily, we allowed
1951	2.3	6.1	16.5	1950 to remain here as it only gave
1975	2.2	12.3	31.5	up a small fraction of its early
1950	2.0	1.7	21.8	January substantial gain.)
1972	1.4	1.8	15.6	
1964	1.3	2.7	13.0	
1961	1.2	6.3	23.1	
1980	0.9	5.8	25.8	
1965	0.7	3.3	9.1	
1952	0.6	1.6	11.8	
1954	0.5	5.1	45.0	
1959	0.3	0.4	8.5	
1971	0.0	4.0	10.8	BULLISH: Loss or neutral at start;
1955	—1.8	1.8	26.4	reversal later.
1985	—1.9	7.4	??	
1984	2.4	—0.9	1.4	BEARISH: Early gain given up in
1973	1.5	—1.7	—17.4	part or entirety. Only 1968 good
1966	0.8	0.5	—13.1	(Johnson's "abdication").
1970	0.7	—7.6	0.1	
1968	0.2	—4.4	7.7	
1960	—0.7	—7.1	— 3.0	BEARISH: Early loss with market
1953	—0.9	—0.7	— 6.6	still in minus column at month's
1957	—0.9	—4.2	—14.3	end despite some improvement.
1974	—1.5	—1.0	—29.7	All bear market years, except 1956
1981	—2.0	—4.6	— 9.7	and 1978, both of which didn't do
1956	—2.1	—3.6	2.6	too much anyway, and 1982, which
1977	—2.3	—5.1	—11.5	changed from bear to bull status in
1982	—2.4	—1.8	14.8	August.
1969	—2.9	—0.8	—11.4	
1962	—3.4	—3.8	—11.8	
1978	—4.6	—6.2	1.1	* Based on S&P Composite Index.

1956 and 1978 were up just a smidgen.

Do a little forecasting on your own! Use Standard & Poor's composite index. Remember, though, that five days is a brief span and that some extraordinary event (such as the imminence of the Vietnam cease-fire in early January 1973) could affect the market's normal indication.

THE JANUARY BAROMETER CHECK AND BALANCE SYSTEM

By comparing the percentage changes of January's first five trading days to those of the entire month, I was able to devise a method which almost gives the January Barometer a perfect record. See if you agree with my interpretations!

Table 43 divides the last thirty-six years into four classifications —two bullish, two bearish. The two bullish categories contain the twenty best years. The dominant pattern is that the initial rise was followed by gains the remainder of the month. Three years started off negatively but then experienced bullish reversals during January's remaining days and the rest of the year.

Our first bearish category consisted of five years in which January lost all or part of its early gain. The eleven years in which January began with a loss and ended with a loss were put into the second bearish category. Only 1982 was far off the mark.

SOLID PROOF JANUARY BAROMETER OUTPERFORMS ALL OTHER MONTHLY BAROMETERS

Since I developed the January Barometer years ago, I have had to defend it from critics on occasion. The two chief complaints were: 1) January's performance was unfairly included in the year as a whole and 2) I failed to include results prior to 1950. The first point is valid, but Table 44 shows that the J.B. works just as well or better using "subsequent eleven-month performance." As for the second point, I have always dismissed the first third of the century and have demonstrated in Table 41 that prior to the passage of the Lame Duck Amendment to the Constitution in 1933, the J.B. did not work at all.

An article in *Barron's* (March 1984) made light of the J.B. and contended other months had a better track record. This is untrue! By hand and computer using the S&P index, I calculated results for each month as a barometer of its own fiscal year, and of its subsequent eleven months. I then tallied the 34½-year performance for all months. January is still king!

Some critics claim a $10,000 buy and hold strategy for the 34½-year period would have left you better off. Investing $10,000 with the J.B. for subsequent eleven-month periods would have pyramided to $148,724 in 34½ years. In the same time period, a holder's $10,000 would have grown to $98,407.

TABLE 44

JANUARY BAROMETER VS. OTHER MONTHLY BAROMETERS

Net Gains January 1950-June 1984 (34½ Years)

	12 Months (Month Included)	Subsequent 11 Months	Ranked by 11-Months Performance		
			Barometer	11 Months	12 Months
JAN	460.7%	305.0%	JAN	305.0%	460.7%
FEB	152.2	72.1	APR	175.4	308.4
MAR	179.3	86.7	NOV	128.9	245.0
APR	308.4	175.4	MAR	86.7	179.3
MAY	111.4	4.9	FEB	72.1	152.2
JUN	101.9	— 5.3	DEC	42.4	137.6
JUL	141.8	16.0	JUL	16.0	141.8
AUG	142.2	13.5	AUG	13.5	142.2
SEP	41.2*	— 74.9	MAY	4.9	111.4
OCT	81.9	— 43.6	JUN	— 5.3	101.9
NOV	245.0	128.9	OCT	— 43.6	81.9
DEC	137.6	42.4	SEP	— 74.9	41.2

9
12-MONTH
SEASONAL STRATEGIST

TWELVE-MONTH SEASONAL
STRATEGIST

In nineteen annual editions of the *Stock Trader's Almanac* I have made many accurate forecasts for coming years. My sense of timing evolved out of my study of the recurring patterns within these covers. As you become familiar with the political/stock market cycle, the concept of "contrary opinion," the Stoken System, the January Barometer and market bias at certain times of the day, week, month, and year, it is my firm belief that you, the reader, will be able to forecast many market trends with accuracy and confidence.

I have laid out the Twelve-Month Seasonal Strategist chronologically to help you keep track of the market on a month-by-month basis:

• *Monthly Almanac* lists the idiosyncrasies of the month, its record, seasonality.

• *Ten years of daily price changes* shows how much the Dow Jones industrials were up or down for each day of that month over the past ten years.

• *Market probability chart* for the month and both the months before and after, shows the chance of the market rising on any particular trading day.

• *Seasonal phenomena* recurring within the month follow on additional pages.

FIGURE 37

JANUARY DAILY PROBABILITY CHART

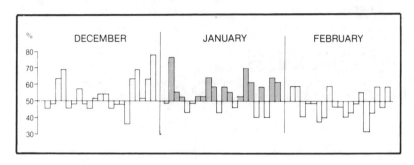

THE JANUARY ALMANAC

• AS JANUARY GOES, SO GOES THE YEAR

• GREATEST CONCENTRATION OF TURNDOWNS SINCE 1949 OCCURRED IN MONTH'S FIRST SIX TRADING DAYS

• WORST FIVE LOSERS OF THIRTY DOW JONES IN- DUSTRIALS TEND TO OUTPERFORM BEST FIVE IN LAST-THROUGH-THE-FIRST WEEKS OF YEAR

• JANUARY BAROMETER OUTPERFORMS ALL OTHER MONTHLY BAROMETERS (See Table 44)

• PURCHASES IN JANUARY FOR ONE-, TWO-, THREE-, OR SIX-MONTH PERIODS HAVE PRO- DUCED JUST AVERAGE GAINS FOR MOST YEARS. THIS HAS AMOUNTED TO AN AVERAGE CHANGE OF 0.56% PER MONTH

• JANUARYS OFTEN PERFORM WELL FOLLOWING BEAR MARKET YEARS

• TEN OF THE LAST ELEVEN JANUARYS HAD MUCH LARGER PERCENT CHANGES THAN THE PREVIOUS TWENTY-FIVE YEARS—JANUARY IS MORE VOLATILE THAN ALL OTHER MONTHS

• THE ONLY JANUARY IN A PRESIDENTIAL ELEC-
TION YEAR THAT PRODUCED A GIANT GAIN WAS
1976, UP 122.87 DOW POINTS FOR A GAIN OF 14.4%.
OTHER SIZEABLE GAINERS IN THIS CENTURY
WERE: 1908 (6.7%), 1924 (5.4%), AND 1980 (4.4%). THE
DOW WAS DOWN 3.0% IN 1984

• ALL ELEVEN PRE-ELECTION YEAR JANUARYS
SINCE THE THIRTIES HAVE SEEN A RISE IN THE
DOW, THE LAST SIX HAVE GAINED 6.3% ON
AVERAGE, EQUAL TO 86 DOW POINTS AT CUR-
RENT LEVELS.

• NOT ONE LOSING PRE-ELECTION YEAR SINCE
1939 AND JUST ONE BAD LOSS (1931) SINCE 1907,
AVERAGE CHANGE 16.8%

TABLE 45

JANUARY DAILY POINT CHANGES DOW JONES INDUSTRIALS

	1976	1977	1978	1979	1980	1981	1982	1983	1984	1985
Previous Month Close	852.41	1004.65	831.17	805.01	838.74	963.99	875.00	1046.54	1258.64	1211.57
1	H	H	H	H	H	H	H	H	H	H
2	6.30	—	—	6.41	−14.17	8.79	—	—	—	−12.70
3	—	− 4.90	−13.43	5.97	− 4.26	—	—	−19.50	− 5.90	− 9.05
4	—	−11.88	− 4.16	8.75	8.53	—	7.52	19.04	16.31	− 4.86
5	19.12	− 9.81	− 8.66	4.59	—	19.88	−17.22	− 1.19	13.19	—
6	12.99	1.83	−11.43	—	—	12.03	− 4.28	26.03	4.40	—
7	7.87	3.24	—	—	3.16	−23.80	0.76	5.15	—	5.63
8	9.29	—	—	− 2.59	19.71	−15.19	4.75	—	—	1.11
9	3.15	—	− 8.93	3.29	− 1.62	2.99	—	—	− 0.42	11.04
10	—	3.74	− 3.03	− 6.50	8.87	—	—	16.28	− 7.74	20.76
11	—	−10.22	− 5.63	3.12	− 0.43	—	−16.07	− 8.56	− 1.16	− 5.41
12	11.26	− 8.40	2.25	8.23	—	0.08	− 2.76	− 0.18	1.99	—
13	− 9.45	7.90	− 2.42	—	—	− 3.67	− 8.75	− 9.66	− 9.21	—
14	16.69	− 3.99	—	—	5.04	1.37	3.33	6.70	—	16.45
15	− 5.12	—	—	12.39	5.03	3.50	5.32	—	—	− 3.75
16	5.12	—	− 3.99	−13.08	− 3.41	3.32	—	—	− 2.51	− 0.11
17	—	− 4.91	7.28	− 1.39	− 1.62	—	—	3.96	3.87	− 1.99
18	—	− 4.82	7.28	4.94	3.58	—	7.52	− 5.16	− 2.09	− 1.33
19	14.09	6.24	− 7.63	− 1.65	—	− 2.30	− 7.71	−11.59	− 3.35	—
20	6.14	− 9.64	− 1.73	—	—	−20.31	− 1.52	2.76	− 6.91	—
21	− 3.62	3.40	—	—	5.63	− 4.43	2.38	−17.84	—	34.01
22	− 2.76	—	—	1.04	− 6.57	− 5.81	− 3.24	—	—	− 1.87
23	10.47	—	− 6.24	8.32	11.35	− 0.25	—	—	−14.66	15.23
24	—	1.17	0.87	− 0.44	2.39	—	—	−22.81	− 1.57	− 4.30
25	—	2.32	0.87	8.23	− 3.84	—	− 2.28	11.86	−10.99	5.63
26	7.56	− 7.39	− 9.10	5.11	—	− 1.28	− 1.24	− 4.04	− 2.20	—
27	− 3.70	− 3.99	0.78	—	—	10.58	1.15	25.66	0.31	—
28	− 6.46	2.99	—	—	2.39	− 6.91	21.59	1.10	—	1.77
29	17.40	—	—	− 3.98	− 4.10	6.31	6.85	—	—	14.79
30	6.53	—	8.32	− 3.99	7.51	− 1.62	—	—	− 8.48	− 4.74
31	—	− 3.16	− 2.52	−12.56	− 6.06	—	—	10.95	− 0.94	− 1.11
Close	975.28	954.37	769.92	839.22	875.85	947.27	871.10	1075.70	1220.58	1286.77
Change	122.87	−50.28	−61.25	34.21	37.11	−16.72	− 3.90	29.16	−38.06	75.20

COMBINING THE SANTA CLAUS RALLY WITH THE JANUARY BAROMETER

Since many readers may attempt to combine the Santa Claus Rally and the January Barometer into a series of indicators, I am making it easier by placing the pertinent data on one page. For additional clarity, twelve bear market years have been screened. These, plus six others, have

TABLE 46
_____

FROM SANTA CLAUS RALLY
THROUGH JANUARY BAROMETER

Previous Santa Claus Rally	Year	1st 5 Days Change	January Change	Year's Change
1.8%	1953*	−0.9%	−0.7%	− 6.6%
1.3	1954	0.5	5.1	45.0
3.8	1955	−1.8	1.8	26.4
−1.2	1956*	−2.1	−3.6	2.6
0.5	1957*	−0.9	−4.2	−14.3
3.3	1958	2.5	4.3	38.1
4.1	1959*	0.3	0.4	8.5
2.3	1960*	−0.7	−7.1	− 3.0
1.7	1961	1.2	6.3	23.1
0.4	1962*	−3.4	−3.8	−11.8
1.7	1963	2.6	4.9	18.9
2.1	1964	1.3	2.7	13.0
0.6	1965*	0.7	3.3	9.1
0.7	1966*	0.8	0.5	−13.1
−1.2	1967	3.1	7.8	20.1
0.5	1968*	0.2	−4.4	7.7
−1.1	1969*	−2.9	−0.8	−11.4
3.6	1970*	0.7	−7.6	0.1
1.9	1971	0.0	4.0	10.8
1.0	1972	1.4	1.8	15.6
3.1	1973	1.5	−1.7	−17.4
6.6	1974*	−1.5	−1.0	−29.7
7.1	1975	2.2	12.3	31.5
4.3	1976	4.9	11.8	19.1
0.9	1977*	−2.3	−5.1	−11.5
0.0	1978*	−4.6	−6.2	1.1
3.2	1979	2.8	4.0	12.3
−2.1	1980*	0.9	5.8	25.8
1.9	1981*	−2.0	−4.6	− 9.7
−1.8	1982*	−2.4	−1.8	14.8
1.3	1983	3.2	3.3	17.3
1.8	1984	2.4	−0.9	1.4
−0.6	1985*	−1.9	7.4	26.3

% —All % changes based on S&P composite index
* —Denotes loss or less than 1% gain in 2 of 3 periods
Grey Screen—Bear market years

asterisks signifying that two of their three indicators (S.C. Rally, the first five days of Jan., and the J.B.) had losses or minuscule gains of less than 1%.

The sixteen best years, with double-digit gains, have no asterisks, except 1980, 1982, and 1985. The fifteen years, marked with asterisks, had either losses for the entire year or only single-digit gains. One exception was 1973. The S.C. Rally and the first five days of January were bullish because of the euphoria of the Vietnam Armistice, but the year as a whole was down. Another exception was 1984.

Bear markets of the fifties and sixties lasted less than a year, and the last year of the bull markets that followed had single digit gains: 1956, 2.6%; 1959, 8.5%; 1965, 9.1%; and 1968, 7.7%.

The unholy trinity of Vietnam, Watergate, and OPEC caused longer bear markets thereafter. However, the bull market that erupted in August 1982 erased the year's loss and then some.

The data from Table 46 has been rearranged into three groups in chronologic order: the best (double-digit gains), the next best (single-digit gains), and the worst (mostly first or second years of a bear market).

In the last column I have awarded points to the three periods in the following manner: Santa Claus rally—one point; the first five days—two points; full month of January—three points. Gains of more than 1%, add allotted points. Gains of less than 1% or losses, subtract allotted points. Election years receive one added point. Post-election years, deduct one point.

Best years have double-digit gains, solid Januarys, and not more than one bad period. (Three exceptions: the Iranian situation affected the market at the start of 1980; a bear market carried over into 1982 for eight additional months; and 1985 fooled those expecting the usual post-election bear year.) Other years, except 1973 and 1984, have at least two bad periods. The election cycle may be too well known, with too many trying to anticipate its usual tendencies. As the market in 1984 and 1985 did the opposite of what was expected, perhaps people will ignore the elction cycle and not play the anticipation game for a while.

TABLE 47

SANTA CLAUS RALLY/JANUARY POINT SYSTEM

Santa Claus Rally/January Point System	Year	1st 5 Days Change	January Change	Year's Change	Points
		GROUP (1) THE 15 BEST YEARS			
1.3%	1954	0.5%	5.1%	45.0%	2
3.8	1955	—I.8	1.8	26.4	2
3.3	1958	2.5	4.3	38.1	6
1.7	1961P	1.2	6.3	23.1	5
1.7	1963	2.6	4.9	18.9	6
2.1	1964E	1.3	2.7	13.0	7
—1.2	1967	3.1	7.8	20.1	4
1.9	1971	0.0	4.0	10.8	2
1.0	1972E	1.4	1.8	15.6	7
7.1	1975	2.2	12.3	31.5	6
4.3	1976E	4.9	11.8	19.1	7
3.2	1979	2.8	4.0	12.3	6
—2.1	1980E	0.9	5.8	25.8	1
—1.8	1982	—2.4	—1.8	14.8	—6
1.3	1983	3.2	3.3	17.3	6
0.6	1985	—1.9	7.4	26.3	—1
		GROUP (2) THE 5 NEXT BEST YEARS			
—1.2	1956E	—2.1	—3.6	2.6	—5
4.1	1959	0.3	0.4	8.5	—4
0.6	1965P	0.7	3.3	9.1	—1
0.5	1968E	0.2	—4.4	7.7	—5
1.8	1984E	2.4	—0.9	1.4	1
		GROUP (3) THE 12 WORST YEARS			
1.8	1953P	—0.9	—0.7	—6.6	—5
0.5	1957P	—0.9	—4.2	—14.3	—7
2.3	1960E	—0.7	—7.1	—3.0	—3
0.4	1962	—3.4	—3.8	—11.8	—6
0.7	1966	0.8	0.5	—13.1	—6
—1.1	1969P	—2.9	—0.8	—11.4	—7
3.6	1970	0.7	—7.6	0.1	—4
3.1	1973P	1.5	—1.7	—17.4	—1
6.6	1974	—1.5	—1.0	—29.7	—4
0.9	1977P	—2.3	—5.1	—11.5	—7
0.0	1978	—4.6	—6.2	1.1	—6
1.9	1981P	—2.0	—4.6	—9.7	—5

% — All % changes based on S&P composite index
E — Election year
P — Post-election year

FIGURE 38

FEBRUARY DAILY PROBABILITY CHART

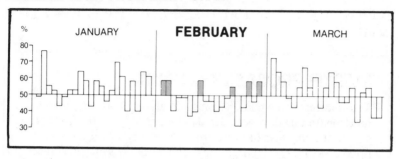

THE FEBRUARY ALMANAC

• SHARP JANUARY MOVES TEND TO CONSOLIDATE IN FEBRUARY

• IF JANUARY IS UP, STAY IN; IF DOWN, MOVE TO SIDELINES

• FEBRUARY BOX SCORE: 17 UP, 19 DOWN

• BEST GAINS IN 1975 (+6.0%) AND 1970 (+5.3%)

• FEBRUARY'S AVERAGE CHANGE IS -0.5%, SECOND WORST MONTH NEXT TO MAY SINCE 1950

• MANY ANALYSTS MAY REVISE ANNUAL FORECASTS AT THE BEGINNING OF FEBRUARY BASED ON WHETHER THE MARKET GAINED OR LOST GROUND IN JANUARY, AS THE REST OF THE YEAR FOLLOWS THE LEAD OF THE FIRST MONTH'S PERFORMANCE, ESPECIALLY IN ODD YEARS

• BUYING IN FEBRUARY FOR 30- OR 60-DAY PERIODS HAS PRODUCED ABOVE-AVERAGE RESULTS IN THE PAST

• AIRLINE STOCKS TEND TO TURN IN THEIR BEST PERFORMANCE IN THE FIRST QUARTER. AEROSPACE STOCKS TEND TO HAVE A SEASONAL BIAS OF RISING THROUGH THE FALL AND PEAKING IN JANUARY IN ANTICIPATION OF WHAT

NEWLY ELECTED CONGRESSES MIGHT DO

• FEW IMPORTANT MOVES BEGIN OR END IN THIS MONTH

MARKET PROBABILITY CHART

The chances of the market rising on any of February's typical nineteen trading days is depicted in Figure 38. Both the first and second trading days of one third of a century's Februarys were up 57.6% of the time; in contrast, the third day's up percentage was 39.4% and the fifth from last was up only 30.3% of the time. A composite of such percentages for all months since May 1952 is presented in Figure 39. Upward bias for the beginnings and endings of most months can be seen at a glance. A Market Probability Calendar for each day in 1986 appears as well (Table 49).

TABLE 48

FEBRUARY DAILY POINT CHANGES DOW JONES INDUSTRIALS

Previous Month Close	1976 975.28	1977 954.37	1978 769.92	1979 839.22	1980 875.85	1981 947.27	1982 871.10	1983 1075.70	1984 1220.58	1985 1286.77
1	—	3.99	4.42	1.65	5.63	—	— 19.41	— 15.91	— 8.27	— 9.05
2	— 3.93	— 5.57	1.04	— 6.24	—	— 15.02	0.86	2.85	1.57	—
3	1.26	— 5.65	— 4.42	—	—	9.13	— 7.52	2.02	— 16.85	—
4	4.01	0.75	—	—	— 6.39	0.60	2.00	13.25	—	12.36
5	— 11.81	—	—	— 10.65	1.53	4.78	4.00	—	—	— 4.85
6	— 9.91	—	— 2.34	— 1.13	5.21	5.54	—	—	— 22.72	— 4.64
7	—	— 1.58	10.23	— 6.84	3.66	—	—	9.19	6.18	9.49
8	—	— 4.07	3.81	2.86	10.24	—	— 17.60	— 11.77	— 24.19	— 0.11
9	2.28	— 8.40	— 4.85	3.46	—	— 5.12	— 2.86	— 7.91	— 3.56	—
10	11.57	4.08	— 1.82	—	—	1.45	6.09	20.33	7.96	—
11	3.15	— 6.40	—	—	— 6.14	— 6.14	— 1.99	— 1.25	—	— 13.91
12	— 5.12	—	—	2.51	9.39	— 5.89	— 0.86	—	—	0.55
13	— 8.42	—	— 1.56	5.37	4.86	— 5.03	—	—	— 10.57	21.31
14	—	6.81	— 9.27	— 0.43	— 10.07	—	—	10.60	13.71	— 10.04
15	—	5.99	— 3.47	— 0.69	— 8.79	—	H	— 4.00	— 5.13	— 5.86
16	H	3.98	— 8.40	— 2.08	—	H	— 2.47	— 5.67	— 3.77	—
17	— 7.79	— 4.57	— 0.60	—	—	8.11	— 3.71	1.48	— 6.07	—
18	9.52	— 3.49	—	—	H	7.42	1.33	3.91	—	H
19	15.67	—	—	H	— 8.96	— 13.74	— 4.66	—	—	— 1.43
20	12.04	—	H	7.54	10.84	2.73	—	—	H	2.54
21	—	H	— 3.38	n/c	— 18.34	—	—	H	— 9.53	— 4.09
22	—	— 0.33	— 0.26	— 5.98	0.25	—	— 13.04	— 12.42	— 5.13	— 3.20
23	— 2.52	— 1.66	1.90	— 5.29	—	9.14	1.72	16.54	0.42	—
24	8.27	— 5.65	5.29	—	—	0.87	13.79	24.87	30.47	—
25	1.02	0.83	—	—	— 8.96	8.30	— 0.95	— 0.87	—	1.66
26	— 15.74	—	—	— 2.16	4.44	12.41	— 1.43	—	—	8.61
27	— 6.22	—	— 7.89	— 14.12	— 9.13	7.77	—	—	14.86	— 5.08
28	—	2.99	— 6.23	1.82	— 0.68	—	—	— 8.32	— 22.82	2.98
29	—				8.70				— 2.51	
Close	972.61	936.42	742.12	808.82	863.14	974.58	824.39	1112.62	1154.63	1284.01
Change	— 2.67	— 17.95	— 27.80	— 30.40	— 12.71	27.31	— 46.71	36.92	— 65.95	— 2.76

TABLE 49

1986 MARKET PROBABILITY CALENDAR

The chances of the market rising on any trading day of the year.
(Based on the number of times the market rose
on a particular trading day during the period May 1952—June 1985)

Date	Jan.	Feb.	Mar.	Apr.	May	June	July	Aug.	Sept.	Oct.	Nov.	Dec.
1	H	SAT	SAT	63.6	50.0	SUN	63.6	54.5	H	39.4	SAT	45.4
2	48.4	SUN	SUN	48.4	73.5	52.9	66.7	SAT	66.7	75.8	SUN	48.4
3	75.8	57.6	72.7	51.5	SAT	52.9	63.6	SUN	63.6	57.6	60.6	63.6
4	SAT	57.6	63.6	51.5	SUN	58.8	H	42.4	63.6	SAT	60.6	69.7
5	SUN	39.4	57.6	SAT	64.7	64.7	SAT	51.5	45.4	SUN	75.8	45.4
6	54.5	48.4	48.4	SUN	52.9	52.9	SUN	57.6	SAT	66.7	48.4	SAT
7	51.5	48.4	42.4	63.6	55.9	SAT	60.6	60.6	SUN	57.6	45.4	SUN
8	42.4	SAT	SAT	60.6	50.0	SUN	60.6	36.4	45.4	51.5	SAT	48.4
9	48.4	SUN	SUN	69.7	41.2	50.0	60.6	SAT	48.4	45.4	SUN	57.6
10	51.5	36.4	54.5	54.5	SAT	32.4	42.4	SUN	48.4	42.4	57.6	48.4
11	SAT	39.4	66.7	54.5	SUN	64.7	30.3	57.6	60.6	SAT	72.7	45.4
12	SUN	57.6	54.5	SAT	47.1	58.8	SAT	45.4	45.4	SUN	60.6	51.5
13	51.5	45.4	60.6	SUN	35.3	50.0	SUN	54.5	SAT	39.4	48.4	SAT
14	63.6	45.4	42.4	57.6	44.1	SAT	63.6	57.6	SUN	39.4	45.4	SUN
15	57.6	SAT	SAT	54.5	47.1	SUN	54.5	54.5	54.5	39.4	SAT	54.5
16	42.4	SUN	SUN	54.5	50.0	52.9	36.4	SAT	48.4	57.6	SUN	54.5
17	54.5	H	54.5	57.6	SAT	47.1	45.4	SUN	51.5	45.4	60.6	45.4
18	SAT	39.4	63.6	51.5	SUN	47.1	39.4	45.4	45.4	SAT	51.5	48.4
19	SUN	42.4	57.6	SAT	32.4	52.9	SAT	45.4	54.5	SUN	69.7	48.4
20	54.5	48.4	45.4	SUN	44.1	50.0	SUN	54.5	SAT	57.6	66.7	SAT
21	45.4	54.5	45.4	45.4	50.0	SAT	48.4	39.4	SUN	48.4	54.5	SUN
22	51.5	SAT	SAT	54.5	50.0	SUN	51.5	42.4	54.5	36.4	SAT	48.4
23	69.7	SUN	SUN	39.4	44.1	50.0	48.4	SAT	51.5	33.3	SUN	36.4
24	60.6	30.3	54.5	57.6	SAT	38.2	42.4	SUN	54.5	51.5	72.7	63.6
25	SAT	42.4	33.3	63.6	SUN	47.1	45.4	45.4	54.5	SAT	54.5	H
26	SUN	57.6	51.5	SAT	H	52.9	SAT	33.3	57.6	SUN	54.5	69.7
27	39.4	45.4	54.5	SUN	41.2	52.9	SUN	51.5	SAT	30.3	H	SAT
28	57.6	57.6	H	39.4	32.4	SAT	54.5	51.5	SUN	54.5	54.5	SUN
29	39.4	—	SAT	39.4	52.9	SUN	54.5	75.8	39.4	57.6	SAT	51.5
30	63.6	—	SUN	57.6	58.8	58.8	57.6	SAT	33.3	45.4	SUN	63.6
31	60.6	—	36.4	—	SAT	—	63.6	SUN	—	48.4	—	78.8

FIGURE 39

MARKET PROBABILITY CHART

The chances of the market rising on any trading day of the year.
(Based on the number of times the market rose
on a particular trading day during the period May 1952—June 1985)

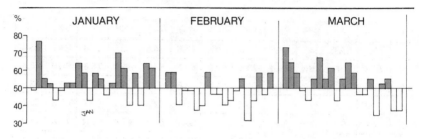

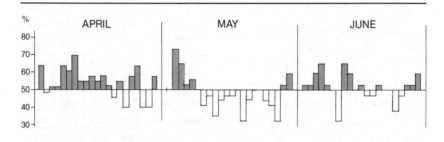

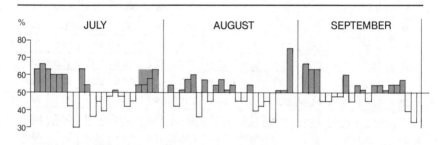

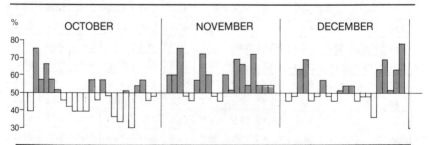

Shows the usual number of trading days in each month (Saturdays, Sundays and holidays excluded)

FIGURE 40

MARCH DAILY PROBABILITY CHART

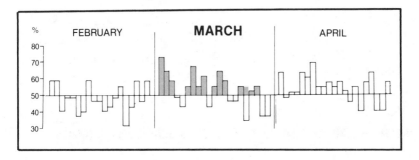

THE MARCH ALMANAC

• "IN LIKE A LION, OUT LIKE A LAMB" DESCRIBES STRONGER FIRST HALF THAN SECOND

• ELEVEN SUBSTANTIAL RALLIES OF AT LEAST 5% STARTED HERE SINCE 1949, THE LAST IN 1984. THE MARKET TURNAROUND CALENDAR (Table 52 Just Ahead) SHOWS IN WHICH MONTHS ALL POST—WORLD WAR II RALLIES AND DECLINES BEGAN

• AVERAGE S&P 500 GAIN 1.0%, SIXTH BEST

• GAIN OF 197.96 DOW POINTS FIFTH BEST OVER THIRTY-FIVE YEARS

• PRECEDES BEST PERFORMING DOW MONTH, APRIL, WITH 464.06 POINTS GAINED

• THIS MONTH IS ONE OF THE BEST BUYING TIMES FOR A THIRTY-DAY PERIOD

• MARCH TENDS TO BE A DOWN MONTH IN DECLINING YEARS

• THE LAST FEW DAYS OF THE MONTH ARE OFTEN GOOD BUYING POINTS

• IF THE MARKET HAS BEEN MOSTLY DOWN SINCE THE BEGINNING OF THE YEAR, PREPARE

YOURSELF FOR A SPRING RALLY THIS MONTH OR NEXT

• IRISH INVESTORS WILL BE PLEASED TO KNOW THAT TWENTY OF THE LAST TWENTY-NINE ST. PATRICK'S DAYS HAVE SEEN A RISE IN THE DOW JONES INDUSTRIALS

TABLE 50

MARCH DAILY POINT CHANGES DOW JONES INDUSTRIALS

Previous Month Close	1976	1977	1978	1979	1980	1981	1982	1983	1984	1985
	972.61	936.42	742.12	808.82	863.14	974.58	824.39	1112.62	1154.63	1284.01
1	2.75	8.31	1.21	7.02	—	—	4.00	18.09	4.81	15.35
2	9.76	− 2.66	3.12	− 0.09	—	3.41	− 2.57	4.35	12.04	—
3	− 6.29	6.57	0.86	—	− 8.79	−11.97	−10.66	3.00	—	—
4	− 8.19	4.82	—	—	2.13	5.42	− 7.61	2.90	—	− 9.83
5	2.28	—	—	11.61	−11.60	− 6.82	− 0.19	—	− 6.28	2.32
6	—	—	− 4.59	− 0.78	−16.81	N/C	—	—	−12.67	−11.48
7	—	1.66	4.07	7.71	− 7.51	—	—	0.78	− 8.90	− 8.84
8	15.82	− 3.08	4.08	10.56	—	—	−11.89	−21.96	3.46	− 1.87
9	4.96	− 9.14	− 0.87	− 1.99	—	11.80	8.37	12.86	− 7.33	—
10	1.58	3.83	8.58	—	− 1.62	− 3.76	1.05	−11.70	—	—
11	8.03	0.99	—	—	7.51	− 4.99	0.67	− 3.20	—	− 1.11
12	−15.67	—	—	1.82	− 6.91	22.15	− 8.19	—	15.60	3.20
13	—	—	1.38	2.25	− 9.98	− 4.05	—	—	9.42	−10.05
14	—	10.64	2.60	− 1.56	2.13	—	—	− 3.29	1.26	− 1.65
15	−13.14	6.65	− 3.98	1.65	—	—	3.62	10.07	1.36	−12.70
16	8.97	2.99	4.24	5.80	—	17.02	− 2.66	− 8.52	16.96	—
17	2.52	− 3.16	5.89	—	−23.04	−10.26	− 2.48	0.97	—	—
18	− 6.14	− 3.82	—	—	12.97	1.53	9.42	0.77	—	2.32
19	H	—	—	4.77	− 0.68	− 7.48	0.38	—	−12.98	21.42
20	—	—	5.11	− 7.28	−11.86	6.22	—	—	4.39	− 5.85
21	—	− 7.48	−11.00	7.45	− 3.93	—	—	7.55	− 4.92	2.98
22	2.44	− 2.58	− 5.28	3.55	—	—	13.89	− 2.32	−14.97	− 0.77
23	13.14	− 8.64	− 1.04	− 1.56	—	11.43	7.13	17.90	− 1.04	—
24	13.78	− 6.65	H	—	−19.71	− 8.10	− 3.33	5.03	—	—
25	− 7.08	− 6.81	—	—	2.39	19.09	4.29	− 5.81	—	− 7.51
26	1.33	—	—	− 4.93	− 5.71	− 9.46	− 9.71	—	− 1.89	− 0.22
27	—	—	− 3.29	16.54	− 2.14	−10.98	—	—	1.36	5.19
28	—	− 2.75	5.63	− 5.11	17.67	—	—	− 6.77	20.31	− 4.20
29	− 6.06	5.90	2.94	0.52	—	—	5.90	− 2.13	− 3.87	6.07
30	− 5.27	−10.80	− 2.16	− 4.59	—	− 2.62	0.67	12.10	− 5.86	—
31	7.32	− 2.08	− 2.26	—	8.10	11.71	− 1.72	−13.26	—	—
Close	999.45	919.13	757.36	862.18	785.75	1003.87	822.77	1130.03	1164.89	1266.78
Change	26.84	−17.29	15.24	53.36	−77.39	29.29	− 1.62	17.41	10.26	−17.23

MARKET BULLISH ON ST. PATRICK'S DAY—THE LUCK OF THE IRISH!

Leprechauns on Wall Street? While the Dow Jones industrial average has risen on only 52% of all the days since 1947, strange that the market has done significantly better on St. Patrick's Day by rising 60.0% of the time—up twenty St. Patrick's Days out of twenty-nine.

It would be more than a bit of blarney to attribute the market's good fortune on March 17 to Irish elves. What then could account for such bullish behavior?

One observation: There is a large Irish population in New York City. Many work in the Wall Street area. The happiness of the celebrants on their holiday is highly infectious. Quite a few non-Irish individuals participate in this "fun" holiday by wearing something green and having a drink or two with Irish friends and associates. We can only deduce that the euphoria generated on this day spills over into the market. (Readers will be spared a closing sentence in an Irish brogue!)

THE MARKET TURNAROUND CALENDAR

The seasonal tendency of major turning points is revealed in the thirty-four-year (1949-1983) composite calendar. All months were adjusted to an average twenty-one days and show precisely where declines and rallies of at least 5% began in the Dow industrials.

During thirty-four years, 105 markets turned down from tops and 105 turned up from bottoms. The greatest concentration of turndowns (ten) occurred within January's first six trading days as investors locked up profits in the new year. Many rallies began near the tail ends of fall months. October was the "bear-killer." Most major bear markets (1946, 1957, 1960, 1962, 1966, 1974) ended here. March and June were likely months for spring and summer rallies to begin.

TABLE 51

MARKET PERFORMANCE ON ST. PATRICK'S DAY

Year	Day of Week	Closing Data March 17	Change From Previous Day	% Change
1947	Monday	173.35	0.98	0.57%
1948	Wednesday	166.24	0.85	0.51
1949	Thursday	176.33	0.80	0.46
1950	Friday	207.57	0.32	0.15
1951	Saturday	249.03	0.41	0.16
1952	Monday	264.08	− 0.35	−0.13
1953	Tuesday	290.64	1.12	0.39
1954	Wednesday	298.31	0.22	0.07
1955	Thursday	405.23	2.09	0.52
1956	Saturday	—	—	—
1957	Sunday	—	—	—
1958	Monday	448.23	− 4.81	−1.06
1959	Tuesday	612.69	4.81	0.79
1960	Thursday	615.09	− 1.64	−0.27
1961	Friday	676.48	6.10	0.91
1962	Saturday	—	—	—
1963	Sunday	—	—	—
1964	Tuesday	818.16	1.68	0.21
1965	Wednesday	899.37	0.47	0.05
1966	Thursday	919.32	3.29	0.36
1967	Friday	869.77	1.28	0.15
1968	Sunday	—	—	—
1969	Monday	904.03	− 0.28	−0.03
1970	Tuesday	767.42	2.37	0.31
1971	Wednesday	914.02	− 0.62	−0.07
1972	Friday	942.88	6.17	0.66
1973	Saturday	—	—	—
1974	Sunday	—	—	—
1975	Monday	786.53	13.06	1.69
1976	Wednesday	985.99	2.52	0.26
1977	Thursday	964.84	− 3.16	−0.33
1978	Friday	768.71	5.89	0.77
1979	Saturday	—	—	—
1980	Monday	788.65	−23.04	−2.84
1981	Tuesday	992.53	−10.26	−1.02
1982	Wednesday	795.85	− 2.48	−0.31
1983	Thursday	1116.97	0.97	0.09
1984	Saturday	—	—	—
1985	Sunday	—	—	—

TABLE 52

THE MARKET TURNAROUND CALENDAR

Trading Days	JAN	FEB	MAR	APR	MAY	JUNE	JULY	AUG	SEPT	OCT	NOV	DEC
1	**1955** **1956** **1960** **1977**	1981	1978		1952 1960			**1959**	**1969**	1956 1975	**1978**	**1968** **1975**
2	**1953** 1967	**1958**									**1980**	
3	**1957** **1974** **1981**			1983		**1963** 1967	1978				**1981**	1950 **1957** 1973
4			**1955**	**1976**	**1951**	**1978**	1970		**1961**	1974 **1979**	**1956** **1974** 1980 **1982**	**1978** **1981**
5	**1949**				**1982** **1983**	1976			**1971**			**1982**
6	**1968**			**1956**	**1967**			1968 1982	**1975** **1978**	1966	**1969**	1974 1975
7			1960		1972 **1976**	**1960** **1974** 1983		**1952** 1955 **1956** 1971	1980	1955 1969 **1981**	1976	
8	**1973** **1983**	**1951** 1957 1974		**1970** **1972** 1976 **1979**	1981	**1950** 1953	1950 **1968** **1976**	**1967**				
9		**1980**	1982					**1953**		**1978**	**1977**	1980
10			1955 1969 **1974**		**1965** **1969**	1949 1975	**1957** **1975**	**1972**	**1951** 1953		**1958** **1961** 1978	
11			1951 1966	**1960**	**1975**	**1966** **1981**		**1980**	**1966**	**1960** **1980**	**1966**	1982
12	1955		**1975**		1966	1961	1972			1972		1957
13	**1966**					1982	**1982**				**1980**	1978
14	1956					**1970**	1963				1967	
15							1960	**1962** 1975	1959 **1976** 1978 **1982**	1979	1981	
16	1983		1968		**1961** 1983			**1960** 1973	**1955** **1980**	1952 1957 1962 **1982**		
17				**1966**		1962			1961	1960 1977 1981	**1950** 1951 1971 1982	
18	**1979**	1958		**1981**	1970		**1955**		**1967**	1982	1963	
19	**1952**		1975 1980	**1971**	**1983**	1973	**1973**	1967 1976	1981	**1963** **1973**	1958	
20					1956 **1972**	1965	1969	1966	**1960** 1980	1978	1956	
21	1970	1979	**1983**		1949 1979	1951			1982	1980		
Total Tops	15	3	4	9	11	8	7	9	13	8	13	6
Total Bottoms	5	5	10	2	10	12	7	9	8	17	11	8

Trading days 1–11: 73 Tops/46 Bottoms

Mid-Month

Trading days 11–21: 32 Tops/59 Bottoms

Trading days 1–7: 45 Tops/31 Bottoms

Trading days 8–14: 37 Tops/28 Bottoms

Trading days 15–21: 23 Tops/46 Bottoms

Key: **Black,** market turned down, grey, market turned up

FIGURE 41

APRIL DAILY PROBABILITY CHART

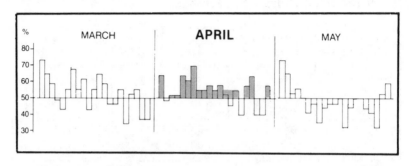

THE APRIL ALMANAC

• MORE GROUND IS GAINED IN THE TWO WEEKS PRIOR TO THE APRIL 15 FEDERAL TAX DEADLINE THAN IN THE LAST TWO

• WHEN A COMPANY'S FIRST QUARTER EARNINGS DOUBLE, ITS STOCK TENDS TO SCORE A 25.2% GAIN IN THE PREVIOUS THIRTY DAYS AND ONLY 5.0% MORE IN THE NEXT THIRTY

• APRIL BOX SCORE: TWENTY-FIVE UP, ELEVEN DOWN

• FIRST QUARTER EARNINGS TEND TO BE POORER FOLLOWING BEAR MARKET YEARS, AND ARE USUALLY DISCOUNTED BY RISING MARKETS

• THOUGH APRIL IS ONE OF THE BEST PERFORMING MONTHS, IT RANKS AT BOTTOM WHEN ONE PURCHASES STOCKS FOR ONE-, TWO-, THREE-, OR SIX-MONTH HOLDING PERIODS

• MACHINE TOOL STOCKS OFTEN TOP OUT AT THIS TIME OF THE YEAR

• SHARP MOVES IN THE SECOND AND/OR THIRD WEEKS OF APRIL IN RECENT YEARS MAY BE DUE TO THE OPTION EXPIRATION DATE

NUMERO UNO....APRIL

The hottest month in recent years has been April, with 464.06 Dow points gained since 1950. Over 120 of these points were netted in 1982 and 1983, probably due to the newly enacted legislation making IRA accounts more attractive. This may have triggered a massive inflow of funds.

Here's why: Few people realize that the forty million existing IRA accounts must now have their contributions deposited by April 15. This means that some $30 to $40 billion hit the banks and the mutual funds, with a chunk of it surely winding up in the stock market.

Consider also that of the billions already in IRAs any year end, a good portion are in maturing certificates of deposit which need to be rolled over. If interest rates are low or falling and stocks are buoyant, you can bet some of that money will find its way to Wall Street. If you add the billions in money market funds at a time of shrinking interest rates, the possibilities for the market become mind-boggling. And if the decision to invest is held up temporarily, pressures can build up which can rocket the Dow as it did in August 1984 up 109 points or in May and June 1985 up 77 points.

TABLE 53

APRIL DAILY POINT CHANGES DOW JONES INDUSTRIALS

Previous Month Close	1976	1977	1978	1979	1980	1981	1982	1983	1984	1985
	999.45	919.13	757.36	862.18	785.75	1003.87	822.77	1130.03	1164.89	1266.78
1	− 5.35	8.23	—	—	− 1.28	10.27	10.47	H	—	5.97
2	− 2.52	—	—	− 6.93	3.33	− 5.13	5.33	—	−11.73	− 7.07
3	—	—	− 6.32	13.08	− 3.67	− 1.90	—	—	− 4.40	− 7.62
4	—	−11.80	4.33	1.47	H	—	—	− 2.42	− 0.20	0.99
5	12.51	0.58	7.71	7.80	—	—	− 3.24	− 7.45	−18.01	H
6	− 2.44	− 1.41	0.87	− 1.91	—	−12.87	4.00	− 6.67	1.67	—
7	−15.43	4.15	5.63	—	−15.79	− 1.35	− 2.48	4.16	—	—
8	− 9.13	H	—	—	6.66	0.54	6.09	7.06	—	− 6.07
9	− 8.81	—	—	− 1.99	10.92	5.40	H	—	1.68	0.88
10	—	—	4.07	5.02	5.55	1.44	—	—	4.40	6.08
11	—	5.22	− 3.47	− 7.01	0.08	—	—	17.12	− 7.33	3.75
12	2.99	13.06	− 3.89	− 1.21	—	—	− 1.62	3.49	26.17	1.99
13	12.99	1.02	8.92	H	—	− 7.11	− 0.28	11.32	− 7.01	—
14	− 9.61	8.82	19.92	—	− 6.65	− 4.06	− 2.95	8.61	—	—
15	5.83	0.76	—	—	− 1.54	12.61	1.52	6.09	—	1.10
16	H	—	—	−10.05	−12.11	3.87	3.81	—	10.15	2.77
17	—	—	14.99	− 2.52	− 2.39	H	—	—	4.29	2.76
18	—	− 5.00	− 6.85	2.34	− 5.46	—	—	11.90	− 8.06	− 7.18
19	7.63	− 3.99	4.77	− 5.02	—	—	2.66	− 8.70	1.57	1.43
20	15.35	3.82	6.50	1.73	—	10.36	− 5.52	16.93	H	—
21	7.56	− 6.79	− 1.74	—	− 4.27	−10.00	2.86	− 3.20	—	—
22	− 3.31	− 8.73	—	—	30.72	1.08	9.70	8.03	—	n/c
23	− 7.00	—	—	3.12	− 0.60	3.25	9.04	—	− 8.58	12.15
24	—	—	13.26	6.76	7.85	10.08	—	—	13.40	− 0.22
25	—	−12.47	7.53	0.60	6.48	—	—	− 9.09	0.63	6.29
26	2.05	1.02	3.38	− 6.49	—	—	3.42	22.25	11.72	− 9.60
27	− 7.25	8.14	−10.05	− 4.33	—	3.70	− 8.08	− 1.06	− 6.18	—
28	5.20	3.56	10.40	—	1.88	− 7.12	− 4.86	11.12	—	—
29	1.42	− 0.42	—	—	5.63	−12.61	− 7.70	6.68	—	−15.46
30	− 5.28	—	—	− 1.74	5.97	− 6.57	3.42	—	1.68	− 1.66
Close	996.85	926.90	837.32	854.90	817.06	997.75	848.36	1226.20	1170.75	1258.06
Change	− 2.60	7.77	79.96	− 7.28	31.31	− 6.12	25.59	96.17	5.86	− 8.72

FIRST HALF OF APRIL
OUTPERFORMS SECOND HALF

Most people believe Uncle Sam has a chilling effect on stock prices in early April. They suppose many investors must sell some of their holdings to pay income taxes. Once the April 15 tax deadline passes, they assume the market will turn up as taxselling ceases.

However, the obvious is seldom true in investing. From 1955 through 1985, **the first half of April outperformed the second half twenty-three out of thirty-one times.** The former gained 1.5% on average compared to an average loss of 0.1% for the latter.

TABLE 54

MARKET PERFORMANCE IN APRIL

	End Of March	Mid-April Tax Deadline	End of April	April 1-15	April 16-30
1955	36.58*	37.96*	37.96*	3.8%	0.0%
1956	48.48	47.96	48.38	—1.1	0.9
1957	44.11	44.95	45.74	1.9	1.8
1958	42.10	42.43	43.44	0.8	2.4
1959	55.44	56.98	57.59	2.8	1.1
1960	55.34	56.59	54.37	2.3	—3.9
1961	65.06	66.68	65.31	2.5	—2.1
1962	69.55	67.60	65.24	—2.8	—3.6
1963	66.57	69.09	69.80	3.8	1.1
1964	78.98	80.09	79.46	1.4	—0.8
1965	86.16	88.15	89.11	2.3	1.1
1966	89.23	91.99	91.06	3.1	—1.0
1967	90.20	91.07	94.01	1.0	3.2
1968	90.20	96.59	97.59	7.1	1.0
1969	101.51	101.53	103.69	0.0	2.1
1970	89.63	86.73	81.52	—3.2	—6.0
1971	100.31	103.52	103.95	3.2	0.4
1972	107.20	109.51	107.67	2.2	—1.7
1973	111.52	111.44	106.97	—0.1	—4.0
1974	93.98	94.36	90.91	0.4	—4.3
1975	83.36	86.30	87.30	3.5	1.2
1976	102.77	100.67	101.64	—2.0	1.0
1977	98.42	101.04	98.44	2.7	—2.6
1978	89.21	94.45	96.83	5.9	2.5
1979	101.59	101.12	101.76	—0.5	0.6
1980	102.09	102.63	106.29	0.5	3.6
1981	136.00	134.70	132.81	—1.0	—1.4
1982	111.96	116.35	116.44	3.9	0.1
1983	152.96	158.75	164.42	3.8	3.6
1984	159.18	158.32	160.05	—0.5	1.1
1985	180.66	180.92	179.83	0.1	—0.6

*S & P Composite Index   **Average 1.5%   —0.1%**

Several of the few Aprils with no market gains in the first half of the month were in bear market years. However, these declining years had more of an adverse effect on the last two weeks of the month.

The table begins with 1955. As in prior years, March 15 was the income tax deadline. On occasions when April 15 falls on the weekend and the IRS extends the deadline, I have used the following Monday's market average in my calculations.

STRONGEST TWO-DAY RALLY OF THE YEAR USED TO BE THE EASTER RALLY

The market's two strongest consecutive days of the year used to be the Wednesday and Thursday prior to Easter Sunday. (The market is closed on Good Friday.) In a period of 22 years, the market chalked up an average .631% gain for these two days. This is equivalent to 6.31 points in the Dow Jones industrial average, using 1000 as a base. Only six times during bearish periods —1969, 1974, 1976, 1978, 1979, and 1980—did the market fail to advance. Even individually, these two days compared most favorably to such other strong days as the day before July Fourth, the second trading day in January, and the last market day of the year.

One might reasonably assume that this bullishness derived from the usual consumer buying spree prior to Easter. It is interesting that while the market had risen only 59% since 1960, average pre-Easter gains were twice what they were in the fifties, when the market climbed 150%. But professionals seemed to be selling into this seasonal bias, so I stopped tracking it. The Dow declined prior to three of the four subsequent Easters. You can kiss any obvious short-term pattern goodbye once it is widely circulated.

TABLE 55

MARKET PERFORMANCE PRIOR TO EASTER

Dow Jones Industrial Average			Good Friday	Points Gained/Lost Based on D.J. 1000	
Tuesday	Wednesday	Thursday		Thursday	Both Days
626.50	626.50	630.12	Apr. 15, 1960	5.78	5.78
669.58	676.41	676.63	Mar. 31, 1961	0.32	10.53
688.43	691.01	694.25	Apr. 20, 1962	4.68	8.45
706.03	704.35	708.45	Apr. 12, 1963	5.82	3.43
811.43	813.16	815.91	Mar. 27, 1964	3.38	5.52
908.01	912.86	911.91	Apr. 16, 1965	−1.04	4.30
944.71	945.26	945.76	Apr. 8, 1966	0.53	1.11
866.59	870.55	876.67	Mar. 24, 1967	7.03	11.63
884.42*	892.63	905.69	Apr. 12, 1968	14.63	24.05
933.08	930.92	927.30	Apr. 4, 1969	−3.89	−6.20
773.76	790.13	791.05	Mar. 27, 1970	1.16	22.34
912.73	918.49	920.39	Apr. 9, 1971	2.07	8.39
937.01	933.02	940.70	Mar. 31, 1972	8.23	3.94
953.42	958.31	963.20	Apr. 20, 1973	5.10	10.26
846.84	843.71	844.81	Apr. 12, 1974	1.30	−2.40
747.89	766.19	770.26	Mar. 28, 1975	5.31	29.91
984.26	974.65	980.48	Apr. 16, 1976	5.98	−3.84
916.14	914.73	918.88	Apr. 8, 1977	4.54	2.99
762.82	757.54	756.50	Mar. 24, 1978	−1.37	−8.28
878.72	871.71	870.50	Apr. 13, 1979	−1.39	−9.36
784.47	787.80	784.13	Apr. 4, 1980	−4.66	−0.43
989.10	1001.71	1005.58	Apr. 17, 1981	3.86	16.66
			Average Points Gained	**3.07**	**6.31**

*Tuesday holiday, Monday's close

FIGURE 42

MAY DAILY PROBABILITY CHART

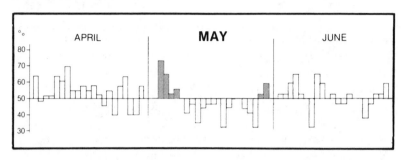

THE MAY ALMANAC

• MAY MARKETS TEND TO COME IN LIKE BULLS, EXIT LIKE BEARS

• AIRLINES HAVE OFTEN HIT SEASONAL HIGHS IN MAY

• MAY IS A "DISASTER" MONTH AND MOST "HAZARDOUS TO ONE'S WEALTH"

• MAY BOX SCORE: UP TEN, DOWN FIVE 1950-64; UP SIX, DOWN FIFTEEN 1965-85

• WORST MONTH IN S&P 500, OFF 0.6% ON AVERAGE; IN DOW, DOWN 324.38 POINTS

• MAY RANKS NEXT TO LAST AMONG ALL THE MONTHS IN PURCHASING STOCKS FOR ONE-, TWO-, THREE-, AND SIX-MONTH HOLDING PERIODS; APRIL IS THE WORST

• AS APRIL HAS IMPROVED ITS SEASONAL PER-FORMANCE IN RECENT YEARS, MAY HAS BECOME INCREASINGLY VULNERABLE. THIS IS NOT UNLIKE THE JULY-AUGUST RELATIONSHIP, OR THAT OF JANUARY-FEBRUARY—GAINS IN THE EARLIER MONTH, CONSOLIDATION OR TOPPING OUT IN THE FOLLOWING MONTH

• IF THE MARKET HAS BEEN VERY STRONG IN RE-CENT MONTHS, IT MIGHT NOT BE A BAD IDEA TO NAIL DOWN SOME PROFITS, SELL OPTIONS ON SOME STOCKS, SHORT AGAINST THE BOX, OR SELL INDEX FUTURES

TABLE 56

MAY DAILY POINT CHANGES DOW JONES INDUSTRIALS

Prev. Month Close	1976 996.85	1977 926.90	1978 837.32	1979 854.90	1980 817.06	1981 997.75	1982 848.36	1983 1226.20	1984 1170.75	1985 1258.06
1	—	—	7.01	0.61	— 8.27	— 2.16	—	—	12.25	—16.01
2	—	4.32	— 4.15	n/c	2.13	—	—	—21.87	3.56	0.22
3	— 6.53	2.97	—11.35	2.08	—	—	0.67	3.68	—5.03	4.97
4	3.38	6.53	— 4.42	—10.05	—	—16.48	5.42	4.64	—16.22	—
5	— 7.24	2.72	4.68	—	5.38	— 6.67	n/c	7.07	—	—
6	3.07	— 6.70	—	—	— 0.26	0.90	8.75	12.87	—	0.55
7	6.69	—	—	—14.12	5.21	5.05	6.00	—	1.25	4.97
8	—	—	—4.51	1.47	— 6.06	— 1.99	—	—	9.74	— 2.98
9	—	— 3.65	— 2.51	3.73	— 9.39	—	—	— 4.36	—10.78	10.49
10	11.26	3.05	0.09	— 9.70	—	—	— 8.28	1.45	1.67	13.91
11	— 0.87	— 9.24	12.04	1.64	—	—12.96	4.95	— 9.96	—10.05	—
12	— 0.94	— 1.36	6.50	—	— 0.60	7.38	— 0.10	— 5.32	—	—
13	— 4.57	2.80	—	—	11.69	— 3.06	— 6.66	4.35	—	3.32
14	— 8.50	—	—	— 5.54	2.73	5.31	— 1.33	—	— 6.07	— 4.20
15	—	—	6.06	0.86	2.91	12.88	—	—	— 0.21	0.22
16	—	4.16	7.54	2.60	4.35	—	—	—15.77	2.30	4.53
17	— 4.96	3.98	4.07	14.47	—	—	—12.46	2.81	—10.89	7.29
18	1.81	5.43	— 7.45	— 1.04	—	— 0.18	— 4.47	— 2.23	— 8.48	—
19	— 0.55	— 5.43	— 4.07	—	4.01	— 5.76	— 4.95	—12.19	—	—
20	8.37	— 6.02	—	—	1.62	— 3.15	— 3.42	— 1.35	—	19.54
21	— 6.52	—	—	0.52	— 1.45	— 0.27	3.42	—	— 8.48	4.82
22	—	—	8.57	2.94	11.86	— 4.87	—	—	— 8.69	— 5.94
23	—	—13.40	—10.13	— 7.97	11.18	—	—	10.54	— 2.82	— 7.05
24	—19.22	— 4.66	— 7.37	0.26	—	—	0.48	18.48	—10.37	5.26
25	0.16	— 9.16	— 2.51	— 1.38	—	H	— 1.81	9.97	3.67	—
26	— 3.06	4.83	— 3.72	—	H	12.24	— 5.80	— 5.52	—	—
27	— 3.06	— 9.24	—	—	3.66	9.18	— 3.81	— 7.35	—	H
28	9.66	—	—	H	2.56	1.11	— 5.42	—	H	— 0.45
29	—	—	H	— 3.73	—14.07	— 2.50	—	—	— 5.86	1.46
30	—	H	2.51	—10.39	4.60	—	—	H	1.35	2.80
31	H	— 0.17	6.41	0.17	—	—	H	—16.16	2.26	9.63
Close	975.23	898.66	840.61	822.33	850.85	991.75	819.54	1199.98	1104.85	1315.41
Change	—21.62	—28.24	3.29	—32.57	33.79	— 6.00	—28.82	—26.22	—65.90	57.35

WARNING: MAY AND JUNE MIGHT BE HAZARDOUS TO YOUR WEALTH

Not once in the ten years 1965-1974 was the Dow Jones industrial average able to chalk up a net gain between May 1 and June 30. Then came 1975, and the May-June market curse was finally crushed. However, it took the greatest half-year gain in history (265.75 Dow points) to break the spell.

While June had been the weakest market month since the early fifties, May has been getting clobbered with monotonous regularity in recent years. As a result, May has conquered last place in the performance derby. In the last twenty-one years, the market in May as measured by the Dow has lost ground sixteen out of twenty-one times, in contrast to the 1955-1964 period when May was a loser only thrice.

In Table 57, the figures show an average 1.8% decline for May since 1965. June also has been a loser with a smaller average decline of 0.3%. Translated into Dow Jones points (using a D.J. base of 1300), this would mean an average loss of four points in June and twenty-three points in May. Peering down the performance columns of the two months, you can see that, in most years, if one month didn't get you the other did (1975, 1980, and 1985 were exceptions).

I tried to pinpoint the reason for the market's weakness in May in those years and noted that a number of unsettling incidents occurred during the month: a political crisis in Saigon (1966); the prelude to the Arab-Israeli War (1967); France paralyzed by civil violence (1968); Cambodian Invasion (1970); a massive peace protest in several major U.S. cities (1971); and Watergate (1973). The most logical reason for weak Mays, in my opinion, is that the market tends to rise sharply in bull years through the first quarter and into April, becoming overextended in May. In bear years, declines start slowly and pick up steam in May and June.

TABLE 57

THE MAY-JUNE DISASTER AREA

	End of Month Dow Jones Industrials			Net % Change		Both
	April	May	June	May	June	Months
1965	922.31	918.04	868.03	−0.5%	−5.4%	−5.9%
1966	933.68	884.07	870.10	−5.3	−1.6	−6.8
1967	897.05	852.56	860.26	−5.0	0.9	−4.1
1968	912.22	899.00	897.80	−1.4	−0.1	−1.6
1969	950.18	937.56	873.19	−1.3	−6.9	−8.1
1970	736.07	700.44	683.53	−4.8	−2.4	−7.1
1971	941.75	907.81	891.14	−3.6	−1.8	−5.4
1972	954.17	960.72	929.03	0.7	−3.3	−2.6
1973	921.43	901.41	891.71	−2.2	−1.1	−3.2
1974	836.75	802.17	802.41	−4.1	0.0	−4.1
1975	821.34	832.29	878.99	1.3	5.6	7.0
1976	996.85	975.23	1002.78	−2.2	2.8	0.6
1977	926.90	898.66	916.30	−3.0	2.0	−1.1
1978	837.32	840.61	818.95	0.4	−2.6	−2.2
1979	854.90	822.33	841.98	−3.8	2.4	−1.5
1980	817.06	850.85	867.92	4.1	2.0	6.2
1981	997.75	991.75	976.88	−0.6	−1.5	−2.1
1982	848.36	819.54	811.93	−3.4	−0.9	−4.3
1983	1226.20	1199.98	1221.96	−2.1	1.8	−0.3
1984	1170.75	1104.85	1132.40	−5.6	2.5	−3.3
1985	1258.06	1315.41	1335.46	4.6	1.5	6.2
			Average Change	−1.8%	−0.3%	−2.1%

A MAY/JUNE DISASTER
LEAST LIKELY IN
PRESIDENTIAL YEAR

The accompanying table presents a very positive picture for stocks during May and June in presidential years and even the months beyond:

   • Only three of the last nine presidential Mays were down, in 1956, 1976, and 1984. During two of the years, the market was in the process of topping out.

   • Only one June (1972) in the presidential series was a loser. The market moved higher in the others.

   • Combining Mays and Junes shows only four losing months out of eighteen. Comparing month-end June with month-end April shows losses only in 1956, 1972, and 1984, for the sixty-day period.

   • Looking at the nine Julys in the cycle, four were losers (1960, 1968, 1976, and 1984). Three were years when at convention time no strong incumbent was running for reelection, which created a climate of uncertainty. Note that April through July periods had only two losers. That was in 1972, and by a small margin at that—twenty-eight cents on the S&P composite, or equal to just two to three current Dow points—and in 1984.

   • For a longer perspective, we've extended the table out to December and see only one losing eight-month period in an election year between April and December of 3.5% in 1956. The other years had gains of 4.5 to 27.7%.

TABLE 58

LAST EIGHT MONTHS OF ELECTION YEARS BULLISH

Election Year	April	May	June	July	December	Change April to Dec.
		Monthly Closings, Standard & Poors Composite Index				
1952	23.32	23.86	24.96	25.40	26.57	13.9%
1956	48.38	45.20	46.97	49.39	46.67	− 3.5
1960	54.37	55.83	56.92	55.51	58.11	6.9
1964	79.46	80.37	81.69	83.18	84.75	6.7
1968	97.59	98.68	99.58	97.74	103.86	6.4
1972	107.67	109.53	107.14	107.39	118.05	9.6
1976	101.64	100.18	104.28	103.24	107.46	5.7
1980	106.29	111.24	114.24	121.67	135.76	27.7
1984	160.05	150.55	153.18	150.66	167.24	4.5

```
              6up/3down  7up/2down  5up/4down
              |_____|
                    6up/3down
       |_____|
                   7up/2down
```

FIGURE 43

JUNE DAILY PROBABILITY CHART

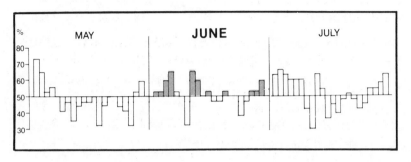

THE JUNE ALMANAC

• AFTER RISING JUST ONCE BETWEEN 1965 AND 1974, THE MARKET ROSE IN EIGHT OF THE FOLLOWING ELEVEN JUNES

• AUTOS OFTEN BEGIN MAJOR MOVES HERE

• JUNE BOX SCORE: VERY LITTLE GROUND GAINED IN THIRTY-FIVE JUNES (S&P)

• 74.52 DOW POINTS LOST SINCE 1950

• MANY SHARP SPRING DECLINES ACCELERATE INTO JUNE

• JUNE IS THE LEADING RALLYING POINT AFTER OCTOBER DURING BOTH BULL AND BEAR MARKETS. SEVERAL DECLINES THAT HAVE STARTED IN JUNE HAVE BEEN HALTED BY THE STRONG MIDYEAR REINVESTMENT PERIOD IN JULY

• JUNE IS A GOOD BUYING MONTH FOR ONE-, TWO-, THREE-, AND SIX-MONTH HOLDING PERIODS RANKING FIFTH AMONG ALL MONTHS

• THE SOFT DRINK GROUP TENDS TO START TURNING DOWN AS THE MERCURY STARTS CLIMBING

- BAD PERFORMING MARKETS IN MAY OVER THE LAST TWENTY YEARS HAVE MADE THE MAY-JUNE PERIOD A DISASTER AREA IN MOST YEARS

- IF YOUR PORTFOLIO HADN'T BEEN MAULED IN MAY, IT USED TO GET CLIPPED IN JUNE

- SINCE THE MARKET ROSE OUT OF DEPTHS OF DOW 570 IN DECEMBER 1974, JUNE HAS BEEN A BETTER PERFORMER RISING 1.5% ON AVERAGE WHILE THE DOW HAS BEEN TACKING ON A THOUSAND POINTS

TABLE 59

JUNE DAILY POINT CHANGES DOW JONES INDUSTRIALS

	1976	1977	1978	1979	1980	1981	1982	1983	1984	1985
Previous Month Close	975.23	898.66	840.61	822.33	850.85	991.75	819.54	1199.98	1104.85	1315.41
1	— 2.10	7.89	0.09	— 1.12	—	6.21	— 4.57	2.23	19.50	—
2	2.80	— 3.40	6.84	—	— 3.50	—10.48	1.91	9.23	—	—
3	— 2.13	9.08	—	—	— 3.58	2.23	— 0.38	1.60	—	— 4.48
4	— 9.90	—	—	0.69	14.25	— 2.97	—11.52	—	7.22	4.37
5	—	—	16.29	9.44	0.68	7.05	—	—	— 6.68	5.26
6	—	— 9.16	2.68	4.16	2.82	—	—	1.20	8.95	6.72
7	— 5.81	5.60	— 4.59	1.47	—	—	— 0.95	—19.33	— 1.40	—10.86
8	1.88	4.32	0.17	— 1.82	—	1.85	— 1.80	— 9.41	— 1.19	—
9	— 1.88	— 3.14	— 2.86	—	— 0.85	— 1.20	— 6.66	3.50	—	—
10	6.30	0.94	—	—	3.32	— 0.56	3.14	7.11	—	2.02
11	14.41	—	—	2.43	8.71	13.54	11.03	—	—15.64	— 4.60
12	—	—	— 2.51	7.71	— 0.09	— 1.14	—	—	— 5.08	— 7.50
13	—	1.61	0.26	— 3.12	3.76	—	—	24.44	N.C.	—16.24
14	12.44	10.17	— 2.42	0.17	—	—	— 7.89	6.71	—12.92	10.86
15	— 5.32	— 5.00	—10.31	0.96	—	5.71	— 0.58	10.02	—10.71	—
16	2.70	2.88	— 7.28	—	1.36	— 8.66	— 4.37	11.02	—	—
17	14.57	N/C	—	—	1.54	3.23	— 5.42	— 6.11	—	— 2.57
18	— 1.31	—	—	— 3.90	2.64	—11.41	— 2.86	22.75	—	6.38
19	—	—	1.65	N/C	—11.01	1.04	—	—	6.18	— 7.39
20	—	3.82	— 8.58	0.43	— 1.19	—	—	— 3.01	15.80	2.35
21	5.57	4.33	— 5.11	3.81	—	—	1.33	8.22	— 4.42	24.75
22	— 9.82	— 2.29	2.77	5.46	—	— 1.99	9.71	— 1.71	3.86	—
23	— 1.07	— 0.94	— 4.68	—	4.10	12.46	13.51	— 3.90	—	—
24	7.21	4.33	—	—	3.49	— 7.33	— 2.76	— 0.10	—	— 3.92
25	— 3.93	—	—	— 4.85	10.24	— 2.56	— 7.33	—	— 0.55	2.47
26	—	—	—10.74	— 6.59	— 4.09	— 3.90	—	—	— 7.73	0.78
27	—	— 5.60	5.03	2.86	— 1.62	—	—	—12.22	— 6.07	8.40
28	— 2.46	— 8.48	2.60	2.52	—	—	8.85	—20.24	9.83	3.25
29	3.27	— 2.29	1.73	— 1.06	—	— 8.28	0.28	4.61	5.85	—
30	2.13	2.97	— 2.69	—	—13.91	— 7.71	— 0.28	8.12	—	—
Close	1002.78	916.30	818.95	841.98	867.92	976.88	811.93	1221.96	1132.40	1335.46
Change	27.55	17.64	—21.66	19.65	17.07	—14.87	— 7.61	21.98	27.55	20.05

A RALLY FOR ALL SEASONS

In any year in which the market has been a disappointment, you can expect to hear talk of a summer rally. Parameters for this "rally" were defined by the late Ralph Rotnem (Smith Barney) as the lowest close in the Dow Jones industrial average in May or June to the highest close in July, August, or September. Such a big deal is made of the "summer rally" that one might get the impression the market puts on its best razzle-dazzle performance in the summertime. Nothing could be further from the truth! Not only does the market "rally" in every season of the year, but it does so with more gusto in the winter, spring, and fall than in the summer.

Winters in the past two decades have seen an average 11.7% gain as measured from the low in November or December to the first quarter closing high. The 10.7% gain in fall ranked second, followed by the 9.4% spring gain. Last and least was the average 8.8% "summer rally."

Nevertheless, no matter how thick the gloom or grim the outlook, never despair! There's a rally for all seasons

TABLE 60

SEASONAL GAINS IN DOW JONES INDUSTRIALS

	WINTER RALLY Nov/Dec Low to 1 Q. High	SPRING RALLY Feb/Mar Low to 2 Q. High	SUMMER RALLY May/Jun Low to 3 Q. High	FALL RALLY Aug/Sep Low to 4 Q. High
1964	15.3%	6.2%	9.4%	8.3%
1965	5.7	6.6	11.6	10.3
1966	5.9	4.8	3.5	7.0
1967	11.6	8.7	11.2	4.4
1968	7.0	11.4	5.2	13.3
1969	0.9	7.7	1.9	6.7
1970	5.4	6.2	22.5	19.0
1971	21.6	9.4	5.5	7.4
1972	19.1	7.7	5.2	11.4
1973	8.6	4.8	9.7	15.9
1974	13.1	8.2	1.4	11.0
1975	36.2	24.2	8.2	8.7
1976	23.3	6.4	5.9	4.6
1977	8.2	3.1	2.8	2.1
1978	2.1	16.8	11.8	5.2
1979	11.0	8.9	8.9	6.1
1980	13.5	16.8	21.0	8.5
1981	11.8	9.9	0.4	8.3
1982	4.6	9.3	18.5	37.8
1983	15.7	17.8	6.3	10.7
1984	5.9	4.6	14.1	9.7
1985	11.7	7.1	9.5	19.7
Totals	258.2%	206.6%	194.5%	236.1%
Average	11.7%	9.4%	8.8%	10.7%

SEASONAL TRADING MAP

The graphs below represent the seasonal patterns of the five industry groups in a computer study. This classic example measures in essence a group's average performance for each month in the March 1953-June

FIGURE 44

SEASONAL TENDENCIES

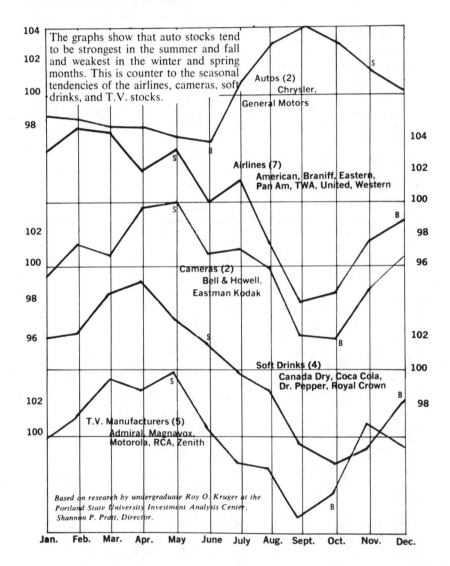

The graphs show that auto stocks tend to be strongest in the summer and fall and weakest in the winter and spring months. This is counter to the seasonal tendencies of the airlines, cameras, soft drinks, and T.V. stocks.

Autos (2)
Chrysler,
General Motors

Airlines (7)
American, Braniff, Eastern,
Pan Am, TWA, United, Western

Cameras (2)
Bell & Howell,
Eastman Kodak

Soft Drinks (4)
Canada Dry, Coca Cola,
Dr. Pepper, Royal Crown

T.V. Manufacturers (5)
Admiral, Magnavox,
Motorola, RCA, Zenith

Based on research by undergraduate Roy O. Kruger at the Portland State University Investment Analysis Center, Shannon P. Pratt, Director.

Jan.   Feb.   Mar.   Apr.   May   June   July   Aug.   Sept.   Oct.   Nov.   Dec.

1966 period. The area above the 100 line indicates a tendency towards rising prices; below the 100 line is where a group tends towards declining prices. Where the best buy and sell points might have been in the past is shown for each group. Nowadays, only autos and airlines are relatively still pure groups; the others have become too diversified.

The graphs show that auto stocks tended to be strongest in the summer and fall and weakest in the winter and spring months. This was counter to the seasonal tendencies of the airline, camera, soft drink, and T.V. stocks.

FIGURE 45

JULY DAILY PROBABILITY CHART

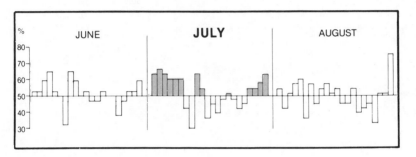

THE JULY ALMANAC

• LAST THIRTY-SIX YEARS HAD JULY UP FOURTEEN TIMES IN FIRST SEVENTEEN YEARS, UP ONLY SEVEN TIMES IN NEXT NINETEEN YEARS

• FIRST THIRD FAR OUTPERFORMS REMAINDER OF MONTH

• JULY FIFTH BEST IN S&P 500, UP 1.1% ON AVERAGE SINCE 1950

• SEVENTH BEST ON DOW WITH 96 POINTS GAINED

• STOCKS IN JULY HAVE TENDED TO GO IN THE OPPOSITE DIRECTION IN LAST NINE YEARS DURING THE WEEK FOLLOWING OPTION EXPIRATION FRIDAY, COUNTER TO WHAT THE MARKET DID IN THE PREVIOUS WEEK

• DISREGARD MOST COMMENTARIES IN FINANCIAL COLUMN REGARDING "SUMMER RALLIES"! THE "EXPECTED" RALLY IS NONSENSICAL! SURE, THE MARKET WILL LIKELY MOVE UP A BIT IN ANY THREE-MONTH PERIOD—SUMMER, WINTER, SPRING, OR FALL (Table 60)

TABLE 61

JULY DAILY POINT CHANGES DOW JONES INDUSTRIALS

Previous Month Close	1975	1976	1977	1978	1979	1980	1981	1982	1983	1984
	878.99	1002.78	916.30	818.95	841.98	867.92	976.88	811.93	1221.96	1132.40
1	− 1.57	− 7.94	− 3.65	—	—	4.35	− 9.22	− 8.66	3.30	—
2	− 7.04	5.00	—	—	− 7.94	3.75	− 8.47	− 6.28	—	− 2.32
3	1.41	—	—	− 6.06	1.54	12.89	—	—	—	4.20
4	H	H	H	H	H	H	H	H	H	H
5	—	—	0.94	− 7.10	0.17	—	—	—	−16.73	− 9.72
6	—	− 8.03	− 5.86	1.38	10.41	—	− 9.89	1.91	12.12	− 1.99
7	−10.71	− 0.65	1.78	5.29	—	9.30	4.85	0.76	−10.21	—
8	− 3.29	0.82	− 1.52	—	—	− 0.86	− 0.67	5.32	− 3.21	—
9	14.08	11.13	—	—	6.83	− 0.08	5.52	9.14	—	11.48
10	N/C	—	—	4.33	− 2.65	−11.35	− 3.33	—	—	− 7.17
11	− 0.78	—	− 2.46	4.50	− 6.48	5.21	—	—	8.31	−18.33
12	—	8.10	− 2.12	3.64	− 7.00	—	—	10.75	−17.02	− 3.98
13	—	− 5.15	− 0.42	− 0.17	− 3.33	—	− 1.33	− 0.67	− 0.70	5.30
14	4.77	− 0.90	H	15.07	—	14.42	− 6.09	4.19	6.51	—
15	5.95	− 7.70	2.96	—	—	− 4.01	5.90	− 1.05	−12.02	—
16	− 9.70	− 4.25	—	—	1.37	2.90	1.33	1.33	—	6.96
17	− 7.83	—	—	− 0.78	− 6.40	10.66	3.42	—	—	6.07
18	− 1.87	—	4.65	−10.05	0.08	8.88	—	—	− 2.41	−11.26
19	—	− 2.38	8.67	11.70	− 1.28	—	—	− 2.57	7.22	− 8.72
20	—	− 2.54	1.21	− 2.08	0.77	—	−18.36	7.33	30.74	− 1.55
21	− 7.67	1.15	1.30	− 5.20	—	4.69	− 6.08	− 1.24	1.51	—
22	− 7.98	1.64	1.64	—	—	− 1.37	− 9.80	− 0.19	1.80	—
23	−10.09	− 0.17	—	—	2.56	1.28	3.90	− 1.43	—	− 4.75
24	3.60	—	—	− 1.82	4.27	− 2.47	8.18	—	—	−10.05
25	− 6.18	—	− 9.18	7.97	9.73	− 8.02	—	—	1.70	10.38
26	—	0.60	− 6.06	7.62	0.25	—	—	− 5.13	10.82	10.60
27	—	− 7.38	−19.75	3.38	n/c	—	9.13	− 2.67	−13.22	7.07
28	− 6.26	− 2.80	1.56	5.72	—	7.34	− 6.47	−10.94	−14.12	—
29	− 2.97	− 2.04	0.08	—	—	6.48	− 2.00	0.38	−17.13	—
30	6.80	5.35	—	—	− 1.02	4.27	7.71	− 3.61	—	− 4.64
31	− 0.15	—	—	5.98	7.68	− 0.86	7.23	—	—	5.30
Close	831.51	984.64	890.07	862.27	846.42	935.32	952.34	808.60	1199.22	1115.28
Change	− 47.48	− 18.14	− 26.23	43.32	4.44	67.40	− 24.54	3.33	− 22.74	−17.12

MIDYEAR RALLY VS. REST OF JULY

For the past century or longer, members of the financial community have come to expect a healthy rally some time during the summer. But ·statistics show that a clearly identifiable summer rally simply does not occur with any reasonable consistency. The only honest-to-goodness rally that investors can often count on is the midyear rally. Setting an arbitrary trading period of five trading days prior to and five after the holiday, as in Table 62, produces an average gain of 1.33 percent. This averages out to a 1½ to 2 point daily gain in the Dow Jones industrials for the nine-day period. Bear market years can produce a negative result here.

The best day precedes Independence Day, except in bear years. In column five (midyear rally), only nine years were on the minus side (seven were in bear years). What is most significant in column six is that after the midyear rally, very little is left for the last two-thirds of July.

TRADING VS. INVESTING IN SEASONAL STOCKS

Some years ago, Merrill Lynch found seven industries in which investors would have done over *three times better,* in the 1954-1964 period, by trading in and out of these same industries on a seasonal basis than by having bought and held for the decade. The traders gained 235.0% on average; the holders, 70.1%.

For example, $10,000 invested in air conditioning stocks would have grown to $16,340 during the ten-year period. However, a strategy of selling your air conditioning stocks every March and reinvesting the entire proceeds each following October for the same ten-year period would have run your original $10,000 up to $44,720! (While the latter figure excludes the extra commissions and taxes involved, it also does not take into account the interest or profits the proceeds could have generated during the seven months it was withdrawn from the air conditioning stocks.)

We calculated the S&P average monthly prices for these groups in the 1965-1975 decade (MLPFS used month-end prices) and found that trading seasonally still worked. Taking into consideration that market prices more than doubled in the earlier decade but fell about one third in the following decade, the seasonal trading only gained 82.3% on average, while the ten-year holders lost 11.9%. Meat packers had best twenty-year record.

Air-conditioning and meat packing were discontinued as groups by Standard & Poor's in recent years as pure plays because there were

TABLE 62

THE MIDYEAR MARKET

Year	Five Days Prior To July 4	Five Days After July 4	Change Day Before July 4	Nine Day Net Change	Change Rest of July	Total July Change
1954	29.28*	30.12*	1.30%	2.87%	2.52%	5.7%
1955	40.99	42.75	0.39	4.29	1.80	6.1
1956	47.07	48.69	0.83	3.44	1.44	5.2
1957	47.26	48.86	1.22	3.39	−1.94	1.1
1958	44.90	45.72	0.33	1.82	3.22	4.3
1959	57.98	59.91	0.53	3.33	1.00	3.5
1960	57.33	56.87	0.25	−0.80	−2.39	−2.5
1961	64.47	65.69	0.88	1.89	1.63	3.3
1962	52.60	57.73	1.13	9.75	0.87	6.4
1963	69.07	69.76	0.69	1.00	−0.90	−0.3
1964	81.46	83.36	0.40	2.33	−0.22	1.8
1965	81.60	85.69	0.80	5.01	−0.51	1.3
1966	86.08	87.45	1.03	1.59	−4.40	−1.3
1967	91.30	92.48	0.30	1.29	2.45	4.5
1968	99.98	102.26	1.17	2.28	−4.42	−1.8
1969	97.33	95.77	0.68	−1.60	−4.11	−6.0
1970	73.47	74.57	−0.16	1.50	4.67	7.3
1971	97.74	100.82	0.00	3.15	−5.00	−4.1
1972	107.37	107.32	0.33	0.00	0.06	0.2
1973	103.62	105.80	−1.00	2.10	2.29	3.8
1974	86.31	79.89	−0.06	−7.47	−0.73	−7.8
1975	94.81	94.66	0.19	−0.16	−6.24	−6.8
1976	103.43	105.90	0.50	2.39	−2.32	−0.8
1977	100.98	99.55	−0.37	−1.42	−0.70	−1.6
1978	94.98	95.93	−0.46	1.00	4.95	5.4
1979	102.27	103.64	0.10	1.34	0.16	0.9
1980	116.00	117.84	0.28	1.59	3.25	6.5
1981	132.56	129.37	−0.87	−2.41	1.20	−0.2
1982	110.26	109.57	−0.95	−0.98	−2.26	−2.3
1983	168.46	168.11	0.48	−0.21	−3.30	−3.3
1984	151.64	150.56	0.33	−0.71	0.06	−1.6
1985	191.23	192.95	−0.29	0.90	−1.05	−0.5
		Averages	0.31%	1.33%	−0.28%	0.8%

*S & P Composite Index

TABLE 63

10-YEAR PROFITS

Industry	Seasonal Strategy BUY	SELL	1954-1964 Trading Seasonally	1954-1964 Holding 10 Years	1965-1975 Trading Seasonally	1965-1975 Holding 10 Years
Air Conditioning	Oct.	March	347.2%	63.4%	48.1%	−27.3%
Meat Packing	Sept.	Feb.	313.8	81.9	149.6	16.0
Machine Tools	Sept.	April	235.8	82.5	117.0	−41.6
Property/Liability Insur.	Oct.	Feb.	222.5	104.6	56.4	45.1
Aerospace	Sept.	Jan.	215.7	36.8	62.6	−51.8
Eastern Railroads	Oct.	Feb.	165.4	49.3	64.0	−22.0
Agricultural Machinery	Oct.	Feb.	145.0	72.5	78.6	− 1.4
	Average Profit*		235.0%	70.1%	82.3%	−11.9%

*Excluding all commissions and taxes

fewer and fewer due to mergers and takeovers. Eastern railroads ceased being a separate group in the previous period. Agricultural machinery was a disaster for holders due to the misfortunes of International Harvester and Massey Ferguson. However, since 1976 traders were trounced by holders of the three remaining groups: machine tools, 746.0% vs. 332.0%, insurance 84.9% vs. 4.7%; aerospace, 281.5% vs. 73.8%. This turnabout was due to low index prices at the start of the period and the big bull surge that began in August 1982, one to two months before the seasonal buy points of these groups.

FIGURE 46

AUGUST DAILY PROBABILITY CHART

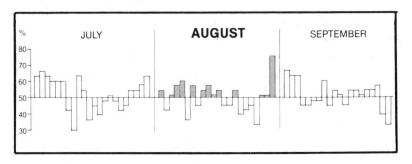

THE AUGUST ALMANAC

• IGNORE ARTICLES EXTOLLING AUGUST BULLISHNESS SINCE 1900—AUGUST WAS UP 80% OF THE TIME IN THE FIRST HALF CENTURY BUT ONLY HALF OF THE TIME THEREAFTER

• EXCLUDING 1982, CHANCE FOR WEAKNESS GREATEST IN LATTER PART OF MONTH

• LAST THREE DAYS BEFORE LABOR DAY UP TWENTY TIMES IN TWENTY-FOUR YEARS

• BEST AUGUST GAINS HAVE OCCURRED IN DOWN YEARS, WHEN JANUARY AND JULY HAVE ALSO DECLINED, AND IN BULL YEARS WITH SHORT, EARLY SUMMER RALLIES

• PURCHASING STOCKS IN AUGUST FOR SHORT-TERM HOLDING PERIODS SEEMS TO PRODUCE BELOW-AVERAGE GAINS. PROSPECTS FOR SIX-MONTH PERIODS ARE MORE FAVORABLE

• SPECTACULAR GAINS OF 92 DOW POINTS IN 1982 AND 109 IN 1984 ARE UNTYPICAL. PREVIOUS MAJOR TURNAROUND IN AUGUST WAS IN 1971 BUT WAS RELATED TO A SPECIFIC MONETARY ACTION TAKEN BY PRESIDENT NIXON

TABLE 64

AUGUST DAILY POINT CHANGES DOW JONES INDUSTRIALS

Previous Month Close	1975 831.51	1976 984.64	1977 890.07	1978 862.27	1979 846.42	1980 935.32	1981 952.34	1982 808.60	1983 1199.22	1984 1115.28
1	− 5.01	—	1.74	− 1.56	3.92	− 3.84	—	—	− 5.01	19.33
2	—	− 2.38	− 4.42	22.78	− 2.39	—	—	13.51	− 6.21	31.47
3	—	8.07	− 1.39	3.38	− 1.79	—	− 6.09	− 5.71	9.82	36.00
4	−8.45	1.95	2.17	1.56	—	− 0.42	− 0.28	−12.94	−14.73	—
5	− 7.90	− 5.60	0.52	—	—	− 1.28	7.61	− 7.61	0.20	—
6	3.52	− 0.68	—	—	2.39	8.45	− 0.67	−11.51	—	0.88
7	2.12	—	—	− 3.38	11.26	12.71	−10.37	—	—	1.66
8	1.95	—	− 9.27	4.16	3.33	3.75	—	—	−20.23	− 8.51
9	—	− 2.54	N/C	2.42	− 4.86	—	—	− 3.99	5.21	27.94
10	—	9.97	7.62	− 6.15	8.78	—	1.14	− 1.05	7.71	− 5.96
11	6.02	− 6.64	− 9.61	5.37	—	9.39	5.62	− 2.09	− 1.59	—
12	4.78	0.33	− 6.33	—	—	−11.69	− 4.09	− 0.29	8.44	—
13	− 7.98	3.07	—	—	8.20	− 3.16	− 0.86	11.13	—	1.99
14	− 3.52	—	—	− 2.68	1.45	13.40	− 7.42	—	—	− 5.97
15	8.60	—	3.03	− 1.04	9.13	4.09	—	—	10.67	−15.13
16	—	2.58	− 4.85	7.45	− 1.80	—	—	4.38	− 3.05	10.16
17	—	6.57	− 4.59	5.54	− 0.68	—	−10.18	38.81	16.05	2.76
18	− 2.89	− 4.33	− 0.43	− 3.29	—	−18.09	− 2.38	− 1.81	−14.02	—
19	−14.24	−11.13	− 0.78	—	—	− 8.78	2.09	9.14	1.73	—
20	−15.25	− 9.81	—	—	3.16	5.46	1.91	30.72	—	5.08
21	− 1.57	—	—	− 7.88	− 0.51	9.72	− 7.80	—	—	22.75
22	13.07	—	3.81	3.46	− 0.17	3.16	—	—	8.94	− 7.95
23	—	− 2.58	− 1.73	4.59	− 5.46	—	—	21.88	−10.26	0.66
24	—	− 8.56	− 2.69	0.35	− 0.18	—	−20.46	−16.27	− 8.64	4.09
25	7.58	7.90	− 8.75	− 1.82	—	− 1.96	1.72	9.99	0.81	—
26	− 9.23	−10.39	1.30	—	—	− 2.82	− 2.57	7.52	7.01	—
27	3.91	3.49	—	—	5.21	−10.32	−10.18	− 8.94	—	− 8.61
28	22.45	—	—	−10.65	− 0.77	−12.71	3.14	—	—	4.19
29	5.87	—	8.67	− 4.68	0.26	2.21	—	—	2.04	− 5.19
30	—	4.99	− 5.20	0.52	− 1.20	—	—	9.83	1.93	− 3.64
31	—	4.82	2.60	− 3.90	3.93	—	−10.75	8.01	20.12	1.10
Close	835.34	973.74	861.49	876.82	887.63	932.59	881.47	901.31	1216.16	1224.38
Change	− 3.83	−10.90	− 28.58	14.55	41.21	− 2.73	− 70.87	92.71	16.94	109.10

APRIL-TO-AUGUST-TO-DECEMBER INDICATOR: A PERFECT RECORD FOR TWENTY-THREE YEARS

For twenty-three straight years, if the market on August 31 was higher (or lower) than it was on April 30, the trend continued through to December 31. If not, it did so by the following August. But before you hock your house, spouse, and kids, bear in mind that no indicator is infallible. In fact, in the previous fourteen years (1949-1962) this "Tinker-to-Evers-to-Chance" indicator erred twice: in 1953, and in 1962, both years with short bear markets. Moreover, during the first forty-eight years of the century (1901-1948) there were thirteen errors.

We can think of no explanation for the recent flawless* twenty-three-year record.

LAST THREE DAYS BEFORE LABOR DAY UP TWENTY-ONE TIMES IN TWENTY-FIVE YEARS

Summer is drawing to a close. Vacationers are returning home or taking one last fling. Spirits have been rejuvenated. A new business season and school year are about to begin. The air is filled with a sense of anticipation, optimism, and even euphoria. A happy setting indeed, and very likely the simple reason for eighteen straight years of rising markets during the three-day period prior to Labor Day, until 1978. My publicizing this phenomenon may have jinxed it.

Chances of an up market on these Mondays or Tuesdays have been about one in three (twenty out of fifty). In contrast, on Wednesday, Thursday or Friday, the odds were four to one the market would rise on any of the three days (fifty-three out of seventy-four).

A phenomenal parallel exists between the calendar year starting New Year's Day and the new business season starting Labor Day. Both are preceded by periods exhibiting strong bullish tendencies: The Santa Claus Rally and the Pre-Labor Day Rally. The first five days of January (January Early Warning System) tend to correctly anticipate the entire month's market performance (January Barometer). The record of both indicators in leading the full year is abundantly clear.

Similarly, Labor Day Week anticipates the market over the following 30 days quite well and acts as a reverse indicator just as the September "Reverse" Barometer. Strength in the fourth quarter tends to follow weakness during Labor Day Week and September—and vice versa.

* Dow fell below 1216 first day of September 1984 and was below in most prior months.

TABLE 65

END-OF-MONTH DOW JONES INDUSTRIALS

	APRIL	AUGUST	DECEMBER	FOLLOWING AUGUST
1949	174.16	178.66	200.13	
1950	214.33	216.87	235.41	
1951	259.13	270.25		275.04
1952	257.63	275.04	291.90	
1953	274.75	261.22		335.80
1954	319.33	335.80	404.39	
1955	425.63	468.18	488.40	
1956	516.12	502.04	499.47	
1957	494.36	484.35	435.69	
1958	455.86	508.63	583.65	
1959	623.75	664.41	679.36	
1960	601.70	625.99		719.94
1961	678.71	719.94	731.14	
1962	665.33	609.18		729.32
1963	717.70	729.32	762.95	
1964	810.77	838.48	874.13	
1965	922.31	893.10		788.41
1966	933.68	788.41	785.69	
1967	897.05	901.29	905.11	
1968	912.22	896.01		836.72
1969	950.18	836.72	800.36	
1970	736.07	764.58	838.92	
1971	941.75	898.07	890.20	
1972	954.17	970.05	1020.02	
1973	921.43	887.57	850.86	
1974	836.75	678.58	616.24	
1975	821.34	835.34	852.41	
1976	996.85	973.74		861.49
1977	926.85	861.49	831.17	
1978	837.32	876.82		887.63
1979	854.90	887.63		932.59
1980	817.06	932.59	963.19	
1981	997.75	881.47	875.00	
1982	848.36	901.31	1046.54	
1983	1226.20	1216.16		122.38
1984	1170.75	1224.38		1334.04
1985	1258.06	1334.01	1546.67	

TABLE 66

WEEK BEFORE LABOR DAY
DAILY DOW POINT CHANGES

YEAR	MON	TUES	WED	THURS	FRI	WEEK'S CLOSE	CHANGE LAST 3 DAYS
1961	− 0.69	− 1.86	2.75	3.04	1.25	721.19	7.04
1962	− 1.17	− 7.32	− 2.01	− 0.92	6.86	609.18	3.93
1963	1.03	− 4.29	5.19	1.33	2.92	729.32	9.44
1964	− 0.61	5.52	1.08	0.94	2.29	848.31	4.31
1965	− 0.33	− 2.53	0.50	6.80	7.57	907.97	14.87
1966	−13.53	8.69	12.69	3.68	− 4.40	787.69	11.97
1967	0.64	0.05	− 1.04	7.57	− 0.11	901.18	6.42
1968	3.79	− 2.48	Closed	0.68	1.68	896.01	2.36
1969	− 5.81	− 7.92	1.26	3.63	8.31	836.72	13.20
1970	− 1.23	− 6.43	− 1.51	8.63	5.88	771.15	13.00
1971	− 6.72	− 3.36	0.95	1.61	12.12	912.75	14.68
1972	− 2.41	− 2.25	3.16	5.87	6.32	970.05	15.35
1973	7.22	1.36	11.36	− 0.90	5.04	887.57	15.50
1974	− 1.33	−16.59	− 4.93	− 9.77	21.74	678.58	7.04
1975	7.58	− 9.23	3.91	22.45	5.87	835.34	32.23
1976	4.99	4.82	12.21	− 1.16	4.32	989.11	15.37
1977	8.67	− 5.20	2.60	3.37	7.45	872.31	13.42
1978	−10.65	− 4.68	0.52	− 3.90	2.51	879.33	− 0.87
1979	5.21	− 0.77	0.26	− 1.20	3.93	887.63	2.99
1980	− 0.68	− 0.25	− 1.06	− 1.17	0.25	932.59	− 1.98
1981	−10.75	1.24	1.52	−17.22	− 5.33	861.68	−21.03
1982	9.83	8.01	−6.26	14.35	15.73	940.49	23.82
1983	2.04	1.93	20.12	−9.35	8.64	1215.45	19.41
1984	− 8.61	4.19	− 5.19	− 3.64	1.10	1224.38	− 7.73
1985	− 0.67	4.82	8.62	4.04	− 1.12	1334.01	11.54
UP	10	10	7	15	21		21
DOWN	15	15	7	10	4		4

FIGURE 47

SEPTEMBER DAILY PROBABILITY CHART

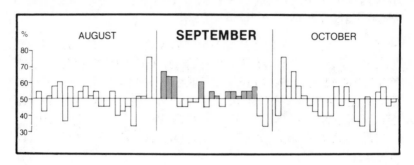

THE SEPTEMBER ALMANAC

• FIRST HALF TENDS TO BE STRONGER THAN SEC-OND

• SEPTEMBER IS THE WORST MONTHLY BAROM-ETER OF THE NEXT ELEVEN OR TWELVE MONTHS SINCE 1950 (JANUARY HAS THE BEST RECORD)

• SEPTEMBER BOX SCORE: UP SIXTEEN, DOWN NINETEEN ON S&P; UP THIRTEEN, DOWN TWENTY-TWO ON DOW

• AVERAGE SEPTEMBER LOSES 0.3%

• CHANCES OF STOCK PRICES RISING DURING LABOR DAY WEEK AND THE MONTH AS A WHOLE TEND TO BE PRACTICALLY NIL IN A BEAR MARKET

• THE LAST SOLID BULL SEPTEMBER WAS IN 1973, WHEN THE MARKET TEMPORARILY BOT-TOMED IN THE PREVIOUS MONTH. THE OTHER UP SEPTEMBERS DURING THE SEVENTIES WERE 1970 and 1976; MOST RECENTLY, 1980 WAS UP 2.5%, 1982 0.8%, AND 1983 1.0%

• SOME OF THE GROUPS THAT TEND TO HIT SEA-SONAL LOWS DURING THE MONTH ARE AERO-SPACE, AND MACHINE TOOLS. AEROSPACE

STOCKS TEND TO START MOVING UP IN ANTICI-
PATION OF JANUARY'S DEFENSE BUDGET IN
WASHINGTON

• THE LAST TWO TRADING DAYS OF THE MONTH
HAVE RISEN FEWER TIMES SINCE 1952 THAN ANY
OTHER MONTH. THEY WERE BOTH UP IN 1985 BUT
HURRICANE GLORIA CLOSED THE NEW YORK
STOCK EXCHANGE ON WHAT WOULD HAVE BEEN
THE NEXT-TO-LAST TRADING DAY OF THE
MONTH

TABLE 67

SEPTEMBER DAILY POINT CHANGES DOW JONES INDUSTRIALS

Previous Month	1975	1976	1977	1978	1979	1980	1981	1982	1983	1984
Close	835.34	973.74	861.49	876.82	887.63	932.59	881.47	901.31	1216.16	1224.38
1	H	12.21	3.37	2.51	—	H	1.24	− 6.26	− 9.35	—
2	−11.65	− 1.16	7.45	—	—	8.19	1.52	14.35	8.64	—
3	8.60	4.32	—	—	H	12.38	−17.22	15.73	—	H
4	6.02	—	—	H	−15.02	− 4.35	− 5.33	H	—	−12.03
5	− 2.34	—	H	7.28	−6.48	− 7.85	H	—	H	− 3.32
6	—	H	0.96	9.18	1.19	—	—	—	23.27	9.83
7	—	7.48	3.12	− 2.08	6.83	—	—	−10.85	5.39	−11.48
8	4.14	− 3.65	8.23	14.03	—	−12.38	−10.56	1.47	2.03	—
9	−12.36	− 6.07	−11.09	—	—	6.15	2.76	− 3.22	− 6.40	—
10	−10.09	1.49	—	—	2.73	3.75	8.56	− 5.71	—	− 4.86
11	− 5.00	—	—	N/C	− 7.17	2.82	10.37	—	—	− 4.53
12	− 3.37	—	− 2.69	− 1.30	1.19	− 4.78	—	—	−10.67	2.32
13	—	− 5.07	0.18	− 6.84	− 0.17	—	—	11.87	− 4.98	27.94
14	—	− 4.65	4.15	−12.56	8.37	—	− 6.66	4.32	5.38	9.27
15	− 6.10	0.67	2.08	− 8.49	—	1.11	− 7.80	7.45	−14.43	—
16	− 8.06	8.64	− 3.98	—	—	8.27	− 6.75	− 2.66	10.67	—
17	3.92	7.15	—	—	2.21	15.36	−11.51	−10.86	—	− 0.44
18	15.56	—	—	8.40	− 7.16	− 4.78	− 3.90	—	—	−10.82
19	15.18	—	− 5.29	− 8.58	2.30	7.26	—	—	8.23	−13.25
20	—	− 0.59	0.26	− 4.41	17.24	—	—	− 0.64	15.25	3.53
21	—	20.28	−10.82	3.98	0.25	—	10.37	18.49	− 5.90	−14.80
22	− 9.39	− 0.74	− 1.82	1.30	—	10.83	− 0.86	− 7.18	14.23	—
23	− 0.55	− 3.25	n/c	—	—	−12.54	− 4.76	− 1.84	− 1.93	—
24	6.34	− 1.49	—	—	− 8.10	2.73	− 5.80	− 6.25	—	3.32
25	−5.95	—	—	− 0.09	0.34	− 8.79	−11.13	—	—	2.10
26	− 1.64	—	2.51	5.81	0.17	−15.87	—	—	5.18	4.96
27	—	3.82	− 5.80	− 7.97	1.11	—	—	1.38	−12.80	4.64
28	—	−18.20	− 1.13	1.12	− 8.88	—	18.55	− 1.57	− 6.00	−10.05
29	−13.37	− 3.74	5.37	4.51	—	−18.17	5.33	−13.06	− 1.83	—
30	−11.35	− 1.00	7.02	—	—	10.49	2.09	−10.02	− 7.01	—
Close	793.88	990.19	847.11	865.82	878.58	932.42	849.98	896.25	1233.13	1206.71
Change	−41.46	16.45	−14.38	−11.00	− 9.05	− 0.17	−31.49	− 5.06	16.97	−17.67

THE LABOR DAY WEEK FORECASTER RIGHT TWENTY TIMES IN TWENTY-SIX YEARS

Watch what happens to stock prices during the short four-day week following Labor Day. Should the market decline that week, postpone your purchases for thirty days. If there is a net gain that week, buy at once, knowing the market will probably be higher thirty days later. This strategy would have put you on the "right side" of an average change in twenty of the last twenty-six years, equivalent to 28 points in the Dow Jones industrial average at Dow 1500.

The market rose during Labor Day week in twelve of the last twenty-six years. One month later except in 1975, 1978, and 1985, the D.J. average tacked on additional points. During fourteen other years, the opposite occurred. Losses in the Labor Day week were followed by an additional loss thirty days later. The year 1970 was a lemon. The 1979 October Massacre began one day after period ended. The indicator in 1982 was off base. A powerful new bull market began in 1982 and swept

TABLE 68

THE LABOR DAY WEEK FORECASTING RECORD

	Previous Week	Labor Day Week	Point Change	One Month Later	Point Change	% Gain
1960	625.22	614.22	−11.00	587.31	−26.91	4.4
1961	721.19	720.91	− 0.28	705.42	−15.49	2.2
1962	609.18	600.86	− 8.32	586.09	−14.77	2.5
1963	729.32	735.37	6.05	743.86	8.49	1.2
1964	848.31	867.13	18.82	878.08	10.95	1.3
1965	907.97	918.95	10.98	942.65	23.70	2.6
1966	787.69	775.55	−12.14	744.32	−31.23	4.0
1967	901.18	907.54	6.36	933.31	25.77	2.8
1968	896.01	921.25	25.24	956.68	35.43	3.8
1969	836.72	819.50	−17.22	809.40	−10.10	1.2
1970	771.15	761.84	− 9.31	764.24	2.40	− 0.3
1971	912.75	911.00	− 1.75	891.94	−19.06	2.1
1972	970.05	961.24	− 8.81	948.75	−12.49	1.3
1973	887.57	898.63	11.06	977.65	79.02	8.8
1974	678.58	677.88	− 0.70	607.56	−70.32	10.4
1975	835.34	835.97	0.63	819.66	−16.31	− 1.9
1976	989.11	988.36	− 0.75	940.82	−47.54	4.8
1977	872.31	857.07	−15.24	840.26	−16.81	2.0
1978	879.33	907.74	28.41	893.19	−14.55	− 1.6
1979	887.63	874.15	−13.48	884.04	9.89	− 1.1
1980	932.59	940.96	8.37	965.70	24.74	2.6
1981	861.68	872.81	11.13	873.00	0.19	0.1
1982	925.13	906.82	−18.31	986.85	80.03	− 8.8
1983	1215.45	1239.74	24.29	1284.65	44.91	3.6
1984	1224.38	1207.38	−17.00	1177.89	−29.49	2.4
1985	1334.01	1335.69	1.68	1324.37	−11.32	− 0.8

* Original research, Newton D. Zinder (E.F. Hutton)

over this indicator.

One might note that six substantial Labor Day week losers—1960, 1962, 1966, 1969, 1970 and 1977—were all bear years. An obvious line of reasoning is that when the market declines during Labor Day week and is down further one month later in a bear market year, it is merely continuing its downward direction.

THE SEPTEMBER "REVERSE" BAROMETER

September always had special significance to Wall Streeters, as it was the start of a new business year. During the first sixty years of this century, the stock market in the final quarter of the year often took its cue from its own behavior in September and followed a similar course two-thirds of the time. As a result, September market activity was naturally regarded as a useful barometer and became folklore.

However, starting with 1960, an incredible transformation occurred. September became a **reverse barometer**. Bearish Septembers tended to be followed by bullish fourth quarters, and vice-versa. In the last twenty-six years, seventeen Septembers were losers or gained less than one percent. They preceded average fourth quarter gains of 5.8%. The other nine Septembers ending in the plus column preceded fourth quarters gaining 1.7%, on average.

Even more incredible is September's record as a reverse barometer giving us advance notice of what the market will do in the following year. Six of the nine Septembers, with gains of 1.0% or more in Standard & Poor's composite index, were followed by bear market years (1974, 1969, 1966, 1981, 1977 and 1984 through August). The average loss for the nine years was 5.2%. Sixteen other Septembers were down, flat or slightly up and their following years gained 13.1% on average. There were only two losing years—1973 and 1962—and neither was recession-induced. The former was caused by the market drop after Watergate's Saturday Night "Massacre" and OPEC's world-shattering boost in oil prices; the latter by Kennedy's stare-down with Big Steel.

TABLE 69

AS SEPTEMBER GOES, BE CONTRARY!

	Fourth-Quarter Performance		
Year	1st Day in October	2nd Day in January	4th Quarter % Change
1960	53.36*	58.36*	9.4%
1961	66.77	71.13	6.5
1962	55.49	63.72	14.8
1963	72.22	75.50	4.5
1964	84.08	84.63	0.7
1965	89.90	92.26	2.6
1966	74.90	80.55	7.5
1967	96.32	95.67	−0.7
1968	102.86	103.99	1.1
1969	92.52	93.46	1.0
1970	84.32	91.80	8.9
1971	98.93	102.09	3.2
1972	110.16	119.57	8.5
1973	108.21	99.80	−7.8
1974	63.39	70.71	11.5
1975	82.93	92.58	11.6
1976	104.17	105.70	1.5
1977	96.74	93.52	−3.3
1978	102.96	97.80	−5.0
1979	108.56	105.22	−3.1
1980	127.13	137.97	8.5
1981	117.08	120.05	2.5
1982	121.97	141.35	15.9
1983	165.80	166.78	0.6
1984	164.62	164.57	0.0
1985	185.07	210.88	13.9

*S & P Composite Index

Previous Septembers Bullish

Year	Sept Change	4th Q Change	Next Year's Change
1973	4.0%	− 7.8%	− 29.7%
1968	3.9	1.1	− 11.4
1967	3.3	− 0.7	7.7
1970	3.3	8.9	10.8
1965	3.2	2.7	− 13.1
1964	2.9	0.7	9.1
1980	2.5	8.5	− 9.7
1976	2.3	1.5	− 11.5
1983	1.0	0.6	1.4
Averages	2.9%	1.7%	− 5.2%

Previous Septembers Bearish

Year	Sept Change	4th Q Change	Next Year's Change
1982	0.8%	15.9%	17.3%
1979	0.0	− 3.1	25.8
1977	− 0.2	− 3.3	1.1
1984	− 0.4	0.0	26.3
1972	− 0.5	8.5	− 17.4
1978	− 0.7	− 5.0	12.3
1966	− 0.7	7.5	20.1
1971	− 0.7	3.2	15.6
1963	− 1.1	4.5	13.0
1961	− 2.0	6.5	− 11.8
1969	− 2.5	1.0	0.1
1985	− 3.5	13.9	??
1975	− 3.5	11.6	19.1
1962	− 4.8	14.8	18.9
1981	− 5.4	2.5	14.8
1960	− 6.0	9.4	23.1
1974	−11.9	11.5	31.5
Averages	−2.5%	5.8%	13.1%

FIGURE 48

OCTOBER DAILY PROBABILITY CHART

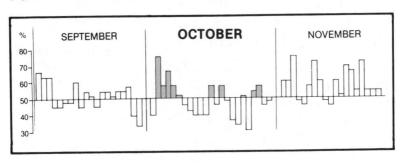

THE OCTOBER ALMANAC

• OCTOBER, THE "BEAR-KILLER," HAS TURNED THE TIDE IN SIX MAJOR BEAR MARKETS: 1946, 1957, 1960, 1962, 1966, AND 1974

• MARKET CRASH IN OCTOBER 1929 GAVE THE MONTH A BAD NAME

• RECENT NOTORIETY INCLUDED BACK-TO-BACK "MASSACRES" IN 1978 AND 1979

• BARGAIN MONTH AND BEST BUYING TIME, OCTOBER PRECEDES MOST BULLISH THREE-MONTH SPAN (NOVEMBER, DECEMBER, AND JANUARY)

• SINCE 1960, FOURTEEN DOWN LABOR DAY WEEKS PRECEDED AVERAGE 5.9% GAINS IN FOURTH QUARTER; ELEVEN WINNERS PRECEDED AVERAGE 1.7% GAINS

• OCTOBER OUTRANKS ALL OTHER MONTHS AS A BUYING TIME FOR ONE-, TWO-, THREE-, AND SIX-MONTH BUYING PERIODS. IT SHOULD BE THE FAVORITE MONTH FOR PURCHASERS OF CALL OPTION CONTRACTS, WRITERS OF PUT OPTIONS, AND INDEX FUTURES BUYERS

• THIRD FRIDAYS OF OCTOBER (OPTION EXPIRA-TION DAY) IN PAST TEN YEARS HAVE BEEN DOWN EIGHT TIMES AND UP JUST A TAD TWICE

• NORMALLY ONE OF MARKET'S BEST DAYS IS THE LAST TRADING DAY OF THE MONTH WHICH RISES ABOUT 57% OF THE TIME. BUT ON HALLO-WEEN, IF YOU'RE CURIOUS, THE MARKET IN TWENTY YEARS HAS ONLY RISEN FOUR TIMES OUT OF FOURTEEN (28.5%). THE HOLIDAY FELL ON A WEEKEND SIX TIMES

TABLE 70

OCTOBER DAILY POINT CHANGES DOW JONES INDUSTRIALS

Previous Month	1975	1976	1977	1978	1979	1980	1981	1982	1983	1984
Close	793.88	990.19	847.11	865.82	878.58	932.42	849.98	896.25	1233.13	1206.71
1	− 9.72	−10.30	—	—	− 5.63	7.00	2.28	11.49	—	− 7.73
2	10.39	—	—	5.54	12.37	2.82	8.47	—	—	− 7.62
3	18.66	—	4.85	− 3.46	− 0.17	8.44	—	—	− 1.83	− 8.50
4	—	− 1.91	− 9.96	6.06	4.95	—	—	− 4.13	5.39	4.53
5	—	−11.22	− 4.68	2.51	7.51	—	− 0.86	3.58	13.51	− 4.86
6	6.45	− 7.07	4.76	3.55	—	15.02	− 3.61	37.07	18.60	—
7	−3.15	5.40	− 1.73	—	—	− 5.03	12.46	21.71	3.35	—
8	7.40	−12.71	—	—	−13.57	3.32	9.42	20.88	—	− 4.64
9	0.63	—	—	13.17	−26.45	− 5.03	− 5.14	—	—	− 2.76
10	− 0.63	—	− 0.09	− 1.56	− 8.27	− 8.28	—	—	12.50	2.10
11	—	−11.56	− 7.88	9.79	− 4.70	—	—	25.94	−19.51	5.85
12	—	− 8.47	− 8.40	− 4.68	− 5.63	—	− 3.52	− 9.11	−5.49	7.62
13	13.86	15.95	− 5.81	0.35	—	9.22	− 3.90	11.40	1.73	—
14	− 2.52	−12.38	3.47	—	—	2.30	−14.93	−18.21	2.14	—
15	1.97	1.08	—	—	− 7.93	10.24	5.61	− 3.77	—	12.26
16	0.63	—	—	−21.92	− 1.54	−13.74	− 4.57	—	—	− 5.19
17	− 5.67	—	− 1.30	− 8.83	1.20	− 2.56	—	—	5.18	− 1.88
18	—	9.56	0.17	− 6.67	− 0.60	—	—	26.12	−17.89	29.49
19	—	3.41	− 8.31	−13.26	−15.44	—	− 4.56	− 5.42	− 4.06	0.55
20	10.07	4.90	2.60	− 8.40	—	4.70	4.75	20.32	4.77	—
21	4.57	− 9.97	− 6.50	—	—	− 6.40	− 0.85	2.86	− 2.64	—
22	2.75	− 6.15	—	—	− 5.55	0.68	− 2.76	− 5.52	—	− 8.73
23	5.59	—	—	1.65	− 2.30	−15.61	−10.28	—	—	− 4.19
24	−14.64	—	− 5.98	− 7.11	1.53	4.09	—	—	0.10	3.42
25	—	− 0.75	− 0.78	− 2.34	− 2.90	—	—	−36.33	3.46	− 5.41
26	—	10.14	11.87	− 9.09	3.84	—	− 7.03	10.94	− 8.46	− 6.07
27	− 2.04	7.98	5.20	−15.07	—	−11.86	7.42	0.28	− 1.73	—
28	12.98	− 3.49	4.07	—	—	0.85	− 0.77	−15.36	−18.59	—
29	−12.83	12.30	—	—	− 0.68	− 3.41	− 4.66	0.73	—	− 3.54
30	0.79	—	—	5.80	15.19	−11.43	19.60	—	—	15.90
31	− 3.38	—	− 4.33	−19.40	− 8.11	6.74	—	—	1.72	− 9.93
Close	836.04	964.93	818.35	792.45	815.70	924.49	852.55	991.72	1225.20	1207.38
Change	42.16	−25.26	−28.76	−70.37	−62.88	− 7.93	2.57	95.47	− 7.93	0.67

BEST SHORT-TERM BUYING TIMES

October, without a doubt, has been the best buying month for short-term traders since 1949. The chief reason for its success as a favorable buying time has been that most major market declines seem to choose this time of the year to turn around. October also precedes the most bullish three-month span of the year.

In one-, two-, three- and six-month time periods, October ranked number one in performance over the other months, with average gains of 1.1%, 2.2%, 4.3%, and 6.3%. November was second, with December and September placing third and fourth. The worst showings were made by May and April.

TABLE 71

WHAT THE MARKET DID IN ALL 1, 2, 3 AND 6 MONTH PERIODS

(34-Year Record, 1949-1983)
Average Percent Change Between Any Month And

	30 days Later	Rank	60 days Later	Rank	90 days Later	Rank	6 months Later	Rank
January	0.2%	10	0.9%	8	2.1%	5	2.6%	11
February	0.7	6	1.9	4	2.1	6	2.8	8
March	1.3	2	1.5	5	0.9	11	2.8	9
April	0.1	11	−0.2	12	0.4	12	1.5	12
May	−0.4	12	0.4	11	0.8	8	2.7	10
June	0.8	5	1.3	7	1.6	9	4.4	6
July	0.5	7	0.8	9	1.2	10	5.2	3
August	0.3	9	0.7	10	1.8	7	5.0	4
September	0.5	8	1.5	6	2.6	4	5.5	2
October	1.1	3	2.2	2	4.3	1	6.3	1
November	1.1	4	2.8	1	3.2	2	5.0	5
December	1.6	1	2.0	3	2.7	3	3.8	7
Avg. Chg.	0.7%		1.3%		2.0%		4.0%	
	Average 30-day change		Average 60-day change		Average 90-day change		Average 6-month change	

Based on average monthly prices of Standard & Poor's Composite Index

The average percentage change per month for all periods ranked in order were: 1. October (1.16); 2. November (1.01); 3. December (0.84); 4. September (0.84); 5. June (0.68); 6. August (0.65); 7. July (0.64); 8. February (0.63); 9. March (0.54); 10. January (0.48); 11. May (0.29); 12. April (0.15).

GOLDS GREAT BUYS SINCE 1963 DURING FOURTH QUARTERS

Fourth quarters in most of the years since 1963 have produced attractive buying opportunities for gold stocks. I noted in 1975 that catching these seasonal lows in ASA and selling at the spring or summer highs would have produced an average annual gain of 87.8% for the prior decade.

FIGURE 49

ASA, LTD. (ASA)

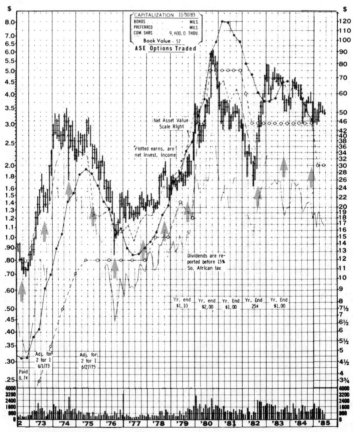

Chart courtesy Security Research Co.

The annual International Monetary Fund meetings in the fall and weakness in gold shares appeared to have some correlation. Arrows on the ASA chart illustrate most of the annual seasonal buy points. Ian McAvity of *Deliberations* has identified a six-year gold cycle with tops in 1967-68 (after tripling), 1973-74 (after quintupling) and 1979-80 (after quadrupling).

Is a fourth cycle forthcoming? The first three were accompanied by the inflationary Vietnam escalation and OPEC's crippling oil price increases in 1973 and 1979. Is inflation dead or will it rise again? And what will trigger a gold rush this time?

FIGURE 50

NOVEMBER DAILY PROBABILITY CHART

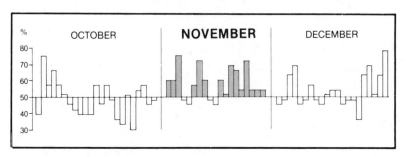

THE NOVEMBER ALMANAC

• GREATEST PERCENTAGE GAINER IN THIRTY-FIVE YEARS BASED ON STANDARD & POOR'S COMPOSITE INDEX

• UP AN AVERAGE 1.8% PER YEAR

• TOTAL GAIN OF 289 DOW POINTS IS BEHIND APRIL'S 464 AND DECEMBER'S 314

• UP TWENTY-THREE TIMES, DOWN TWELVE, BUT ONLY THREE LOSSES OVER 2.0% (1969, -3.5%; 1973, -11.4%; AND 1974, -5.3%)

• TAX SELLING MAY HAMPER BIG GAINERS AND BIG LOSERS

• EXPECT TURNDOWNS IN FIRST HALF OF MONTH, TURNUPS LATER

- THE PERIOD OF FIVE TRADING DAYS PRE-CEDING AND THREE TRADING DAYS FOLLOWING ELECTION DAY GAINS 0.2% ON AVERAGE IN ODD ELECTION YEARS, COMPARED TO 1.2% FOR PRES-IDENTIAL YEARS AND 3.0% FOR MIDTERM ELEC-TION YEARS

- NOVEMBER RANKS SECOND TO OCTOBER AS A BEST BUYING TIME FOR ONE-, TWO-, THREE-, AND SIX-MONTH PERIODS

- AUTO STOCKS TEND TO TURN DOWN SEASON-ALLY IN NOVEMBER

- THE DAY BEFORE AND THE DAY AFTER THANKSGIVING COMBINED HAVE AVERAGED A NINE—POINT GAIN ON THE DOW FOR TWENTY STRAIGHT YEARS WITHOUT A LOSS

TABLE 72

NOVEMBER DAILY POINT CHANGES DOW JONES INDUSTRIALS

Previous Month Close	1975 836.04	1976 964.93	1977 818.35	1978 792.45	1979 815.70	1980 924.49	1981 852.55	1982 991.72	1983 1225.20	1984 1207.38
1	—	1.16	—11.44	35.34	4.44	—	—	13.98	4.07	9.71
2	—	H	— 6.06	—10.83	— 1.20	—	14.27	16.38	8.03	— 0.44
3	—10.32	— 9.56	1.82	6.15	—	12.71	1.90	43.41	—10.17	—
4	4.41	3.91	7.27	—	—	H	— 1.90	—15.27	— 8.84	—
5	6.14	—17.37	—	—	— 6.31	15.96	— 7.71	1.56	—	12.59
6	4.65	—	—	— 8.23	— 6.15	—17.75	— 6.66	—	—	14.91
7	— 5.12	—	6.50	—14.81	— 9.81	— 2.99	—	—	— 3.45	—10.93
8	—	— 9.39	— 0.17	7.54	0.94	—	—	—14.34	0.10	— 4.53
9	—	— 2.91	2.16	— 3.64	8.87	—	2.76	22.81	17.58	— 9.72
10	— 0.32	— 6.73	14.12	3.12	—	1.37	— 1.23	—15.73	3.35	—
11	3.07	7.39	13.34	—	—	10.24	3.14	10.21	14.33	—
12	13.70	— 3.74	—	—	15.45	20.90	3.42	—14.81	—	0.22
13	— 1.02	—	—	—15.08	— 7.85	17.49	— 4.66	—	—	—12.59
14	2.44	—	— 7.53	— 6.75	2.47	3.93	—	—	3.87	0.33
15	—	7.73	4.42	0.34	4.78	—	—	—18.49	— 6.10	— 0.77
16	—	— 0.08	— 5.72	8.58	— 5.63	—	—10.85	—13.43	3.35	—18.22
17	2.99	2.74	— 5.20	3.55	—	— 0.09	5.14	19.50	3.35	—
18	— 1.42	12.05	3.90	—	—	11.69	— 6.09	4.60	— 3.65	—
19	— 7.00	— 1.33	—	—	— 0.43	— 6.91	0.67	—10.85	—	— 2.65
20	— 4.73	—	—	7.88	— 6.05	9.13	8.18	—	—	9.83
21	— 2.75	—	0.35	— 1.56	— 1.80	—10.24	—	—	17.78	6.40
22	—	7.07	6.41	2.95	H	—	—	—21.25	7.01	H
23	—	— 6.57	0.78	H	4.35	—	— 1.14	— 9.01	— 0.20	18.78
24	4.88	1.66	H	3.12	—	—11.18	18.45	9.01	H	—
25	9.76	H	1.12	—	—	3.93	7.90	H	1.83	—
26	3.15	5.66	—	—	16.98	7.00	H	7.36	—	— 7.95
27	H	—	—	3.72	— 2.90	H	7.80	—	—	7.84
28	2.12	—	— 4.85	— 9.70	4.61	3.66	—	—	— 7.62	—14.80
29	—	— 6.57	—12.30	—14.03	1.28	—	—	— 4.51	17.38	—11.93
30	—	— 2.83	2.43	8.92	— 9.39	—	—	3.04	36.43	—11.18	— 4.52
Close	860.67	947.22	829.70	799.03	822.35	993.34	888.98	1039.28	1276.02	1188.94
Change	24.63	—17.71	11.35	6.58	6.65	68.85	36.43	47.56	50.82	—18.44

MIDTERM ELECTION TIME
UNUSUALLY BULLISH

It may only be coincidence, but midterm election years—the even years falling between presidential election years—seem to produce an unusual amount of bullishness around election time compared to other years in the presidential cycle. From the fifth trading day preceding to the third trading day following Election Day during 1950, 1954, 1958, 1962, 1966, 1970, 1974, 1978, and 1982, the market averaged a 3.0% gain. This is equal to a jump from 1300 to 1339 in the Dow Jones industrial average.

The average gain for these eight trading days in the last nine presidential election years was 1.2%, while all the odd years since 1949—there were nineteen of them—produced average gains of only 0.2 percent.

Four earlier midterm election years—1934, 1938, 1942, and 1946—were also quite bullish.

SURE WAY TO WIN
THE TURKEY SHOOT

Easy! Be invested on the day before and after Thanksgiving. These two days combined have gained about nine Dow points on average for nineteen straight years without a loss. In thirty-three years there was only one five-point loss and one loss of less than a point. Strength around Thanksgiving may be attributed to the Holiday spirit if you want, but it may also be due to two other seasonal factors. November has been the number one percentage gainer since 1950 (S&P 500). Then, too, the last chance for one tax strategy comes around Thanksgiving. This allows investors to dump a losing position in late December to establish tax losses for 1985 without losing their position in that stock. Tax laws permit you to sell a stock for a loss as long as you don't purchase it for 31 days before or after the loss is taken. If you buy an additional amount of a "loser" in late November, you can then sell your losing position in that stock in late December. This seasonal tendency can be useful to investors and traders alike as long as it doesn't get around the Street. I would go long prior to the Wednesday before Thanksgiving. As ten of the following Mondays in the past thirteen years lost 12 Dow points on average, I would tend to exit somewhere near the close on the Friday after Thanksgiving.

TABLE 73

BULLS VS. ELEPHANTS AND DONKEYS

	5 Trading Days Before Election Day	3 Trading Days After Election Day	Net % Change During Period
1949	16.04*	16.14*	0.6%
1950	19.61	19.94	1.7
1951	22.69	22.75	0.3
1952	24.09	24.78	2.9
1953	24.31	24.61	1.2
1954	31.96	32.71	2.3
1955	42.34	45.24	6.8
1956	46.49	46.34	—0.3
1957	40.42	40.19	—0.6
1958	50.42	52.26	3.6
1959	56.96	57.60	1.1
1960	53.39	55.87	4.6
1961	68.42	71.07	3.9
1962	55.72	58.78	5.5
1963	74.48	73.36	—1.5
1964	85.00	85.23	0.3
1965	91.67	92.37	0.8
1966	80.20	81.94	2.2
1967	94.79	92.21	—2.7
1968	103.90	103.95	0.0
1969	97.94	98.26	0.3
1970	83.31	84.22	1.1
1971	94.74	94.46	—0.3
1972	111.58	113.73	1.9
1973	109.33	105.30	—3.7
1974	72.83	74.91	2.9
1975	90.51	89.33	—1.3
1976	101.06	100.82	—0.2
1977	92.10	92.29	0.2
1978	93.15	94.77	1.7
1979	102.67	101.51	—1.1
1980	128.05	129.18	0.9
1981	119.29	122.67	2.8
1982	134.48	142.16	5.7
1983	166.47	162.44	—2.4
1984	166.84	167.60	0.4
1985	187.76	193.72	32

*S&P Composite Index

TABLE 74

WHAT DOW JONES INDUSTRIALS DID ON
THE DAY BEFORE AND AFTER THANKSGIVING

	Day Before	Day After	Total Gain Dow Points	Dow Close
1952	1.54	1.22	2.76	283.66
1953	0.65	2.45	3.10	280.23
1954	1.89	3.16	5.05	387.79
1955	0.71	0.26	0.97	482.88
1956	− 2.16	4.65	2.49	472.36
1957	10.69	3.84	14.53	449.87
1958	8.63	8.31	16.94	557.46
1959	1.41	1.42	2.83	652.52
1960	1.37	4.00	5.37	606.47
1961	1.10	2.18	3.28	732.60
1962	4.31	7.62	11.93	644.87
1963	− 2.52	9.52	7.00	750.52
1964	− 5.21	− 0.28	− 5.49	882.12
1965	n/c	− 0.78	− 0.78	948.16
1966	1.84	6.52	8.36	803.34
1967	3.07	3.58	6.65	877.60
1968	− 3.17	8.76	5.59	985.08
1969	3.23	1.78	5.01	812.30
1970	1.98	6.64	8.62	781.35
1971	0.66	17.96	18.62	816.59
1972	7.29	4.67	11.96	1025.21
1973	10.08	− 0.98	9.10	854.00
1974	2.03	− 0.63	1.40	618.66
1975	3.15	2.12	5.27	860.67
1976	1.66	5.66	7.32	956.62
1977	0.78	1.12	1.90	844.42
1978	2.95	3.12	6.07	810.12
1979	− 1.80	4.35	2.55	811.77
1980	7.00	3.66	10.66	993.34
1981	7.90	7.80	15.70	885.94
1982	9.01	7.36	16.37	1007.36
1983	− 0.20	1.83	1.63	1277.44
1984	6.40	18.78	25.18	1220.30
1985	18.92	−3.56	15.36	1472.13

FIGURE 51

DECEMBER DAILY PROBABILITY CHART

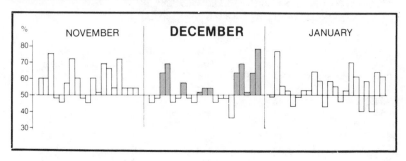

THE DECEMBER ALMANAC

• DECEMBER MARKETS TEND TO GO NOWHERE

• "FREE LUNCH" SERVED ON WALL STREET AT MID-MONTH

• LOW-PRICED STOCKS USUALLY BEAT HIGH QUALITY IN JANUARY

• GOLD GREAT BUY IN FOURTH QUARTERS

• DECEMBER BOX SCORE: UP TWENTY-FOUR, DOWN TEN

• DECEMBER IS THIRD BEST MONTH, WITH AVERAGE 1.4% GAIN ON S&P 500 AND 291.55 TOTAL DOW POINTS SINCE 1950

• PROSPECTS FOR DECEMBER 1986 ARE EXCELLENT, AS NINE PREVIOUS DECEMBERS PRIOR TO A PRE-ELECTION YEAR GAINED AN AVERAGE 2.5%—ABOUT 40 DOW POINTS AT CURRENT LEVELS. A SMALL 0.1% LOSS IN 1966 AND ONE OF 2.0% AT THE 1974 BOTTOM PRECEDED THE BIG BULL YEARS OF 1967 AND 1975

• NO LOSING PRE-ELECTION YEAR SINCE 1939 AND JUST ONE BAD LOSS (1931) SINCE 1907, AVERAGE CHANGE 16.8%

• PROSPECTS FOR DECEMBER 1987 ARE GOOD, AS NINE PREVIOUS DECEMBERS PRIOR TO AN ELECTION YEAR GAINED 2.2% ON AVERAGE. SIX WERE UP AND THREE HAD SMALL LOSSES—0.1% IN 1955 AND 1.2% IN 1975, PRIOR TO TOPPING-OUT YEARS; AND 0.9% IN 1983, PRIOR TO A SEVEN-MONTH DECLINE THEN A COMEBACK TO YEAR END

TABLE 75

DECEMBER DAILY POINT CHANGES DOW JONES INDUSTRIALS

Previous Month Close	1975 860.67	1976 947.22	1977 829.70	1978 799.03	1979 822.35	1980 993.34	1981 888.98	1982 1039.28	1983 1276.02	1984 1188.94
1	− 4.33	2.16	− 3.99	12.47	—	−23.89	1.24	− 8.19	− 0.92	—
2	−13.14	− 2.74	− 1.73	—	—	4.95	− 7.61	2.02	− 9.86	—
3	−17.71	3.91	—	—	− 2.73	− 2.13	1.24	− 1.75	—	− 6.52
4	3.62	—	—	− 4.67	5.29	− 1.79	8.84	—	—	2.65
5	−10.31	—	− 2.95	13.68	3.50	−14.25	—	—	5.29	−13.47
6	—	11.22	−14.12	1.39	6.66	—	—	24.29	− 1.22	− 1.11
7	—	− 1.08	0.52	− 5.81	− 1.88	—	− 5.70	1.29	4.47	− 7.28
8	2.83	2.57	− 0.52	− 4.24	—	−22.53	− 5.24	− 9.85	−11.89	—
9	2.52	7.48	8.32	—	—	0.34	6.47	−19.13	− 1.83	—
10	9.84	2.41	—	—	0.68	−17.83	3.81	− 9.20	—	9.05
11	—	—	5.80	− 0.17	− 7.76	− 5.52	—	—	—	6.07
12	0.08	—	0.52	− 2.68	1.97	8.70	—	—	1.53	− 3.20
13	—	1.09	− 0.52	− 5.11	0.42	—	—	5.52	− 5.70	− 6.29
14	—	6.39	7.45	2.68	6.66	—	−15.03	−14.90	− 9.24	7.07
15	3.78	3.16	− 4.77	− 7.19	—	− 5.55	4.47	−16.74	− 9.86	—
16	7.71	− 2.49	− 2.59	—	—	6.49	− 7.23	− 2.39	5.38	—
17	1.97	− 2.24	—	—	1.87	10.41	1.81	21.25	—	0.88
18	5.82	—	—	−17.84	− 5.97	1.70	5.23	—	—	34.78
19	− 7.71	—	− 7.37	2.34	0.26	7.00	—	—	2.44	− 3.53
20	—	− 6.65	− 1.73	3.81	4.43	—	—	− 6.99	− 2.64	− 4.75
21	—	5.98	7.71	1.13	− 4.43	—	− 2.66	25.75	13.01	− 4.31
22	− 5.75	6.15	7.88	13.68	—	—	− 1.14	4.78	− 1.32	—
23	5.12	1.08	8.06	—	—	− 0.51	− 2.29	10.03	− 3.15	—
24	8.19	—	—	—	0.25	4.77	3.71	—	—	11.16
25	H	H	H	H	H	H	H	H	H	H
26	7.87	—	—	—	7.54	− 1.02	3.33	—	—	− 1.22
27	—	10.47	—	− 7.45	1.96	—	—	25.48	13.21	− 6.40
28	—	3.99	− 0.17	− 2.60	− 1.19	—	− 3.04	−11.68	− 0.51	1.65
29	− 3.15	− 5.15	NC	− 0.95	—	− 5.80	− 2.09	0.73	− 3.05	—
30	− 4.25	4.16	0.69	—	—	1.45	4.85	−12.23	− 1.52	—
31	NC	5.56	0.78	—	− 0.17	1.96	1.90	− 0.83	—	7.40
Close	852.41	1004.65	831.17	805.01	838.74	963.99	875.00	1046.54	1258.64	1211.57
Change	− 8.26	57.43	1.47	5.98	16.39	−29.35	−13.98	7.26	−17.38	22.63

MID-DECEMBER NEW LOWS—
THE ONLY FREE LUNCH
ON WALL STREET

Several shrewd observers have noted that many depressed issues sell at "bargain" levels near the close of each year as investors rid their portfolios of these "losers" for tax purposes. What happens thereafter can be seen in Table 76—featured originally in my 1970 *Stock Trader's Almanac*. Stocks hitting new lows for the year around December 15 in 1966, 1967, and 1968 outperformed the market handsomely by February 15 in the following year. The first group of forty-five stocks appreciated 18.0%, twice the 8.9% of the New York Stock Exchange composite index. And while this comprehensive index was suffering declines in the two-month bargain period of 4.7 and 3.4% in the next two years, the "new lows" were advancing 7.4 and 5.0%.

TABLE 76

BARGAIN STOCKS VS. THE MARKET

Period of Dec. 15-Feb. 15	No. of New Lows Around Dec. 15	Net Change by Feb. 15	Net Change in NYSE Composite	Net Gain
1966-67	45	18.0%	8.9%	9.1%
1967-68	45	7.4	—4.7	12.1
1968-69	24	5.0	—3.4	8.4
1974-75	112	48.9	22.1	26.8
1975-76	21	34.9	14.9	20.0
1976-77	2	1.3	—3.3	4.6
1977-78	15	2.8	—4.5	7.3
1978-79	43	11.8	3.9	7.9
1979-80	5	9.3	6.1	3.2
1980-81	14	7.1	—2.0	9.1
1981-82	21	—2.6	—7.4	4.8
1982-83	4	33.0	9.7	23.3
1983-84	13	—3.2	—3.8	0.6
1984-85	32	19.0	12.1	6.9
1985-86	4	—22.5	3.9	(26.4)

I retested this seasonal tendency in my investment newsletter, **Smart Money,** by reproducing the 112 NYSE common stocks hitting new lows in mid-December 1974. As you can see, the average rebound was 48.9% vs. the 22.1% gain for the NYSE composite. The figures for 1975 were 34.9 vs. 14.9%. I have also seen these "unwanted children" outperforming the market in subsequent years—until last year's debacle when oil prices crumbled and three of the four new lows were oils.

Understandably, lower quality stocks tend to bounce back even higher than their bluer chip brethren. Santa Claus seems to reward pre-Christmas "scavengers" on Wall Street.

One small broker/money manager publicly claims to achieve excellent results for his clients by establishing most of his positions during December, when stocks can be acquired at "wholesale" prices.

Examination of December purchases and sales by NYSE members through the years shows they tend to buy on balance during this month contrary to other months of the year. Enjoy the lunch!

THE SANTA CLAUS RALLY

Santa Claus comes to Wall Street nearly every year and brings a short, sweet, respectable rally. In the past thirty-four years, he failed to appear only in 1955, 1966, 1968, 1977, 1979, 1981, and 1984. The rally occurs within the last four days of the year (five starting in 1968 with the new NYSE settlement period) and the first two in January and is good for an average 1.84% gain, equivalent to a three-point rise in the Dow (at Dow 1600) for each of the seven days.

Twenty years had substantial gains of 1.0% to 7.1% during this holiday period. Of the other thirteen years, six had losses and seven had substandard gains of 0.4% to 0.7%. The bear markets of 1957, 1962, 1966, 1969, and 1977 were not preceded by Santa Claus rallies. Six other inferior periods preceded years when stocks could have been purchased at much lower prices later in the year (1956, 1965, 1968, 1978, 1980, and 1982). Just 1966, with tax selling down to the wire, proved to be the exception.

Getting back into the seasonal spirit: **If Santa Claus should fail to call,**
Bears may come to Broad & Wall.

TABLE 77

DAILY % CHANGE IN S&P COMPOSITE INDEX AT YEAR END

	Trading Days Before Year End							First Days in January		
	7	6	5	4	3	2	1	1	2	3
1952	0.6	−0.4	0.1	0.2	0.6	0.7	−0.1	−0.1	0.5	−0.7
1953	−0.8	−0.3	0.4	−0.4	−0.6	0.9	0.2	0.6	0.6	0.2
1954	−0.1	0.1	−0.8	1.0	0.9	0.0	0.7	2.1	−0.9	0.3
1955	0.9	0.2	0.2	−0.6	−0.4	0.2	0.7	−0.7	−0.4	−0.1
1956	−0.2	−0.8	0.7	0.1	−0.1	0.4	0.2	−1.0	0.9	0.1
1957	−0.8	0.0	0.1	1.0	−0.4	−0.5	1.0	0.9	1.3	−0.5
1958	−0.1	−0.7	−0.5	1.3	1.2	0.3	0.5	0.4	0.4	−0.1
1959	−0.2	−0.3	0.1	−0.1	0.5	0.8	0.2	0.1	0.8	−0.4
1960	0.8	−0.3	0.1	0.1	0.5	0.5	0.1	−0.9	1.4	0.4
1961	−0.2	−0.4	0.1	0.2	0.9	0.1	−0.2	−0.8	0.2	−0.7
1962	0.4	−0.3	−0.1	0.6	−0.1	0.1	0.2	−0.7	1.6	0.7
1963	−0.2	−0.7	0.2	0.5	0.2	0.2	0.6	0.5	0.1	0.1
1964	−0.1	−0.2	0.0	−0.1	−0.3	0.6	0.5	−0.6	0.5	0.3
1965	0.3	−0.1	−0.7	0.0	0.3	0.4	0.2	−0.3	0.1	0.7
1966	0.5	0.4	−0.3	−0.6	−0.5	−0.3	−0.1	0.1	0.2	1.3
1967	0.6	0.2	−0.2	0.1	0.7	0.0	0.6	−0.4	−0.5	−0.3
1968	−0.6	−0.1	−0.2	0.1	−0.4	−0.9	0.1	0.1	0.1	−1.5
1969	−0.9	−0.4	1.1	0.8	−0.7	0.4	0.5	1.0	0.5	−0.7
1970	0.1	0.1	0.6	0.5	1.1	0.2	−0.1	−1.1	0.7	0.6
1971	−0.6	−0.4	−0.2	1.0	0.3	−0.4	0.3	−0.4	0.4	1.0
1972	−0.5	−0.3	−0.6	0.6	0.3	0.5	1.0	0.9	0.4	−0.1
1973	−0.3	−1.1	−0.7	3.1	2.1	−0.2	0.0	0.1	2.2	−0.9
1974	−1.1	−1.4	1.4	0.8	−0.4	0.1	2.1	2.4	0.7	0.5
1975	−0.7	0.7	0.8	0.9	−0.1	−0.4	0.5	0.8	1.8	1.0
1976	0.5	0.1	1.2	0.7	−0.4	0.5	0.5	−0.4	−1.2	−0.9
1977	0.6	0.8	1.0	0.0	0.1	0.2	−0.2	−1.4	0.3	−0.8
1978	0.5	0.0	1.7	1.3	−0.9	−0.4	−0.2	0.6	1.1	0.8
1979	0.1	−0.6	0.1	0.1	0.2	−0.1	0.1	−2.0	−0.5	1.2
1980	1.6	−0.4	0.4	0.5	−1.1	0.2	0.3	0.4	1.2	0.1
1981	−0.4	−0.5	0.2	−0.2	−0.5	0.5	0.2	0.2	−2.2	−0.7
1982	0.2	0.6	1.8	−1.0	0.3	−0.6	0.2	−1.6	2.2	0.4
1983	1.0	−0.2	0.0	0.9	0.4	−0.3	0.0	−0.5	1.7	1.2
1984	−0.5	−0.5	0.8	0.2	−0.4	0.3	0.6	−1.1	−0.5	−0.5
1985	0.4.	−1.1	−0.7	0.2	0.9	0.5	0.3	−0.8	0.6	−0.1
Avg.	−0.02	−0.24	0.48*	0.40	0.12	0.13	0.34	−0.11	0.48	0.06

Average 7-Day Gain: 1.84%

*From 1968 to date

10
THE POWER OF CONTRARY THINKING

CONTRARY OPINION: THE MOST POWERFUL INVESTMENT TOOL OF ALL

Many investors have been clobbered by the market in the last decade and have thrown in the towel, convinced that "you can't beat the market." Rubbish! Many people, including most professionals, earn a handsome living off the market. They're bright and gifted, or are disciplined and do lots of homework, or operate as a full-time business. One way to succeed in the market is to specialize in a system that suits your personality, intellect or individual talent. For example, **Contrary Opinion** is number one of all stock market disciplines. If you've got contrarian instincts, I can almost guarantee investment success. While Norman Vincent Peale made a fortune from "The Power of Positive Thinking," if you want to make it in the market, you need the **Power of Contrary Thinking.** A quick example: Glen King Parker, chairman of The Institute For Econometric Research, made a brilliant observation on March 27, 1980, when Bunker Hunt was silverized and the market was pulverized. He confided, "When I heard that Bache and a few other houses might go belly-up, I had a gut feeling that this was a great buying opportunity."

Item: The January 1, 1973 issue of *Barron's* featured an article entitled "Not a Bear Among Them," a compendium of leading market analysts unanimously forecasting a market advance (The Dow was below 1000 then). The following week (Part 2 of the series) was headlined, "1200 on the Dow." By month's end the market embarked on the most severe collapse since the Great Depression.

Item: The December 30, 1974 issue (two years later) of the same publication featured no less than twelve advertisements plugging gold—all of course, in anticipation of the upcoming legalization of gold ownership. Within just a few days, the gold boom ended — the new bull market in stocks thoroughly confirmed. I could find only *one* outright bullish advertisement in that issue.

When *Barron's* boasts a record fat issue, the market is gonna get zonked. Seems that *Barron's*, being the number one advertising medium for investment publications, exotic investments, financial services, and corporations alike, gets fatter and fatter as the market fever heats up. That's when investors, psyched up by the ease with which they have been making money, fill out those coupons for investment services. Advertisers, eager to accommodate them, pack *Barron's* with all kinds of offers. We tracked the size of *Barron's* issues and noted that whenever they trumpeted the "largest issue that *Barron's* has ever published" it coincided with a market top. It happened on May 17, 1971 (92-page issue), May 7, 1973 (96-page issue) and September 17, 1979 (112-page issue). The October 6, 1980 issue hit 128 pages, a new record.

The point? Simply this: At virtually every major turning point for virtually every major investment at virtually any period of time, the vastly preponderant majority is almost certain to be wrong! This axiom held true during the Dutch tulip mania of the seventeenth century, it held true in January 1973, and it will almost certainly hold true tomorrow. Or, to restate, your best strategy at almost all times will be to buck the crowd, to steer your own course, to buy when everyone else is selling and to sell whenever everyone else is buying.

Furthermore, you do not have to guess. Your daily newspapers carry all the "crowd measuring" tools you'll need.

YOU KNOW THE MARKET IS ABOUT TO REVERSE DIRECTIONS...

When newsmagazine cover stories are about Wall Street— As prices plummeted in late September 1974, I was getting ready to issue a buy signal in my newsletter *Smart Money*. Supporting my position was the sudden appearance of Wall Street on the covers of two leading newsweeklies with the expected cover on one of them of a ferocious bear clawing a bull mercilessly. As any contrarian could guess, a classic market bottom was close at hand, and I mailed out my "BUY!" on October 4, 1974, the exact bottom day.

When cartoonists poke fun at Wall Street—Nothing can produce more anxieties among investors than stock prices falling month after month. As the market becomes big news, cartoonists find related ideas popping into their heads. Alert investors with a contrary bent can be sure the worst is about over when cartoons poking fun at investors, brokers, etc., begin appearing.

When the President sets up a special meeting with economic experts as stocks nosedive—A falling market develops its own momentum often pushing stocks down further than they should be going. Hence, a President can easily turn the market around by publicizing a meeting with noted economic advisors. Nixon did it in May 1970 and Ford did it in October 1974.

When *Barron's* **publishes a record-sized issue**—Response to financial ads is greatest when the market has been moving up sharply. So the amount of ads tends to reach a crescendo—*Barron's* ran a record 92-page issue May 17, 1971. The Dow declined 150 points in six months. A 96-pager May 7, 1973 preceded a 108-point slide in three months. 112 pages on September 17, 1979 saw a 112-point slide in one month. On October 6, 1980, a 128-page issue came prior to a 105-point drop in two months.

When investment newsletters advertise superior records— In a strongly rising market, a number of competent stock-picking newsletters pile up impressive performances. Suddenly, three or more of them advertise their superior records in *Barron's*. At that "signal" it is wise to anticipate market weakness.

NEWSMAGAZINE COVER STORIES AS CONTRARY INDICATORS

When the news weeklies feature the stock market, stock prices are usually at an extreme. While the layman might be inclined to load up to the hilt reading a bullish story and dump his holdings in panic reading a bearish cover article, the contrarian instinctively knows it's time to sell on the former news event and buy on the latter. You can see why in "The Cover Story Syndrome" by Patrick J. Regan (V.P. of BEA Associates Inc.) in the January-February 1981 issue of the *Financial Analysts Journal,* reprinted here with permission of the author. Actual titles that appeared on the front covers of *Time* magazine are shown:

TIME MAGAZINE STOCK MARKET COVER STORIES

August 15, 1938—Stock Exchange President William McChesney Martin

Between August 1937 and March 1938, the DJIA dropped nearly 50 percent, from 190 to 98. In the week before the article appeared, the market fell 6.5 percent to 136. It bottomed at 130 a month later and then rallied to 158 by November.

June 14, 1948—Young Bull (Wall Street Breed)—How High Is Up?

The DJIA traded within a narrow band of 165 to 190 for nearly two years, but between March and June 1948 it rose from a low of 165 to a high of 193. The exact high occurred the day after *Time*'s cover story came out on the new bull market. The DJIA then fell to a low of 162 by June of 1949, from which point the postwar bull market began.

June 5, 1950—Wall Street Bull—He Fattened Up On Blue Chips

Between June 1949 and June 1950, the market rose over 40 percent, from 162 to 228. The high took place the week after the article appeared, and in the following month the DJIA dropped nearly 14 percent, to 197.

January 10, 1955—The Bull Market—With a Business Review & Forecast

Between September 1953 and January 1955, the DJIA posted a 60 percent gain, from 255 to 409. It edged slightly higher and traded within a 390 to 430 range for several months until it broke out in a bull market, that carried the Dow to 521 by April 1956.

November 21, 1955—New York Stock Exchange President Funston

Between March 1955 and November 1955, the DJIA rose nearly 100 points, or 25 percent, from 391 to 487. The high occurred the week preceding the article. The market declined approximately five percent in the following three months, before rising to a peak of 521 in April 1956, which was not surpassed until September 1958.

March 24, 1958—Wall Street Bull: Spring 1958

Between October 1957 and March 1958, the market rose nearly 10 percent, to 456. Those gains were digested in the following month and the market then began its 50 percent ascent to the 685 high of January 1960.

December 24, 1958—Wall Street Bull

1958 was one of the best stock market years on record, as the DJIA rose 34 percent to close at 584, an all-time high. The rally continued for all of 1959, with a 685 peak in January 1960, but the major move took place before the article appeared.

June 1, 1962—Bear vs. Bull on Wall Street

Between December 1961 and May 1962, the DJIA fell 21 percent, from 735 to 577. Three weeks after the article appeared, it hit bottom at 536, a 27 percent decline. This paved the way for a four-year bull market that took the Dow to 1,000 by February 1966.

August 10, 1966—Stockbroker James Thomson — Wall Street: The Nervous Market

From a February peak of 1,000 the DJIA tumbled to 767 by August. Six weeks after the article appeared, the Dow hit bottom at 744, paving the way for a 200-point rally to 943 by September 1967.

August 24, 1970—Dreyfus Fund's Howard Stein— Changing Wall Street

The DJIA dropped 36 percent from a peak of 985 in December 1968 to a low of 631 in May 1970. By the time the article appeared it was at 709. In the next eight months it rallied 34 percent.

Time is not the only newsmagazine that has given signals to contrarians in the past. They all have. Months before the Dow began a 500-point sprint in August 1982, *Business Week* ran a cover story entitled, "The Death of Equities!"

HOW CARTOONS PINPOINT MARKET BOTTOMS

Cartoonists are normally oblivious to Wall Street, as is 85 to 90% of the population. However, a bloodbath, rout, debacle, massacre, etc. in the financial community will draw the attention of the nation's cartoonists, especially the "cream" at *New Yorker* magazine. It's time to begin getting back into the market when it becomes subject matter for the cartoonists. The worst crash in history ended in 1932 and inspired the most cartoons. Our favorite appears below:

Just around the corner

New Yorker Jan. 16, 1932

This cartoon tells it all. The steepest decline in history has been progressing relentlessly for twenty-seven months since the October 1929 top. When will it ever end? Here are descriptions of other cartoons in 1932 from *New Yorker:*

CARTOONS AT THE 1932 "BIG BOTTOM"

January 30, 1932
(The ranks of brokers in Wall Street have thinned considerably.)
Scene: One unemployed nattily attired broker, wearing a homburg, is making a pitch for a job to a candy shop owner.
Caption: *"Do you realize what it would mean to have a man with Wall Street experience in the business?"*

February 27, 1932
Scene: A palatial home in Palm Beach, Florida. The millionaire owner is reclining in the shade as his butler approaches and speaks.
Caption: *"Imperial Gas dropped eight points, sir. The temperature in New York today is fifty degrees. Sorry, sir."*

July 30, 1932
(Volume on the N.Y.S.E. had shrivelled to less than a million shares per day on average over the past eight weeks. The final bottom had come on July 8 at Dow 40.56 intraday. Brokerage houses are starving for business.)
Scene: Confetti fills the air at one office as brokers and customers are celebrating. One broker has toppled over in his chair from shock.
Caption: THE TURNING OF THE TIDE
Sub Caption: *A brokerage house receives an order to buy ten shares of Goldman Sachs.*

CARTOONS AT MARKET BOTTOMS IN THE 1970s

May 2, 1970
(The market is in its final plunge three weeks from the bottom.)
Scene: A captionless cartoon shows a woman carrying a shopping bag passing by a storefront brokerage office. Its windows have been dressed not unlike a supermarket's with banners of different shapes and sizes: SALE— PRICES SLASHED—FANTASTIC SAVINGS—U.S. STEEL 25% OFF—AVCO 1/2 PRICE—SHELL OIL SAVE 40%—MANY MORE TO CHOOSE FROM INSIDE!

June 20, 1970
(Though the bottom has occurred, investors are nervous as the Penn Central Railroad has gone bankrupt.)
Scene: A concerned gentleman reading the financial pages on one end of a park bench, two bums sitting on the other. One bum addresses the gentleman.
Caption: *"Cheer up, sir. My friend here thinks we've bottomed out."*

October 22, 1979
(The market is suffering its second October Massacre in a row.)
Scene: Captionless cartoon showing man walking by corner of Broad Street and Wall Street and looking up at the street sign. Sitting on top of the Wall Street sign is a cute, little, grinning Humpty Dumpty. (Humpty Dumpty Sat on a Wall...)

RUN FOR THE HILLS WHEN THEY ANNOUNCE "GOOD NEWS"

"The economy is booming!" "Auto sales are breaking all previous records!" "XYZ Corporation is having its best year ever!" Such announcements may warm an investor's heart — only to break it later. "Good news," in reality, is often "bad news." Consider the following:

• A glance at the past shows that many indicators break records while stock prices are turning down or have even been in a bear trend for many months. People forget that the stock market is a barometer and not a thermometer.

• As I mentioned earlier, whenever two or three advisory publications simultaneously run advertisements in *Barron's* reproducing all their stock selections over the past twelve months and the results shown are sensational — start running! This only happens at the tail end of bull markets, NEVER in bear markets.

• Whenever all your stocks are zooming and the same thing is happening to other friends and associates, start worrying and move to the exit! G.M. Loeb always got scared when things went too well. He said, "It is wise to remember that too much success is in itself an excellent warning."

TEST YOUR CONTRARIAN SAVVY!

How well do you know your way around Wall Street? What would a contrarian do in these situations?

Situation 1) The hottest mutual fund money manager around has launched a new fund and is inundated with several hundred million dollars. Would you be tempted to put some money into his fund?

Situation 2) You notice an impressive full-page investment newsletter ad in *Barron's* showing its performance record for the past two years. Each stock recommendation has gained 87% on average. After you subscribe, should you invest in a few of its forthcoming recommendations?

Situation 3) A publisher at a cocktail party introduces you to his newly-signed author who will be writing a "how-to" investment book. Your hostess whispers that the author-to-be scored a coup by investing $300,000 in an oil stock that grew 4000% in five years to $12 million. When you get him aside later he tells you what stock he likes now. Would you buy it?

Situation 4) *"Wall Street Week"* is on and Louis Rukeyser is talking to the president of a large mutual fund who boasts that his fund had a very sharp increase in the sale of fund shares last month. Would this be a good time to invest in stocks?

If you answered yes to any of the above questions, you flunked the test.

Answer 1) Gerald Tsai was widely acclaimed in the mid-sixties for his stock-picking prowess at the Fidelity group of funds in Boston. When he left and started the Manhattan Fund, $247 million poured in from eager investors. It was in February 1966 when the Dow-Jones industrials were first flirting with the 1000 level. Eight months later the average had sunk 27% to 735. What's more, the worst performing large fund over the next fifteen years (Tsai had left in 1973) turned out to be the Manhattan Fund. (It has a new management and good performance in recent years.)

Answer 2) In a strongly rising market, a number of investment newsletters pile up dazzling performance records. Shortly, light bulbs click on in their minds and advertisements of their success begin appearing in *Barron's*. Seeing several "boasting ads" is usually a sign that the market is about to receive a jolt.

Answer 3) Several lucky hits in major fields combined with OPEC's doubling the price of oil had a lot to do with $300,000 growing to $12 million. However, the tide had turned for oil companies, and one year later the value of the investment shrank 75%.

Answer 4) Mutual fund share sales tend to increase sharply just at the top of a rising market. Thus, no matter what the portfolio manager sitting on a healthy inflow of funds may think of near-term prospects, he may be forced to put the money to work at a time when the outlook is most chancy.

Economist John Kenneth Galbraith hit a bull's-eye with his classic line, "Financial genius is a rising stock market." Don't be influenced by well-publicized success stories in Wall Street. When you hear them it's usually the wrong time to invest.

Contrarian Humphrey Neill had another way of saying it: "Don't confuse brains with a bull market!"

And if you are ever in the fortunate position of seeing the stocks in your portfolio running wild and feel very good about yourself, start nailing down profits, because the market is about to take a tumble.

WHEN EVERYBODY THINKS ALIKE, EVERYBODY IS LIKELY TO BE WRONG

"Buy when everyone else is selling, and hold until everyone else is buying." Billionaire J. Paul Getty made that statement in his book "How To Be Rich." Richard E. Band, editor of Personal Finance, *cleverly takes those words and plasters them across the top of page one of his book* Contrary Investing.

Now that Band has your attention and has given you the essence of contrary thinking in association with one of history's most successful and wealthiest individuals, you are ready to read the finest work written on contrary opinion in the last decade or two. What's important about Contrary Investing *(McGraw Hill) is that Band is a genuine and successful practitioner in the art of contrary opinion. He knows how to recognize C.O., exploit it and make money from other people's mistakes. He describes all the tricks of the trade used by contrarians, the most successful investors in the world. Here are excerpts of some of the brilliance in* Contrary Investing, *without a doubt the best book on contrary opinion of the decade.*

Contrary thinking is the art of thinking for yourself against the pressures of the crowd.

If nobody wants something, it is likely to be cheap. If everybody wants it, it is likely to be dear.

Contrary thinking works in any market because human nature is the same everywhere. Most people are followers, not leaders. In the marketplace, they wait to buy until they see other people buying, and they wait to sell until they see other people selling. As a result, most people buy after prices have already risen, and sell after prices have already fallen.

More than brains, contrary investing takes self-discipline and an ounce of courage. If you have ever been labeled a maverick or a boat rocker, or simply a lone wolf, you may already be a practicing contrarian without even knowing it!

A primary bull market is characterized by rising prices and growing optimism. Likewise, falling prices and growing pessimism characterize a primary bear market. A bull market begins to rise in a climate of **fear**. Later, as the market scores additional gains, fear recedes and an attitude of **caution** takes over in most investors' minds. After prices have climbed substantially, investors start to forget the bad old days of the bear market. **Confidence** reigns. Finally, as prices reach a cyclical peak, **euphoria** sweeps the market. At the top, all but a handful of investors are convinced that the market will keep going up indefinitely.

Contrary investors follow the maxim: "Buy into extreme weakness and sell into extreme strength."

If everyone in the marketplace is looking for prices to go up (a consensus), chances are that everyone who is going to buy has already bought. Likewise, if everyone is counting on the market to go down, everyone who is going to sell has probably already sold.

The majority is often right, especially about the primary trend, for many months at a time. However, the closer it is to a consensus, the more likely that the majority opinion is badly mistaken. As the late Humphrey Neill, the "Vermont ruminator" who is considered the father of contrary investing, used to say: "When everybody thinks alike, everybody is likely to be wrong."

Invariably, just before a high-flying stock collapses, many of the best-known Wall Street analysts will be predicting strong earnings gains for the company into the distant future.

Successful investors can never allow themselves to be married to any widely accepted, pat scenario. They must look for the hidden, potential surprise factors that other forecasters are ignoring. And they must be prepared to change their own forecasts promptly if they see that too many people are adapting their point of view.

The genius of contrary thinking is that it helps you lean the right way at critical market turning points, when emotions drown out reason and other analytical techniques seem to fail. At the irrational moments, when the lunatics are running the asylum, the contrary investor finds the best opportunities for profit.

1. Contrary thinking is really nothing more than thinking for yourself—one of the highest privileges granted to the human species.

2. All the great trail-blazers of history were contrarians who broke out of the narrow mindset of their contemporaries (and often had to face ridicule or persecution for their trouble.)

3. The more frightened you feel when going against the crowd, the better your investment decisions will probably turn out to be.

"Advice from a Contrarian to an Investor"

- Think for yourself.
- Don't settle for pat answers.
- Challenge the conventional wisdom. Be skeptical of experts.
- Look beyond the obvious.
- Steer away from fads.
- Control your emotions, especially fear and hope.
- When the truth is unpleasant, don't try to ignore it. Admit your mistakes while there is time to correct them. Beware of self-deception.

LOW PRICE/EARNINGS RATIO STOCKS OUTPERFORM ALL OTHERS

One investment book that garnered much publicity in 1980 was David Dreman's impressive *Contrarian Investment Strategy* (Random House).

From experience, Dreman "became increasingly convinced that the investment methods in which we are all schooled are not sufficient by themselves to make us consistent winners. Without a grasp of systematic ways to protect ourselves against psychological overreactions, chances are that we will continue to make the same or very similar mistakes time and again."

However, with a contrarian approach, "it is possible to derive successful investment strategies that will allow you to benefit from other people's mistakes." Numerous statistical studies are cited from a forty-year period which "pinpoint investor overreactions in a systematic enough manner so that the investor applying the principles consistently will have a good chance of outdoing the market."

The system, of course, is the selection of stocks selling at low price/earnings ratios which, the author has conclusively proven, outperform the market and the portfolios of nearly all the bank and institutional money managers.

Dreman's startling findings show that "those companies that the market expects will have the best futures as measured by the price/earnings ratios they are accorded have consistently done worse subsequently, while the stocks believed to have the most dismal futures have always provided the best subsequent returns." (Please reread last sentence several times.) Simply, a portfolio of stocks selling at three times earnings is almost guaranteed to outperform a portfolio at fifteen times earnings in any twelve-month period. To really put this concept into perspective, think of two companies earning $3.00 per share, with one's stock selling at 9 and the other's at 45. Most institutional money managers would likely feel it more "prudent" to own the $45 stock. However, the evidence is powerful. Lower P/E ratio stocks are "safer" investments.

I've constructed a table below from the four comprehensive computer studies which Dreman uses to conclusively prove his point. The studies covered a period of forty years. In the first column, you can see that in the twenty-five-year period (1937-1962) the top 20% of stocks most in favor gained only 3% annually, while the lowest quintile (the bottom 20%) had a 16% annual appreciation. Portfolios were reshuffled once per year. The second study shows the "out of favor" stocks outperforming the "popular" stocks 18.4% to 7.7% (1948-1964). The third shows the same result, 16.3% versus 9.6%. Notice the tendency of stocks to do better, the more "unwanted" they become. Finally, to correct criticisms of previous studies, Dreman did his own study of 1,251 of the largest publicly held companies in the flat-to-down 1968-1977 period. Once again, the fifth quintile—"the untouchables"—gained 8.2% annually, on average, while "the elite" (top quintile) suffered an average annual loss of 0.3%. *Caveat emptor!*

TABLE 78

AVERAGE ONE-YEAR PERFORMANCE BY P/E RANKING

P/E Quintile	Nicholson 1937-1962	Miller 1948-1964	Basu* 1957-1971	Dreman* 1968-1977
1 Highest	3%	7.7%	9.6%	—0.3%
2	6	9.2	9.3	2.5
3	7	12.0	11.7	4.8
4	9	12.8	13.6	7.7
5 Lowest	16	18.4	16.3	8.2
* Total return				

11
STOCK SELECTION SYSTEMS: SEARCHING FOR EXCELLENCE

THE HUNDRED GREATEST STOCKS IN RECENT HISTORY

What's the easiest way to spot big stock market winners? By hindsight, of course. Still, you can learn a lot by pulling out one hundred smashing success-story stocks and then searching for common denominators.

William O'Neill & Co. of Los Angeles, publishers of the *Daily Graphs* chart service, put together an attractive chart book several years ago of these one hundred superstocks (eighty were listed on the New York and twenty on the American stock exchanges). Many were well known names, such as Bausch & Lomb, Braniff, Digital Equipment, Engelhard, Hilton, Loews, MGIC, Polaroid, Resorts International, Syntex, Tandy, Teledyne, and Xerox. Most had increases in price of over 1000% in a short time or in a period of several years. Some common characteristics:

• The dominant reason behind the success of almost all of the greatest winners was major increases and acceleration in quarterly earnings per share, on average 70% before their big move.

• Price-to-earnings ratios were irrelevant. Many were on the high side, as those in the know were willing to pay up for anticipated high earnings increases.

• Practically all had less than twenty million shares outstanding during the period of the big upmove.

• Half of the examples were the result of important changes that affected whole industries: new efficient jet engines in the '60s for the airlines (Braniff, Delta, National); oil and coal companies after OPEC struck its mortal blow in 1973; manufactured housing (mobile, shells) after the Federal Reserve introduced "tight money" in 1966 for the first time; retail drug chains; catalog shopping houses; semiconductors; computers.

 • One important factor was the display of greater relative strength than the general market before the spurt in price.

 • The average length of time for the upward explosion in price was about seventeen months between the emerging stage and the peak.

 • Quite a few, after splitting their shares, seemed to stall at the $50 or $100 level, exhausted after a 1000 or 2000% move.

After poring over the charts of these one hundred high flyers, I observed something which could be extremely useful. Many of them began to soar but were interrupted by a sharp decline in the market which triggered frantic profit taking by nervous holders sitting on huge gains. Some were slashed in half, or even more, then bounded back with a vengeance and continued to double, triple, and quadruple ad infinitum.

Next time the market takes a hit, while others are losing their heads, use yours to find a temporarily stalled fallen favorite.

WHAT YOU SHOULD LOOK FOR IN AMERICA'S MOST UNDISCOVERED COMPANIES

Here's another tack if you are intent on being the discoverer of future big winners. There are many small, relatively unknown, and embarassingly undervalued companies poised for a takeoff in good markets and able to withstand nasty declines. Here are the qualifications *Smart Money* requires in a candidate for America's Most Undiscovered Companies:

1. They're **"niche" companies** that have concentrated their relatively limited resources in a narrow yet well-defined market where they can gain an edge in a specialized area of vital products or services with little competition.

2. They have **bright prospects** in a field that's growing fast—and because they're small, they're able to grow even faster.

3. They have existing **innovative products** or services superior to conventional approaches. Especially in the high tech area, they have sufficient command of the technology to foresee changes in advance, and are better able to adapt and capitalize on them.

4. Their **profit margins** are high or potentially so. Their products are low-cost to produce, but of high market value. How? By having proprietary products, services, and processes.

5. They have active and **extensive research and development programs,** with roughly 10% of sales budgeted for R&D. This assures a company's future.

6. **Business is not cyclical** or solely dependent on one customer. Our companies supply the "majors," so they'll thrive regardless of who's on top of the heap.

7. There are **limited shares outstanding,** a small capitalization, and stock trades over the counter.

8. **Management owns a significant proportion** of the shares, providing important incentives and commitment to long-range success.

9. The stock **price is low** relative to company's growth potential and earnings power. Stocks under $10 per share will be favored.

10. The companies are **not widely known** and are not followed by major brokerage houses or securities analysts.

TRACK INSIDERS AND DO TWICE AS WELL AS OTHER INVESTORS

In ten years prior to December 1984, *Insider Indicator* in Portland, Oregon published 828 new insider buy signals on New York Stock Exchange listed companies for their readers. Even if you threw darts at the signals as they were published and purchased any of the stocks and held them for a year, you would have had an average one-year gain of 22.8% versus an average of 10.1% for the NYSE composite investor. If you threw your darts just as their 1982 signals, you would have gained 55% versus 37% for the NYSE.

The Insiders in Fort Lauderdale, Florida is another advisory service that analyzes insider transactions that are reported to the SEC. In a period of three and half years—which included the big bull rise of 1982 and 1983—the service actually purchased twenty-five stocks favored by insiders which gained 62.2% on average. The issues were both listed and over-the-counter stocks.

"Insiders"—corporate officers, directors, and certain large shareholders of publically owned companies—are privy to information regarding the future projects of their own corporations. It follows, then, that investors may well benefit from tracking insider transactions and following the lead.

Insider activity provides the most academically proven, successful stock-selection systems on record. Several services, in addition to the SEC, provide the raw data while other services recommend companies to buy or sell using certain proven parameters. Some individual brokers specialize in tracking insiders and analyzing their company's fundamentals. There is even a mutual fund that constructs its portfolio based on what the insiders are buying and selling.

I have reviewed the results of half a dozen insider studies from universities and most corroborate the fact that investors who follow the insiders and buy their companies do about twice as well as the market. The theory that these insiders have a special opportunity to know about events that affect the fortunes of their companies has been well documented.

To test this theory, Dr. James Lorie, Director for the Center of Research of Stock Prices, and Dr. Victor Niederhoffer, president of Niederhoffer, Cross & Zeckhauser, Inc., examined insider trading that occurred just before large price changes in their company's stock. In the study, "large changes" in the price of stock are defined as changes of 8% or more.

TABLE 79

INSIDER TRADING IN SIX MONTHS
PRIOR TO LARGE CHANGES IN STOCK PRICE

Method	Type of Insider Activity	Number of Price Changes	
		Increases	Decreases
Last Transaction before Large Price Change	Purchase Sale	212 89	86 79
Number of Purchases Minus Number of Sales	Positive Negative	197 81	81 67
Volume of Shares Purchased Minus Volume of Shares Sold	Positive Negative	210 86	116 51

First they analyzed the last transaction that insiders had made before a large price change had occurred in their stock. When the last transaction was a purchase, the chances of a large increase in price were seventy-one out of one hundred. When the last transaction was a sale, there was a 53% chance that a large price decrease had followed.

Next, an examination was made of the relative number of purchases and sales that insiders made during the six months prior to a large price change. When the number of purchases was greater than sales (positive), the odds favoring a large increase was 2.2 times greater than that of a large decrease.

The third inquiry evaluated the relative volume of purchases and sales during the six-month period. Although the evidence is weaker in this case, the greater skill of insiders to foresee large changes in price is demonstrated.

The results show that insiders tend to buy more often than usual before large price increases and sell more than usual before large price decreases. They also prove that it is better to analyze the number of transactions by insiders, rather than the aggregate volume of shares insiders purchase or sell.

Evidence that insider exercise of stock options—normally a bullish factor—can be a bearish omen was found by Lorie and Niederhoffer. They discovered that some insiders exercise the options and soon sell off the stock!

HUGE INSIDER HOLDINGS DETERRENT TO PERFORMANCE

Contrary to what might be expected, closely-held corporations (where insiders own 30% or more of the stock) are not as profitable as more widely-held companies. For the ten one-year periods (1960-1970), the proprietary companies (usually controlled by a family or single individual) were outperformed two to one, on average, by the "nonproprietary" companies of similar size.—*Researched by Patrick J. Regan, University of California at Berkeley.*

INSIDER BOOKS AND SERVICES

Wall Street's Insiders by John C. Boland was published by William Morrow & Co. It's a thorough work on insiders and will provide good background along with excellent hints.

Official Summary is a monthly compilation of trading reports filed by insiders with the SEC. It can run hundreds of pages with entries on thousands of companies and is mailed monthly thirty days or so after the month's closing date. However, insiders have forty days to file, so some of the data can be stale.
Subscription: $70 annually
Superintendent of Documents, Government Printing Office, Washington DC 20402. (202) 783-3238.

Weekly Insider Report gathers insider filings from the SEC the day after they have been filed. The raw data is supplied to many services. Readers receive the tallies days after the SEC. Edwin A. Buck, editor.
Subscription: $85 annually
Vickers Stock Research, Box 59, Brookside NJ 07926. (201) 539-1336.

Insider Indicator utilizes a ten-year insider data base of companies listed on the two major stock exchanges. Their system of stock selection grew out of a benchmark insider study at Portland State University in the 1960s. Twice monthly, J. Michael Reid, editor.
Subscription: $145 annually
Insider Indicator Inc., 2230 NE Brazee Street, Portland OR 97212. (503) 224-8072.

The Insiders is edited by Norman Fosback, who also went to Portland State University and studied under Shannon Pratt, co-author of one of the classic insider studies. Each semi-monthly issue ranks about 2600 stocks.
Subscription: $49 annually
Institute for Econometric Research, 3471 North Federal Highway, Fort Lauderdale FL 33306, (305) 561-5105.

NEW ISSUES: CLOSEST THING
TO A SURE THING ON WALL STREET

Communications Satellite went public in 1964. It was so oversubscribed that shares were allocated, ten to a customer, on the initial offering. Offered at $20 a share, it soared to $71.50 by year end.

Over the years, the new issues market has experienced wide swings in activity. The greatest number of new issues seems to hit the market when investor confidence is strong and price/earnings ratios are on the high side. Not only is it easier to market a new issue under these ebullient market conditions—it also enables the issuer to raise more capital by issuing fewer shares at a higher price.

It stands to reason then that a dearth of new issues are the norm when the market has suffered a serious setback and investor confidence is severely depressed.

New issues vary from era to era. In 1961, the hottest issues were aerospace and electronics stocks. In the mid-60s it was fast foods, computers, semiconductors, and nursing homes.

The zenith for that new issue market was in 1968, as illustrated below. Fortunes were made; some gains exceeded 1000%. But it was all over by 1969, even though the new issue pace doubled.

TABLE 80

10 WENT PUBLIC PER WEEK DURING 1968's NEW ISSUE BOOM

Number of New Issues	Percentage Gains through Dec. 31	Number of New Issues	Percentage Gains through Dec. 31
125	200% or higher	204	20-50%
124	100-200%	35	0-20%
26	50-100%	36	under offering price
		TOTAL 550	

Not all new issues are profitable, and a word of caution is in order as evidenced by the performance of some of these 1961 public offerings. (Note which company fell the least from its high—Mother's Cookie Corp.)

Even the low-spirited 1977-1978 market produced some handsome gains. Of forty-four companies going public in 1977, thirty-six were ahead by June 14, 1978. Initial offerings priced below $2 a share were the biggest gainers, with more than half advancing 100% or more. The trend continued into 1978. Table 82 tells the story and it's a very dramatic one.

Things kept getting better and better but very few people seemed to notice. The number of new issues—known as initial public offerings, or IPOs—and the dollar volume doubled in 1979. Much of what was hap-

TABLE 81

NEW ISSUES
BORN 1961, DIED IN 1962

Company	Date	Initial Price	First Day's Bid	High Bid 1961	Low Bid 1962
Boonton Electronics	3/6/61	5½	12¼	24½	1½
Bristol Dynamics	3/20/61	7	16	23	3½
Geophysics Corp. of Amer.	12/8/60	14	27	58	9
Hydro-Space Technology	7/19/60	3	7	7	1
Mother's Cookie Corp.	3/8/61	15	23	25	7
Seaboard Electronic	7/5/61	5½	8¾	15½	2¼
Universal Electronic Labs	11/25/61	4	4½	18	1½

Source: *A Random Walk Down Wall Street* by Burton G. Malkiel

TABLE 82

ANOTHER NEW ISSUE EXPLOSION IN THE MAKING

Year	Number of New Issues	Monies Raised ($ millions)
1978	45	$ 249
1979	81	506
1980	237	1,397
1981	448	3,215
1982	222	1,446
1983	888	12,604
1984	550	3,834
1985*	431	4,441

*Through November 11

pening was in Denver, Colorado, and the big fad was OIL. The price of oil had skyrocketed again because of the maniacal behavior of the Iranians toward the American hostages.

The Denver fever spread all over the country and in 1980 many individuals were doubling and tripling their money again and again. IPOs and dollar volume tripled the previous year's figures. I was told of one investor in his early 20s who parlayed a stake of several thousand dollars into nearly half a million. While in Denver, I spent some time with the young wizard. I expected to find an individual loaded with raw energy, insight, wisdom and genius, someone with a trigger mind and an exciting story to tell of brilliant maneuvers, a grand strategy, and a well thought out master financial plan.

Nothing could have been further from the truth. I was sadly disappointed. The man was a novice investor, ignorant of the great names in Wall Street, past and present, and was unaware of most major financial publications. He had no secrets. He was just friendly with a few registered representatives in various brokerage houses in a period when new issues were jumping 500% to 1000% practically overnight. They would feed him allotments of promising new issues. He would sell them off after a runup and pyramid his profits with the next group of newcomers, as if he were on a roll at a casino craps table.

The new issue momentum was so powerful that it carried into 1981 and allowed more than twice the capital to be raised than in the previous year. But hard times were upon us. Interest rates were going through the roof, the OPEC oil bubble had burst, third world nations were unable to pay their debts, and penny stock brokers were experiencing anxieties. All the big numbers of 1981 were slashed in half in 1982.

I, too, experienced some of the excitement in one of the years most dazzling performers. A new broker I was acquainted with offered me 150,000 shares of Coal Technology at 10 cents a share. I accepted and sent a check for $15,000. The company was going to be marketing a new kind of log made of coal chips for fireplaces. These logs were expected to burn longer and provide more heat.

The stock moved a few cents higher when it began trading and then stood still for four months. Then, suddenly, it began to move—triggered by possible big deals with GE and a few other comnpanies. First it hit 15¢...then 16¢...17¢...18¢...19¢...20¢. Without benefit of hindsight and with a bear market in most stocks, I got nervous as the company had no revenues. I sold 15,000 shares at 21¢. A week later, 10,000 at 22¢ and 10,000 more at 23¢. Another week went by and I dropped 25,000 more at 25¢. I had sold 75,000 shares for $17,350 and now had my original investment back.

The saga continues. On May 4, 1982 Coal Technology hit 43¢ and I sold 25,000 shares. The following day I sold another 25,000 at 47¢. I kept wondering when "they" were going to pull the plug. Three weeks later I unloaded my final 25,000 at 54¢ and felt relieved. It's hard to comprehend, but this company with no revenues ultimately saw its stock climb miraculously to $4.50 per share.

Stocks exploded in August without warning and the Dow began a five-hundred-point surge. Underwriters were unprepared and had to gear up the new issue machinery again. Lick your lips when you look at the figures for 1983. The number of IPOs quadrupled and dollars raised leaped nine-fold.

All hell broke loose in 1983 and penny stock underwriters had a blast. The Dow Jones industrials kept rolling higher and higher in its first 500-point upmove ever. Millions of investors were mesmerized by the rising Dow and must have said "Yes! Yes! Yes!" each time a penny stock broker called and asked Mr. or Ms. Neophite Investor to buy a piece of this or that exciting new company. The euphoria was contagious and made believers of everyone—investors and entrepreneurs alike. Most individuals felt good about themselves and to many investors in new issues, it was like taking candy from a baby.   Most new issues were sold out on Day One and rose swiftly in the aftermarket. Many brokers in the small underwriting offices were even able to dictate terms to investors clamoring for a piece of the action. Though illegal, the implication was "Buy 500 shares in the aftermarket and I'll give you 500 shares at the public offering price."

No matter how anyone operated in new issues, money was being made by all. It was easy to lull yourself into believing you were another Bernard Baruch or one of the Rothschilds. Few had ever heard of John Kenneth Galbraith's famous expression, "Financial genius is a rising stock market."

No matter how anyone operated in new issues, money was being made by all. It was easy to lull yourself into believing you were another Bernard Baruch or one of the Rothschilds. Few had ever heard of John Kenneth Galbraith's famous expression, "Financial genius is a rising stock market."

The swarm of desperate investors reaching for a piece of the Easy Money Pie stopped at some point. And all the new issues which seemed to have defied gravity and soared out of sight, began to fall. Some are still falling and once again are out of sight. Coal Technology which went up 4400% had only to drop 97.8% to give it all back, which it did. It actually fell to 3 cents per share, a 99.3% decline, but bounced back to 6 cents a share. New management has a technique which may help put an end to acid rain.

You might have read of a number of small underwriters who went under. To operate as a member of the National Association of Security Dealers you have to maintain certain capital requirements. It is common practice to use shares of stocks you underwrote, which are usually in your inventory, as part of your capitalization. Comes a sharp downturn, and you're left holding the bag. You have fallen under the required capitalization and the large NYSE member firm that does your back office work and acts like a bank for you tells you you're out of business. That's it, unless you raise a big chunk of capital, which few can do.

To make matters worse, news of possible internal problems always manages to leak out and the vultures spring into action. As no one wants to be holding any of the stocks the troubled firm has underwritten, massive shorting takes place, hopefully before any of the market makers in those stocks can unload. It's not uncommon for a fallen firm's underwritings to be slashed in half regardless of how well the actual companies are operating.

Initial public offerings slowed down in 1984 and 1985. Even though the insanity of 1983 is nowhere to be seen, the dollar volume will still make 1985 the second biggest year in underwriting history.

WHY I EXPECT A GREEN TIDE
TO SWEEP THROUGH WALL STREET

As I said earlier, making money with new issues is like taking candy from a baby. Or as Norman Fosback, editor of *New Issues,* likes to call them, "the closest thing to a sure thing on Wall Street." OK! So when is the big giveaway starting and when will the GREEN TIDE hit Wall Street?

Remember the negative mood of investors in the summer of 1982? We seemed to be on the verge of a world monetary collapse. Banks and bond houses were declaring bankruptcy. Mexico had just devalued the peso and the fate of many third world nations with huge outstanding debts to American banks was worrisome. We were in the worst recession since the thirties. What happened? Suddenly the stock market, having finally noticed that the discount rate and interest rates had been coming down fast, exploded on the upside. As the Dow was moving up 510 points within a year, the climate changed. Business began to improve rapidly, the new issue market came to life again and investors were enriched $760 billion on their holdings—which translated into an enormous amount of purchasing power that obviously impacted the economy. The point I am making is that we seem to be repeating the pattern again. Enjoy it!

Assuming the Dow continues to move higher in 1986 and 1987, mesmerizing the investment public, what will their reaction be? Isn't it likely that a replay of 1983 is in the cards?

NEW ISSUE CHECKLISTS

How do you capitalize on new issues? By observing some basic rules for selecting and acquiring them and by familiarizing yourself with sources of available information.

Look for companies with:
1) An established or new product line.
2) A record of consistent growth and sales to some of the big-name corporations.
3) An aggressive management that intends to build on a base, not bail out on the offering.
4) Good sponsorship (taken public by a top underwriter).

Avoid companies that:
1) Appear to be using the new issue boom to garner as much capital as possible while "the gettin's good."
2) Have large blocks of unregistered "144" stock that can be sold in less than two years.
3) Are one-dealer offerings lacking sponsorship, unless you research them thoroughly.

4) Are registered intrastate and not SEC. Reporting requirements are minimal for these companies which are often vehicles for entrepreneurs to parlay penny stocks into dollar stocks—for their own benefit, of course!

5) Have underwriting expenses greater than 10% of the proceeds being raised (see page one of prospectus).

How to get new issues:

1) It is often helpful to have an account with a principal underwriter.

2) Accounts with smaller participants can also be an advantage, as they may have less demand for new issues.

3) Some brokerage firms use new issues to lure prospective clients into opening an account. It may be worth your while to accommodate them.

4) Companies going public often have the right to distribute a certain percentage of stock to employees, business associates, and others with a tie to the company.

5) If you are unable to get in on the offering for the amount of shares you desire, watch the aftermarket. The best time to buy is on the first pullback from the premium brought in the aftermarket. Just remember: all hot markets cool down in time.

6) Watch for new issues in a severely depressed market. These usually are good companies with shares reasonably priced so as to assure a successful offering.

NEW ISSUE SERVICES

Going Public is the definitive information service on initial public offerings. Weekly reports on IPOs plus underwriter directories and other special reports. Very comprehensive.
Subscription: $600 annually
The Dealers' Digest, Inc., 150 Broadway, New York, NY 10038 (212) 227-1200

Investment Dealers Digest, a weekly (published every Monday) comprehensive listing of all new issues.
Subscription: $195 annually
The Dealers' Digest, 150 Broadway, New York, NY 10038 (212) 227-1200

New Issues contains a calendar of all new issues each month plus special recommendations. A good track record.
Subscription: $95 annually
Institute for Econometric Research, 3471 North Federal Highway #50, Fort Lauderdale, FL 33306 (305) 561-5101

Value Line New Issues Service is a very comprehensive service. Produced weekly, it has just about everything.
Subscription: $330 annually
Value Line Inc., 711 Third Avenue, New York, NY 10017 (212) 687-3965

The Red Herring is a monthly publication that reviews and rates between 6 to 9 initial public offerings in each issue.
Subscription: $45 annually
The Red Herring, PO Box 1234, Pacifica, CA 94044

12
APPENDIX

A.
_____

MONTHLY PERCENT CHANGES IN STANDARD & POOR'S 500

Year	JAN	FEB	MAR	APR	MAY	JUNE	JULY	AUG	SEP	OCT	NOV	DEC	Yr. Chg.
1950	1.7%	1.0%	0.4%	4.5%	3.9%	-5.8%	0.8%	3.3%	5.6%	0.4%	-0.1%	4.6%	21.8%
1951	6.1	0.6	-1.8	4.8	-4.1	-2.6	6.9	3.9	-0.1	-1.4	-0.3	3.9	16.5
1952	1.6	-3.6	4.8	-4.3	2.3	4.6	1.8	-1.5	-2.0	-0.1	4.6	3.5	11.8
1953	-0.7	-1.8	-2.4	-2.6	-0.3	-1.6	2.5	-5.8	0.1	5.1	0.9	0.2	-6.6
1954	5.1	0.3	3.1	4.5	3.7	0.1	5.7	-3.4	8.3	-1.9	8.1	5.1	45.0
1955	1.8	0.4	-0.5	3.8	-0.1	8.2	6.1	-0.8	1.1	-3.0	7.5	-0.1	26.4
1956	-3.6	3.5	6.9	-0.2	-6.6	3.9	5.2	-3.8	-4.5	0.5	-1.1	3.5	2.6
1957	-4.2	-3.3	2.0	3.7	3.7	-0.1	1.1	-5.6	-6.2	-3.2	1.6	-4.1	-14.3
1958	4.3	-2.1	3.1	3.2	1.5	2.6	4.3	1.2	4.8	2.5	2.2	5.2	38.1
1959	0.4	0.0	0.1	3.9	1.9	-0.4	3.5	-1.5	-4.6	1.1	1.3	2.8	8.5
1960	-7.1	0.9	-1.4	-1.8	2.7	2.0	-2.5	2.6	-6.0	-0.2	4.0	4.6	-3.0
1961	6.3	2.7	2.6	0.4	1.9	-2.9	3.3	2.0	-2.0	2.8	3.9	0.3	23.1
1962	-3.8	1.6	-0.6	6.2	-8.6	8.2	6.4	1.5	-4.8	0.4	10.2	1.3	-11.8
1963	4.9	-2.9	3.5	4.9	1.4	1.6	-0.3	4.9	-1.1	3.2	-1.1	2.5	18.9
1964	2.7	1.0	1.5	0.6	1.1	1.6	1.8	-1.6	2.9	0.8	-0.5	-0.4	13.0
1965	3.3	-0.1	-1.5	3.4	-0.8	-4.9	1.3	2.3	3.2	2.7	-0.9	0.9	9.1
1966	0.5	-1.8	-2.2	2.1	-5.4	-1.6	-1.3	-7.8	-0.7	4.8	0.3	-0.1	-13.1
1967	7.8	0.2	3.9	4.2	-5.2	1.8	4.5	-1.2	3.3	-2.9	0.1	2.6	20.1
1968	-4.4	-3.1	0.9	8.2	1.1	0.9	1.8	1.1	3.9	0.7	4.8	-4.2	7.7
1969	-0.8	-4.7	3.4	2.1	-0.2	-5.6	-6.0	4.0	-2.5	4.4	-3.5	-1.9	-11.4
1970	-7.6	5.3	0.1	-9.0	-6.1	-5.0	7.3	4.4	3.3	-1.1	4.7	5.7	0.1
1971	4.0	0.9	3.7	3.6	-4.2	0.1	-4.1	3.6	-0.7	-4.2	-0.3	8.6	10.8
1972	1.8	2.5	0.6	0.4	1.7	-2.2	0.2	3.4	-0.5	0.9	4.6	1.2	15.6
1973	-1.7	-3.7	-0.1	-4.1	-1.9	-0.7	3.8	-3.7	4.0	-0.1	-11.4	1.7	-17.4
1974	-1.0	-0.4	-2.3	-3.9	-3.4	-1.5	-7.8	-9.0	-11.9	16.3	-5.3	-2.0	-29.7
1975	12.3	6.0	2.2	4.7	4.4	4.4	-6.8	-2.1	-3.5	6.2	2.5	-1.2	31.5
1976	11.8	-1.1	3.1	-1.1	-1.4	4.1	-0.8	-0.5	2.3	-2.2	-0.8	5.2	19.1
1977	-5.1	-2.2	-1.4	0.0	-2.4	4.5	-1.6	-2.1	-0.2	-4.3	2.7	0.3	-11.5
1978	-6.2	-2.5	2.5	8.5	0.5	-1.8	5.4	2.6	-0.7	-9.2	1.7	1.5	1.1
1979	4.0	-3.7	5.5	0.2	-2.6	3.9	0.9	5.3	0.0	-6.9	4.3	1.7	12.3
1980	5.8	-0.4	-10.2	4.1	4.7	2.7	6.5	0.6	2.5	1.6	10.2	-3.4	25.8
1981	-4.6	1.3	3.6	-2.3	-0.2	-1.0	-0.2	-6.2	-5.4	4.9	3.7	-3.0	-9.7
1982	-1.8	-6.1	-1.0	4.0	-3.9	-2.0	-2.3	11.6	0.8	11.0	3.6	1.5	14.8
1983	3.3	-1.9	3.3	7.5	-1.2	3.5	-3.3	1.1	1.0	-1.5	-1.7	-0.9	17.3
1984	-0.9	-3.9	1.3	0.5	-6.0	1.7	-1.6	10.6	-0.4	0.5	-2.0	2.2	1.4
1985	7.3	0.9	-0.3	-0.5	5.4	1.2	-0.5	-12.0	3.5	4.3	6.5	4.5	26.3

B.

MONTHLY CLOSING PRICES IN STANDARD & POOR'S 500

Year	DEC	NOV	OCT	SEP	AUG	JUL	JUN	MAY	APR	MAR	FEB	JAN
1950	20.41	19.51	19.53	19.45	18.42	17.84	17.69	18.78	18.07	17.29	17.22	17.05
1951	23.77	22.88	22.94	23.26	23.28	22.40	20.96	21.52	22.43	21.40	21.80	21.66
1952	26.57	25.66	24.52	24.54	25.03	25.40	24.96	23.86	23.32	24.37	23.26	24.14
1953	24.81	24.76	24.54	23.35	23.32	24.75	24.14	24.54	24.62	25.29	25.90	26.38
1954	35.98	34.24	31.68	32.31	29.83	30.88	29.21	29.19	28.16	26.96	26.15	26.08
1955	45.48	45.51	42.34	43.67	43.18	43.52	41.03	37.91	37.96	36.58	36.76	36.63
1956	46.67	45.08	45.58	45.35	47.51	49.39	46.97	45.20	48.38	48.48	45.34	43.82
1957	39.99	41.72	41.06	42.42	45.22	47.91	47.37	47.43	45.74	44.11	43.26	44.72
1958	55.21	52.48	51.33	50.06	47.75	47.19	45.24	44.09	43.44	42.10	40.84	41.70
1959	59.89	58.28	57.52	56.88	59.60	60.51	58.47	58.68	57.59	55.44	55.41	55.42
1960	58.11	55.54	53.39	53.52	56.96	55.51	56.92	55.83	54.37	55.34	56.12	55.61
1961	71.56	71.32	68.62	66.73	68.07	66.76	64.64	66.56	65.31	65.06	63.44	61.78
1962	63.10	62.26	56.52	56.27	59.12	58.23	54.75	59.63	65.24	69.55	69.96	68.84
1963	75.02	73.20	74.01	71.70	72.50	69.13	69.37	70.80	69.80	66.57	64.29	66.20
1964	84.75	84.42	84.86	84.18	81.83	83.18	81.69	80.37	79.46	78.98	77.80	77.04
1965	92.43	91.61	92.42	89.96	87.17	85.25	84.12	88.42	89.11	86.16	87.43	87.56
1966	80.33	80.45	80.20	76.56	77.10	83.60	84.74	86.13	91.06	89.23	91.22	92.88
1967	96.47	94.00	93.90	96.71	93.64	94.75	90.64	89.08	94.01	90.20	86.78	86.61
1968	103.86	108.37	103.41	102.67	98.86	97.74	99.58	98.68	97.59	90.20	89.36	92.24
1969	92.06	93.81	97.24	93.12	95.51	91.83	97.71	103.46	103.69	101.51	98.13	103.01
1970	92.15	87.20	83.25	84.21	81.52	78.05	72.72	76.55	81.52	89.63	89.50	85.02
1971	102.09	93.99	94.23	98.34	99.03	95.58	99.70	99.63	103.95	100.31	96.75	95.88
1972	118.05	116.67	111.58	110.55	111.09	107.39	107.14	109.53	107.67	107.20	106.57	103.94
1973	97.55	95.96	108.29	108.43	104.25	108.22	104.26	104.95	106.97	111.52	111.68	116.03
1974	68.56	69.97	73.90	63.54	72.15	79.31	86.00	87.28	90.31	93.98	96.22	96.57
1975	90.19	91.24	89.04	83.87	86.88	88.75	95.19	91.15	87.30	83.36	81.59	76.98
1976	107.46	102.10	102.90	105.24	102.91	103.44	104.28	100.18	101.64	102.77	99.71	100.86
1977	95.10	94.83	92.34	96.53	96.77	98.85	100.48	96.12	98.44	98.42	99.82	102.03
1978	96.11	94.70	93.15	102.54	103.29	100.68	95.53	97.29	96.83	89.21	87.04	89.25
1979	107.94	106.16	101.82	109.32	109.32	103.81	102.91	99.08	101.76	101.59	96.28	99.93
1980	135.76	140.52	127.47	125.46	122.38	121.67	114.24	111.24	106.29	102.09	113.66	114.16
1981	122.55	126.35	121.89	116.18	122.79	130.92	131.21	132.59	132.87	136.00	131.27	129.55
1982	140.64	138.54	133.71	120.45	119.51	107.09	109.61	111.88	116.44	111.96	113.11	120.40
1983	164.93	166.40	163.55	166.07	164.40	162.56	168.11	162.39	164.42	152.96	148.06	145.30
1984	167.24	163.58	166.09	166.10	166.68	150.66	153.18	150.55	160.05	159.18	157.06	163.41
1985	211.28	202.17	189.82	182.08	188.63	190.92	191.85	189.55	179.83	180.66	181.18	179.63

C.

MONTHLY POINT CHANGES IN DOW JONES INDUSTRIALS

Year	JAN	FEB	MAR	APR	MAY	JUNE	JUL	AUG	SEP	OCT	NOV	DEC	Year's Close
1950	1.66	1.65	2.61	8.28	9.09	−14.31	0.29	7.47	9.49	−1.35	2.59	7.81	235.41
1951	13.42	3.22	4.11	11.19	−9.48	−7.01	15.22	12.39	0.91	−8.81	1.08	7.96	269.23
1952	1.46	−10.61	9.38	−11.77	5.31	11.32	5.30	−4.52	−4.43	1.38	14.43	8.24	291.90
1953	−2.13	−5.50	−4.40	−5.12	2.47	−4.02	7.12	−14.16	2.83	11.77	5.56	0.47	280.90
1954	11.49	2.15	8.97	15.82	8.16	6.04	14.39	−12.12	24.66	−8.32	34.63	17.62	404.39
1955	4.44	3.04	2.17	15.95	−0.76	26.52	14.47	2.33	1.56	−11.75	28.39	5.14	488.40
1956	−17.66	12.91	28.14	4.33	−38.07	14.73	25.03	−15.77	−26.79	4.60	7.07	26.69	499.47
1957	−20.31	−14.54	10.19	19.55	10.57	1.64	5.23	−24.17	−28.05	−15.26	8.83	−14.18	435.69
1958	14.33	−10.10	6.84	9.10	6.84	15.48	24.81	5.64	23.46	11.13	14.24	26.19	583.65
1959	10.31	9.54	1.79	22.04	20.04	0.19	31.28	−10.47	−32.73	14.92	12.58	20.18	679.36
1960	−56.74	7.50	−13.53	−14.89	23.80	15.12	−23.89	9.26	−45.85	0.22	16.86	18.67	615.89
1961	32.31	13.88	14.55	2.08	18.01	−12.76	21.41	14.57	−18.73	2.71	17.68	9.54	731.14
1962	−31.14	8.05	1.10	−41.62	−51.97	−52.08	36.65	11.25	−30.20	10.79	59.53	2.80	652.10
1963	30.75	−19.91	19.58	35.18	9.26	−20.08	−11.45	33.89	3.47	22.44	−4.71	12.43	762.95
1964	22.39	14.80	13.15	−2.52	9.79	10.94	9.60	−2.62	36.89	2.29	2.35	1.30	874.12
1965	28.73	0.62	−14.43	33.26	−4.27	−50.01	13.71	11.36	37.48	30.24	−14.11	22.55	969.26
1966	14.25	−31.62	−27.12	8.91	−49.61	−13.97	−22.72	−58.97	−14.19	32.85	−15.48	−5.90	785.69
1967	64.20	−10.52	26.61	31.07	−44.49	7.70	43.98	2.95	25.37	−46.92	−3.93	29.60	905.11
1968	−49.64	−14.97	0.17	71.55	−13.22	1.20	−14.80	13.01	39.78	16.60	32.69	−41.33	943.75
1969	2.30	−40.84	30.27	14.70	−12.62	−64.37	−57.72	21.25	−23.63	42.90	−43.69	−11.94	800.36
1970	−56.30	33.53	7.98	−49.50	−35.63	−16.91	50.59	30.46	−3.90	−5.07	38.48	44.83	838.92
1971	29.58	10.33	25.54	37.38	−33.94	−16.67	−32.71	39.64	−10.88	−48.19	−7.66	58.86	890.20
1972	11.97	25.96	12.57	13.47	6.55	−31.69	−4.29	38.99	−10.46	2.25	62.69	1.81	1020.02
1973	−21.00	−43.95	−4.06	−29.58	−20.02	9.70	34.69	−38.83	59.53	9.48	−134.33	28.61	850.86
1974	4.69	4.98	−13.85	−9.93	−34.58	0.24	−44.98	−78.85	−70.71	57.65	−46.86	2.42	616.24
1975	87.45	35.36	29.10	53.19	10.95	46.70	−47.48	3.83	−41.46	42.16	24.63	8.26	852.41
1976	122.87	−2.67	26.84	−2.60	−21.62	27.55	−18.14	−10.90	16.45	−25.26	−17.71	57.43	1004.65
1977	−50.28	−17.95	−17.29	7.77	−28.24	17.64	−26.23	−28.58	−14.38	−28.76	11.35	1.47	831.17
1978	−61.25	−27.80	15.24	79.96	3.29	−21.66	43.32	14.55	−11.00	−73.37	6.58	5.98	805.01
1979	34.21	−30.40	53.36	−7.28	−32.57	19.65	4.44	41.21	9.05	−62.88	6.65	16.39	838.74
1980	37.11	−12.71	−77.39	31.31	33.79	17.07	67.40	−2.73	0.17	7.93	68.85	−29.35	963.99
1981	−16.72	27.31	29.29	6.12	6.00	−14.87	−24.54	−70.87	−31.49	7.93	36.43	−13.98	875.00
1982	−3.90	−46.71	1.62	25.59	−28.82	7.61	−3.33	92.71	5.06	95.47	47.56	7.26	1046.54
1983	29.16	36.92	17.41	96.17	−26.22	21.98	−22.74	16.94	16.97	2.57	50.82	−17.38	1258.64
1984	−38.06	−65.96	10.26	5.86	−65.90	27.55	−17.12	109.10	−17.67	0.67	−18.44	22.63	1211.57
1985	75.20	−2.76	−17.23	8.72	57.35	20.05	11.99	−13.46	−5.38	45.68	97.82	74.54	1546.67
UP	23	18	22	24	15	17	21	20	13	20	24	25	
DOWN	13	18	14	12	21	19	15	16	23	16	12	11	
TOTALS	259.15	−157.77	197.96	464.06	−324.38	−54.47	118.78	113.26	−149.72	101.63	387.15	388.72	

D.

1953 DAILY DOW POINT CHANGES
(Dow Jones Industrial Average)

WEEK #	MONDAY	TUESDAY	WEDNESDAY	THURSDAY	FRIDAY	WEEKLY DOW CLOSE	NET POINT CHANGE
					1952 Close: 291.90		
1				H	0.24	292.14	0.24*
2	1.65	— 1.61	— 1.42	— 0.40	— 2.84	287.52	— 4.62
3	— 2.28	1.61	0.52	0.81	— 1.01	287.17	— 0.35
4	— 0.20	1.03	— 0.40	0.24	— 0.95	286.89	— 0.28
5	— 0.35	0.27	0.58	0.57	1.81	289.77	2.88
6	0.26	0.16	— 1.11	— 2.88	— 3.35	282.85	— 6.92
7	— 0.89	— 0.29	— 0.10	H	1.54	283.11	0.26
8	— 0.93	— 0.67	— 0.37	0.41	0.34	281.89	— 1.22
9	H	1.10	1.46	— 0.10	— 0.08	284.27	2.38
10	0.44	1.28	— 2.29	0.16	0.96	284.82	0.55
11	0.08	0.32	2.80	— 0.02	1.04	289.04	4.22
12	0.48	1.12	— 0.32	— 0.35	— 0.28	289.69	0.65
13	— 2.30	1.44	— 0.85	— 1.38	0.73	287.33	— 2.36
14	— 4.26	— 3.20	0.22	— 0.06	H	280.03	— 7.30
15	— 5.93	1.06	1.68	— 0.61	— 0.73	275.50	— 4.53
16	— 0.77	1.12	1.50	— 0.61	— 2.33	274.41	— 1.09
17	1.58	— 0.51	— 1.93	— 2.82	0.53	271.26	— 3.15
18	1.44	1.26	1.42	— 0.63	0.91	275.66	4.40
19	2.68	— 0.12	— 0.08	— 0.71	0.79	278.22	2.56
20	0.57	— 1.70	— 0.29	1.16	— 0.06	277.90	— 0.32
21	— 0.98	— 1.01	2.13	0.47	— 0.35	278.16	0.26
22	— 0.69	— 1.10	— 2.41	— 2.48	0.80	272.28	— 5.88
23	— 3.88	1.44	— 0.24	— 1.97	0.69	268.32	— 3.96
24	— 0.41	— 4.52	— 0.04	1.64	0.79	265.78	— 2.54
25	— 1.91	— 0.99	2.86	0.12	— 0.06	265.80	0.02
26	1.46	1.22	— 0.69	1.14	0.12	269.05	3.25
27	— 0.85	0.06	1.13	0.84	0.30	270.53	1.48
28	0.35	1.25	0.06	— 0.87	— 0.26	271.06	0.53
29	— 2.54	— 0.46	0.69	0.66	1.55	270.96	— 0.10
30	— 1.22	— 0.75	0.40	0.55	— 0.18	269.76	— 1.20
31	— 1.30	0.67	1.30	2.39	2.56	275.38	5.62
32	0.75	— 0.45	— 0.60	0.69	— 0.23	275.54	0.16
33	— 0.22	— 0.02	1.12	0.32	— 1.03	275.71	0.17
34	— 0.67	— 1.75	— 1.79	0.23	0.20	271.93	— 3.78
35	— 3.23	— 1.25	— 0.94	— 0.83	0.06	265.74	— 6.19
36	— 4.52	1.32	1.42	— 0.35	0.73	264.34	-- 1.40
37	H	1.08	0.06	— 2.60	— 3.17	259.71	— 4.63
38	— 4.22	2.18	1.40	0.81	— 1.10	258.78	— 0.93
39	— 0.77	3.27	1.07	0.10	0.86	263.31	4.53
40	1.48	— 0.02	— 0.73	1.64	1.02	266.70	3.39
41	— 1.22	— 1.22	2.27	0.19	0.32	267.04	0.34
42	H	— 0.95	1.42	3.71	1.58	272.80	5.76
43	0.51	0.59	— 0.16	1.15	0.45	275.34	2.54
44	— 0.91	— 1.08	0.79	2.17	— 0.50	275.81	0.47
45	0.91	H	0.10	2.27	— 0.26	278.83	3.02
46	— 0.57	— 2.37	H	0.34	1.30	277.53	— 1.30
47	— 1.60	— 2.05	0.63	1.58	— 0.04	276.05	— 1.48
48	— 0.63	1.71	0.65	H	2.45	280.23	4.18
49	1.14	— 0.27	1.71	0.44	— 0.54	282.71	2.48
50	— 0.71	— 0.55	— 0.33	— 1.23	0.02	279.91	— 2.80
51	— 0.65	0.26	3.35	— 0.20	0.87	283.54	3.63
52	— 0.55	— 3.00	— 0.15	1.08	H	280.92	— 2.62
53	— 1.01	— 1.61	2.13	0.47	(Year's Close) 280.90		— 0.02*
TOTALS	—37.39	— 6.70	19.63	7.25	6.21		—11.00

*Partial Week

1954 DAILY DOW POINT CHANGES
(Dow Jones Industrial Average)

WEEK #	MONDAY	TUESDAY	WEDNESDAY	THURSDAY	FRIDAY	WEEKLY DOW CLOSE	NET POINT CHANGE
					1953 Close: 280.90		
1	1.99	1.30	— 0.23	— 1.36	— 1.09	281.51	0.61
2	— 1.64	1.64	1.52	1.46	2.23	286.72	5.21
3	— 0.69	2.24	0.87	0.34	0.17	289.65	2.93
4	0.75	2.45	— 0.63	— 0.71	0.88	292.39	2.74
5	— 0.55	— 0.67	1.15	1.71	— 0.06	293.97	1.58
6	— 0.39	0.21	— 0.84	— 0.50	1.54	293.99	0.02
7	— 1.44	— 2.94	0.50	1.40	— 0.44	291.07	— 2.92
8	H	— 1.04	— 0.49	1.87	3.13	294.54	3.47
9	2.01	0.93	— 0.45	0.45	1.97	299.45	4.91
10	— 0.81	0.81	0.14	1.24	— 1.12	299.71	0.26
11	— 0.83	— 0.79	0.22	1.79	1.34	301.44	1.73
12	0.16	— 2.58	— 2.13	— 0.49	2.68	299.08	— 2.36
13	0.98	0.83	2.62	2.76	0.40	306.67	7.59
14	0.37	— 2.78	1.15	2.38	1.60	309.39	2.72
15	— 0.20	— 0.21	2.78	2.01	H	313.77	4.38
16	— 1.99	0.11	— 0.98	0.57	1.89	313.37	— 0.40
17	1.17	— 1.05	0.26	4.47	1.11	319.33	5.96
18	0.02	0.47	— 1.89	2.48	0.89	321.30	1.97
19	0.02	— 1.58	1.87	— 1.22	2.11	322.50	1.20
20	0.83	0.81	— 0.93	0.67	2.21	326.09	3.59
21	n/c	— 1.07	2.09	— 0.74	1.12	327.49	1.40
22	H	1.18	— 0.31	0.27	— 1.00	327.63	0.14
23	0.33	— 6.96	— 1.73	0.85	1.97	322.09	— 5.54
24	0.56	2.56	2.07	— 0.07	0.70	327.91	5.82
25	0.65	0.95	1.21	1.48	0.33	332.53	4.62
26	3.59	0.78	— 3.37	0.59	3.54	337.66	5.13
27	H	3.46	— 0.78	— 0.53	1.44	341.25	3.59
28	— 0.34	— 0.87	0.40	0.62	— 1.10	339.96	— 1.29
29	— 1.32	— 1.02	2.36	2.99	0.51	343.48	3.52
30	— 0.09	1.30	0.42	1.04	1.77	347.92	4.44
31	1.65	0.04	0.13	— 1.95	— 4.73	343.06	— 4.86
32	— 2.19	2.69	2.85	— 0.57	0.80	346.64	3.58
33	2.97	— 1.23	0.13	1.38	0.49	350.38	3.74
34	— 2.74	— 1.32	— 1.72	— 1.25	1.13	344.48	— 5.90
35	— 3.23	— 5.45	2.33	3.02	1.95	343.10	— 1.38
36	H	2.27	0.70	0.66	1.10	347.83	4.73
37	3.27	0.68	— 1.15	1.74	2.95	355.32	7.49
38	— 1.84	2.92	1.96	1.27	2.04	361.67	6.35
39	0.59	1.06	— 1.59	— 1.27	— 0.58	359.88	— 1.79
40	2.85	0.64	1.06	— 0.64	— 0.02	363.77	3.89
41	— 2.34	— 1.86	— 0.66	— 4.22	— 1.49	353.20	—10.57
42	1.15	0.40	2.67	0.66	0.53	358.61	5.41
43	— 2.27	— 0.02	— 0.59	— 1.17	— 2.42	352.14	— 6.47
44	1.82	H	7.54	5.45	— 0.95	366.00	13.86
45	3.46	1.61	0.81	3.03	2.19	377.10	11.10
46	— 0.36	2.65	0.30	— 2.25	0.57	378.01	0.91
47	1.46	3.27	1.89	H	3.16	387.79	9.78
48	0.72	— 1.74	— 2.73	1.59	3.97	389.60	1.81
49	2.88	1.40	— 0.80	— 1.55	— 1.45	390.08	0.48
50	— 0.29	— 2.76	1.89	4.22	1.80	394.94	4.86
51	2.38	0.79	— 1.04	0.08	H	397.15	2.21
52	— 3.27	4.63	3.46	n/c	2.42	404.39	7.24
TOTALS	9.81	9.14	24.31	36.05	44.18		123.49

1955 DAILY DOW POINT CHANGES
(Dow Jones Industrial Average)

WEEK #	MONDAY	TUESDAY	WEDNESDAY	THURSDAY	FRIDAY	WEEKLY DOW CLOSE	NET POINT CHANGE
					1954 Close: 404.39		
1							
2	4.50	− 2.72	− 8.93	− 5.35	3.71	395.60	− 8.79
3	5.29	− 0.64	− 0.47	− 1.44	− 1.80	396.54	0.94
4	− 8.34	2.78	1.33	0.72	2.87	395.90	− 0.64
5	0.10	1.00	4.97	0.63	2.08	404.68	8.78
6	4.15	0.87	− 2.59	− 1.26	3.91	409.76	5.08
7	− 0.17	− 3.89	4.62	2.57	1.10	413.99	4.23
8	− 2.60	0.56	− 1.97	0.49	1.16	411.63	− 2.36
9	0.35	H	0.20	− 1.18	− 0.80	409.50	− 2.13
10	2.37	1.84	3.47	1.15	1.35	419.68	10.18
11	− 2.84	− 7.71	− 4.23	1.93	− 5.75	401.08	−18.60
12	− 9.72	7.92	3.86	2.09	− 0.48	404.75	3.67
13	− 2.35	2.07	6.40	3.62	0.28	414.77	10.02
14	− 1.86	0.82	− 3.60	− 0.43	4.14	413.84	− 0.93
15	− 0.87	2.93	0.52	1.78	H	418.20	4.36
16	0.57	2.17	0.63	0.89	2.99	425.45	7.25
17	2.97	− 0.54	0.74	− 0.17	− 2.93	425.52	0.07
18	1.34	3.78	− 2.54	− 4.91	2.46	425.65	0.13
19	0.65	− 3.52	− 0.24	0.85	0.45	423.84	− 1.81
20	0.48	− 0.52	− 3.51	− 2.09	1.37	419.57	− 4.27
21	− 4.56	− 0.89	3.71	1.89	3.17	422.89	3.32
22	− 2.57	0.07	1.38	3.18	0.71	425.66	2.77
23	H	− 0.80	0.02	0.92	2.73	428.53	2.87
24	2.96	3.06	2.40	− 1.88	2.65	437.72	9.19
25	2.45	− 1.97	3.73	0.55	1.60	444.08	6.36
26	0.30	2.42	0.57	1.45	0.11	448.93	4.85
27	0.93	− 0.84	0.68	1.68	2.44	453.82	4.89
28	H	5.60	7.99	− 7.18	0.95	461.18	7.36
29	3.06	− 1.27	− 5.57	1.09	1.74	460.23	− 0.95
30	− 0.16	− 3.35	1.38	2.97	3.62	464.69	4.46
31	3.33	0.59	− 0.16	− 1.99	− 0.61	465.85	1.16
32	− 5.60	0.57	0.16	− 6.80	2.22	456.40	− 9.45
33	− 2.35	− 5.21	1.45	4.89	1.83	457.01	0.61
34	− 0.92	− 2.83	− 0.41	− 0.32	1.04	453.57	− 3.44
35	− 1.02	4.80	2.04	1.88	2.43	463.70	10.13
36	0.67	0.30	3.51	1.45	2.90	472.53	8.83
37	H	3.71	− 1.04	− 0.14	− 0.47	474.59	2.06
38	1.92	4.42	1.97	− 1.34	2.11	483.67	9.08
39	0.13	− 0.13	2.31	− 0.02	1.49	487.45	3.78
40	−31.89	10.37	6.68	− 3.93	− 2.06	466.62	−20.83
41	−10.92	3.15	2.29	− 2.95	− 3.78	454.41	−12.21
42	−13.27	− 2.55	6.99	− 0.67	− 0.23	444.68	− 9.73
43	1.45	2.45	4.51	4.57	0.81	458.47	13.79
44	2.35	− 2.42	− 2.68	− 1.95	1.08	454.85	− 3.62
45	0.02	0.02	0.03	7.05	5.38	467.35	12.50
46	3.23	H	3.32	− 1.38	4.02	476.54	9.19
47	8.34	2.19	0.31	− 2.12	− 2.35	482.91	6.37
48	− 5.61	4.61	0.71	H	0.26	482.88	− 0.03
49	− 1.92	1.64	0.66	− 1.87	1.33	482.72	− 0.16
50	4.44	− 0.43	− 0.38	1.45	− 0.16	487.64	4.92
51	− 3.92	0.57	− 3.45	− 0.12	1.36	482.08	− 5.56
52	− 0.28	0.04	3.65	0.59	0.51	486.59	4.51
53	H	− 0.78	− 1.59	0.34	3.84	488.40	1.81
TOTALS	−56.09	34.31	45.83	1.18	58.78		84.01

1956 DAILY DOW POINT CHANGES
(Dow Jones Industrial Average)

WEEK #	MONDAY	TUESDAY	WEDNESDAY	THURSDAY	FRIDAY	WEEKLY DOW CLOSE	NET POINT CHANGE
					1955 Close: 488.40		
1	H	− 2.62	− 1.67	− 0.09	1.66	485.68	− 2.72
2	− 5.94	− 3.62	2.30	3.38	n/c	481.80	− 3.88
3	− 5.56	1.49	− 4.84	− 4.40	− 4.09	464.40	−17.40
4	− 2.05	5.53	2.83	− 3.89	− 0.26	466.56	2.16
5	1.00	3.18	2.54	0.15	4.01	477.44	10.88
6	1.13	− 2.01	− 5.33	− 4.01	0.44	467.66	− 9.78
7	− 0.49	− 1.45	4.92	− 1.03	7.44	477.05	9.39
8	− 0.59	0.47	H	4.57	4.16	485.66	8.61
9	− 0.66	0.71	− 2.06	3.04	2.15	488.84	3.18
10	2.84	− 0.27	− 0.15	1.10	5.48	497.84	9.00
11	2.40	− 0.91	4.55	3.62	0.10	507.60	9.76
12	2.16	2.86	− 4.70	3.02	2.09	513.03	5.43
13	− 0.61	− 3.74	1.57	1.54	H	511.79	− 1.24
14	3.31	0.81	2.74	− 2.08	4.48	521.05	9.26
15	− 2.53	− 8.48	2.66	− 3.55	0.84	509.99	−11.06
16	− 0.84	− 1.20	− 1.40	− 2.22	2.87	507.20	− 2.79
17	0.08	− 3.92	− 0.34	4.10	4.91	512.03	4.83
18	4.09	− 2.16	− 1.18	1.25	2.41	516.44	4.41
19	− 3.55	− 3.76	− 0.97	− 6.60	− 0.31	501.25	−15.19
20	− 3.97	− 2.45	− 2.14	3.94	− 0.24	496.39	− 4.86
21	− 4.77	− 7.49	− 3.97	− 6.65	− 1.02	472.49	−23.90
22	− 3.68	8.87	H	0.37	2.58	480.63	8.14
23	2.59	− 0.03	− 2.65	2.45	− 7.70	475.29	− 5.34
24	4.12	6.08	1.59	− 1.56	0.39	485.91	10.62
25	− 2.00	0.61	0.48	3.26	− 0.31	487.95	2.04
26	− 1.52	2.94	2.67	0.46	0.28	492.78	4.83
27	− 0.86	3.82	H	4.80	3.60	504.14	11.36
28	2.38	1.82	1.31	− 2.21	3.66	511.10	6.96
29	1.88	1.45	− 1.04	0.47	0.71	514.57	3.47
30	− 0.96	− 0.44	0.96	1.72	− 3.55	512.30	− 2.27
31	1.12	4.39	0.88	2.26	− 0.68	520.27	7.97
32	− 6.39	2.00	2.86	0.30	− 1.66	517.38	− 2.89
33	− 2.98	2.87	0.43	− 0.51	− 1.40	515.79	− 1.59
34	− 4.55	− 5.81	− 3.09	4.72	0.85	507.91	− 7.88
35	− 2.21	− 2.65	− 2.15	− 4.94	6.08	502.04	− 5.87
36	H	5.62	2.16	− 0.33	− 2.73	506.76	4.72
37	− 1.20	− 3.40	− 2.19	− 0.28	− 0.63	500.32	− 6.44
38	− 1.56	− 5.31	− 4.73	− 1.59	3.20	490.33	− 9.99
39	− 2.63	− 6.62	0.52	1.84	− 4.51	475.25	−15.08
40	− 6.55	6.71	6.63	− 0.80	1.15	482.39	7.14
41	0.99	− 2.06	6.00	0.74	2.13	490.19	7.80
42	− 0.79	− 1.83	− 2.91	1.65	− 0.19	486.12	− 4.07
43	− 0.85	− 0.22	− 2.38	− 1.59	4.98	486.06	− 0.06
44	0.88	− 0.47	− 6.62	7.77	2.85	490.47	4.41
45	4.90	H	− 4.22	− 2.43	− 3.37	485.35	− 5.12
46	1.70	− 0.36	− 4.33	− 2.16	0.47	480.67	− 4.68
47	− 6.11	− 4.49	− 2.16	H	4.65	472.56	− 8.11
48	− 2.27	− 0.11	− 4.08	0.52	6.16	472.78	0.22
49	7.83	0.77	7.17	4.19	2.05	494.79	22.01
50	− 1.61	− 2.82	− 2.85	2.96	1.61	492.08	− 2.71
51	1.67	1.34	− 1.28	− 3.37	3.94	494.38	2.30
52	H	H	2.36	− 0.36	0.03	496.41	2.03
53	3.06				(Year's Close)	499.47	3.06*
TOTALS	− 30.15	−16.36	−15.30	9.86	63.02		11.07

*Partial Week

1957 DAILY DOW POINT CHANGES
(Dow Jones Industrial Average)

WEEK #	MONDAY	TUESDAY	WEDNESDAY	THURSDAY	FRIDAY	WEEKLY DOW CLOSE	NET POINT CHANGE
					1956 Close: 499.47		
1		H	— 3.44	3.17	— 0.98	498.22	— 1.25*
2	— 3.02	— 1.34	— 0.65	2.30	— 1.70	493.81	— 4.41
3	— 4.52	— 4.54	0.30	— 1.04	— 6.55	477.46	—16.35
4	— 1.56	1.59	2.44	1.37	— 2.96	478.34	0.88
5	— 3.75	2.33	3.61	— 1.37	— 1.94	477.22	— 1.12
5	— 0.03	— 7.23	0.85	— 2.10	— 2.42	466.29	—10.93
7	— 8.85	— 2.62	7.32	— 0.58	6.51	468.07	1.78
8	— 0.67	— 0.56	2.16	— 2.07	H	466.93	— 1.14
9	— 0.03	0.82	— 1.46	— 1.64	4.29	468.91	1.98
10	2.57	1.40	1.99	— 0.70	— 2.54	471.63	2.72
11	— 2.13	0.81	2.22	1.40	0.35	474.28	2.65
12	— 1.98	1.63	n/c	0.09	— 1.08	472.94	— 1.34
13	— 1.43	0.73	0.88	1.89	— 0.20	474.81	1.87
14	0.17	2.57	0.76	— 0.88	0.18	477.61	2.80
15	1.43	3.62	2.51	— 0.47	2.02	486.72	9.11
16	— 0.88	— 1.52	0.70	3.01	H	488.03	1.31
17	0.76	3.09	1.78	— 1.37	— 0.79	491.50	3.47
18	2.45	0.41	1.40	2.80	— 1.02	497.54	6.04
19	— 1.22	— 1.64	2.05	0.03	1.54	498.30	0.76
20	3.91	— 1.75	1.52	2.86	0.76	505.60	7.30
21	0.38	0.06	— 1.61	— 0.41	n/c	504.02	— 1.58
22	— 4.81	— 1.49	4.46	H	2.75	504.93	0.91
23	— 1.17	— 0.79	— 0.90	2.48	1.08	505.63	0.70
24	— 1.87	5.72	0.18	1.92	0.21	511.79	6.16
25	1.40	— 1.87	— 5.40	— 2.36	— 3.56	500.00	—11.79
26	— 2.92	4.90	— 1.20	2.25	0.26	503.29	3.29
27	n/c	4.26	5.70	H	3.64	516.89	13.60
28	1.52	— 2.04	3.44	— 1.84	2.80	520.77	3.88
29	— 0.61	— 2.74	— 2.31	0.53	0.09	515.73	— 5.04
30	— 0.41	0.29	0.17	0.91	— 2.10	514.59	— 1.14
31	— 6.34	0.68	— 0.41	— 2.31	— 1.11	505.10	— 9.49
32	— 4.32	— 6.65	4.35	— 1.61	— 0.09	496.78	— 8.32
33	— 4.46	— 0.18	— 6.21	1.37	0.90	488.20	— 8.58
34	— 9.25	4.91	1.28	— 3.68	— 5.72	475.74	—12.46
35	— 5.60	7.41	0.24	— 1.73	8.29	484.35	8.61
36	H	1.78	— 3.53	— 3.09	— 0.88	478.63	— 5.72
37	— 4.35	— 4.05	4.17	6.16	0.46	481.02	2.39
38	— 2.94	0.20	0.32	— 2.48	— 7.70	468.42	—12.60
39	— 9.46	3.91	— 5.92	0.06	— 0.12	456.89	—11.53
40	— 0.59	4.50	4.23	0.79	— 4.12	461.70	4.81
41	— 9.28	— 1.86	0.84	— 9.69	— 0.55	441.16	—20.54
42	2.62	4.12	— 3.97	— 7.06	— 3.04	433.83	— 7.73
43	—10.77	— 3.27	17.34	— 0.73	— 1.25	435.15	1.32
44	— 3.01	3.62	4.52	0.76	— 6.33	434.71	— 0.44
45	— 0.67	H	1.78	3.09	— 4.79	434.12	— 0.59
46	— 0.82	— 5.19	0.32	— 2.13	11.41	439.35	5.23
47	— 4.39	— 3.23	1.64	6.43	2.88	442.68	3.33
48	1.70	— 9.04	10.69	H	3.84	449.87	7.19
40	— 2.96	— 0.36	2.32	0.68	— 2.35	447.20	— 2.67
50	— 3.44	— 4.52	0.12	— 0.88	2.00	440.48	— 6.72
51	— 7.08	— 7.75	0.53	5.08	— 4.06	427.20	—13.28
52	0.88	1.03	H	5.05	— 1.26	432.90	5.70
53	— 1.12	3.91			(Year's Close) 435.69		2.79*
TOTALS	—111.28	— 5.93	64.12	4.26	—14.95		—63.78

*Partial Week

1958 DAILY DOW POINT CHANGES
(Dow Jones Industrial Average)

WEEK #	MONDAY	TUESDAY	WEDNESDAY	THURSDAY	FRIDAY	WEEKLY DOW CLOSE	NET POINT CHANGE
					1957 Close: 435.69		
1			H	3.58	5.29	444.56	8.87*
2	− 2.00	5.23	− 1.18	− 3.37	− 4.56	438.68	− 5.88
3	1.03	2.09	3.40	0.03	− 1.11	444.12	5.44
4	3.17	− 0.65	− 0.94	2.23	2.73	450.66	6.54
5	− 2.20	0.21	2.49	− 1.44	0.30	450.02	− 0.34
6	3.96	4.67	− 3.76	− 1.76	− 4.37	448.76	− 1.26
7	− 2.82	− 3.59	− 1.14	− 0.97	4.20	444.44	− 4.32
8	− 2.17	0.44	0.35	− 3.32	− 0.12	439.62	− 4.82
9	− 2.43	− 0.30	3.53	− 2.62	2.12	439.92	0.30
10	3.46	1.68	1.52	4.38	0.53	451.49	11.57
11	0.41	4.02	− 1.32	− 0.50	− 1.06	453.04	1.55
12	− 4.81	− 0.85	2.58	− 0.50	3.03	452.49	− 0.55
13	1.26	− 2.79	− 1.26	− 1.06	− 0.03	448.61	− 3.88
14	− 1.85	− 1.29	− 4.26	− 0.71	H	440.50	− 8.11
15	− 0.41	2.50	− 0.71	− 0.82	0.18	441.24	0.74
16	2.52	3.82	− 3.23	0.74	4.22	449.31	8.07
17	1.41	− 1.17	0.56	3.31	1.50	454.92	5.61
18	− 0.41	− 2.73	4.08	1.15	2.55	459.56	4.64
19	1.56	2.55	− 0.79	− 0.38	0.06	462.56	3.00
20	− 1.82	− 0.88	− 4.41	2.41	− 0.76	457.10	− 5.46
21	− 1.12	3.85	− 1.33	1.74	0.79	461.03	3.93
22	0.03	− 0.38	− 0.24	2.26	H	462.70	1.67
23	3.41	2.03	0.44	− 0.03	1.05	469.60	6.90
24	− 0.14	− 1.27	− 0.26	3.49	3.35	474.77	5.17
25	1.79	2.41	− 2.32	− 5.08	2.03	473.60	− 1.17
26	− 1.94	− 1.23	1.11	2.47	1.41	475.42	1.82
27	2.76	0.64	1.33	0.02	H	480.17	4.75
28	1.68	− 1.85	− 2.41	1.38	3.88	482.85	2.68
29	− 5.96	1.93	2.18	4.70	0.85	486.55	3.70
30	6.81	1.53	− 0.83	3.06	4.64	501.76	15.21
31	1.05	− 1.43	2.99	− 1.38	2.44	505.43	3.67
32	4.90	− 3.38	− 3.84	2.99	4.03	510.13	4.70
33	2.29	− 4.23	1.03	1.08	− 4.17	506.13	− 4.00
34	− 3.46	0.97	0.32	3.14	1.18	508.28	2.15
35	n/c	1.35	0.76	− 2.66	0.90	508.63	0.35
36	H	3.14	1.94	− 0.27	− 0.67	512.77	4.14
37	2.46	3.41	− 2.44	4.23	− 1.00	519.43	6.66
38	3.97	3.17	− 0.68	− 3.55	4.14	526.48	7.05
39	− 2.47	1.88	2.26	− 2.32	1.00	526.83	0.35
40	2.21	3.05	− 1.15	1.15	1.64	533.73	6.90
41	2.56	3.11	− 0.09	0.30	3.75	543.36	9.63
42	2.59	− 4.23	− 5.58	3.97	6.25	546.36	3.00
43	− 2.17	− 0.47	− 1.41	− 1.59	− 1.20	539.52	− 6.84
44	− 4.52	1.88	5.84	0.59	− 0.09	543.22	3.70
45	1.94	H	5.52	4.17	− 0.59	554.26	11.04
46	3.46	3.41	1.26	− 1.64	3.93	564.68	10.42
47	2.76	− 2.55	1.08	0.27	− 6.67	559.57	− 5.11
48	−14.68	− 4.37	8.63	H	8.31	557.46	− 2.11
49	2.61	− 1.50	0.24	0.29	− 2.35	556.75	− 0.71
50	− 0.67	2.05	6.85	− 1.91	− 0.80	562.27	5.52
51	1.71	1.20	4.20	3.00	0.79	573.17	10.90
52	− 1.94	− 4.84	6.34	H	H	572.73	− 0.44
53	4.58	4.49	1.85		(Year's Close) 583.65		10.92*
TOTALS	**14.36**	**26.73**	**29.10**	**24.25**	**53.52**		**147.96**

*Partial Week

1959 DAILY DOW POINT CHANGES
(Dow Jones Industrial Average)

WEEK #	MONDAY	TUESDAY	WEDNESDAY	THURSDAY	FRIDAY	WEEKLY DOW CLOSE	NET POINT CHANGE
					1958 Close: 583.65		
1				H	3.94	587.59	3.94*
2	2.58	1.20	− 8.22	4.99	4.58	592.72	5.13
3	− 0.08	− 1.94	0.94	3.17	0.94	595.75	3.03
4	− 1.35	1.29	1.97	− 1.97	0.38	596.07	0.32
5	− 3.70	2.29	− 6.13	1.87	3.56	593.96	− 2.11
6	− 1.73	0.11	− 2.96	− 3.26	− 3.79	582.33	−11.63
7	− 7.87	8.19	1.38	− 2.14	6.08	587.97	5.64
8	− 0.06	− 1.20	2.11	6.22	7.17	602.21	14.24
9	H	0.70	− 1.73	0.82	1.50	603.50	1.29
10	1.53	5.75	1.06	0.03	− 2.35	609.52	6.02
11	0.44	1.18	0.35	2.26	0.94	614.69	5.17
12	− 6.81	4.81	− 1.82	− 0.85	0.35	610.37	− 4.32
13	− 4.81	1.17	− 0.26	0.11	H	606.58	− 3.79
14	− 3.93	− 0.94	1.23	4.58	4.41	611.93	5.35
15	− 0.77	− 0.82	− 3.90	− 0.94	0.47	605.97	− 5.96
16	1.79	1.77	2.97	5.08	6.48	624.06	18.09
17	3.02	2.15	− 4.08	− 1.88	4.12	627.39	3.33
18	2.48	− 1.00	− 3.00	− 2.12	1.31	625.06	− 2.33
19	n/c	0.84	− 1.51	− 8.75	5.72	621.36	− 3.70
20	3.67	2.63	5.39	3.99	− 2.51	634.53	13.17
21	− 1.00	1.91	− 3.57	− 0.22	3.09	634.74	0.21
22	− 2.39	0.03	4.30	2.90	4.21	643.79	9.05
23	− 0.28	− 6.06	− 0.06	− 6.85	− 0.56	629.98	−13.81
24	− 8.36	− 4.00	9.55	0.32	− 0.07	627.42	− 2.56
25	− 2.83	− 3.19	6.65	1.36	0.35	629.76	2.34
26	1.95	− 0.98	3.54	2.96	2.02	639.25	9.49
27	3.81	0.54	7.28	3.88	H	654.76	15.51
28	5.33	3.12	0.60	− 0.72	0.47	663.56	8.80
29	− 6.21	0.35	2.87	− 2.28	− 1.16	657.13	− 6.43
30	− 2.59	6.94	2.90	0.25	− 0.91	663.72	6.59
31	5.36	2.96	1.14	0.19	1.51	674.88	11.16
32	3.22	− 1.80	− 3.97	− 0.35	− 3.41	668.57	− 6.31
33	−14.78	4.28	− 2.93	0.29	3.31	658.74	− 9.83
34	− 0.32	− 7.63	− 4.26	8.49	0.37	655.39	− 3.35
35	− 2.17	2.74	1.61	5.77	− 0.28	663.06	7.67
36	1.35	− 8.51	− 0.10	− 9.90	6.28	652.18	−10.88
37	H	− 9.49	− 5.02	− 4.29	3.98	637.36	−14.82
38	− 3.57	− 2.99	1.61	− 3.41	− 3.22	625.78	−11.58
39	− 7.63	− 1.70	7.57	8.83	− 0.26	632.59	6.81
40	3.88	3.63	− 8.42	1.92	2.97	636.57	3.98
41	0.44	− 0.95	− 0.69	− 2.33	3.94	636.98	0.41
42	1.57	− 0.72	− 3.56	3.21	5.74	643.22	6.24
43	− 3.56	− 4.29	− 2.68	− 7.10	7.48	633.07	−10.15
44	4.54	4.57	1.42	1.51	1.49	646.60	13.53
45	− 1.14	H	0.28	1.83	3.35	650.92	4.32
46	n/c	− 2.78	− 0.82	− 3.06	− 2.55	641.71	− 9.21
47	− 7.25	1.16	6.37	1.33	2.14	645.46	3.75
48	1.29	2.94	1.41	H	1.42	652.52	7.06
49	6.66	5.20	− 3.09	1.67	1.04	664.00	11.48
50	1.67	9.72	− 4.13	1.48	− 2.24	670.50	6.50
51	4.57	− 1.29	1.42	− 1.30	2.75	676.65	6.15
52	− 0.73	− 4.10	− 1.64	H	0.51	670.69	− 5.96
53	− 0.92	2.46	4.74	2.39	(Year's Close) 679.36		8.67*
TOTALS	**−35.69**	**20.25**	**4.11**	**19.98**	**87.06**		**95.71**

*Partial Week

1960 DAILY DOW POINT CHANGES
(Dow Jones Industrial Average)

WEEK #	MONDAY	TUESDAY	WEDNESDAY	THURSDAY	FRIDAY	WEEKLY DOW CLOSE	NET POINT CHANGE
					1959 Close: 679.36		
1							
2	− 0.30	6.41	− 2.85	− 4.96	− 1.93	675.73	− 3.63
3	− 8.57	− 6.73	− 3.99	4.09	− 0.85	659.68	−16.05
4	− 5.82	− 8.79	− 1.38	1.74	0.42	645.85	−13.83
5	− 6.78	0.77	− 2.17	− 7.83	− 7.22	622.62	−23.23
6	3.58	10.72	− 5.95	0.17	− 4.37	626.77	4.15
7	− 7.34	9.02	− 5.09	− 4.79	3.66	622.23	− 4.54
8	− 4.65	− 6.25	2.22	8.64	6.26	628.45	6.22
9	H	− 2.26	− 2.46	4.78	3.49	632.00	3.55
10	− 1.88	− 3.25	− 5.50	− 9.32	− 2.26	609.79	−22.21
11	− 5.77	− 4.92	8.06	− 4.85	3.52	605.83	− 3.96
12	0.96	5.39	4.55	− 1.64	1.33	616.42	10.59
13	0.58	1.09	3.97	1.94	− 1.53	622.47	6.05
14	− 0.69	− 1.43	− 0.41	− 3.35	− 0.61	615.98	− 6.49
15	2.56	3.65	6.12	0.72	− 0.93	628.10	12.12
16	− 3.21	1.61	n/c	3.62	H	630.12	2.02
17	0.65	− 4.37	− 7.69	0.44	− 2.83	616.32	−13.80
18	− 5.19	− 0.21	− 0.96	− 5.63	− 2.63	601.70	−14.62
19	− 2.09	8.12	3.26	− 2.67	− 0.70	607.62	5.92
20	− 0.14	− 2.66	1.72	1.33	8.16	616.03	8.41
21	1.36	4.24	1.37	1.68	0.56	625.24	9.21
22	− 1.58	− 2.27	− 0.11	1.51	1.99	624.78	− 0.46
23	H	0.72	− 0.61	2.98	1.11	628.98	4.20
24	7.94	8.66	4.77	6.07	− 1.54	654.88	25.90
25	0.97	− 0.97	− 5.46	− 1.15	2.62	650.89	− 3.99
26	− 3.37	− 2.59	0.43	2.05	− 0.40	647.01	− 3.88
27	− 4.52	− 5.03	0.93	2.23	0.68	641.30	− 5.71
28	H	− 0.39	− 0.54	4.52	2.02	646.91	5.61
29	− 6.47	− 6.32	− 2.01	− 0.79	− 1.08	630.24	−16.67
30	− 4.24	− 1.22	− 0.65	− 7.50	− 6.76	609.87	−20.37
31	− 8.19	5.07	− 4.99	3.91	11.06	616.73	6.86
32	1.12	− 4.17	− 4.99	0.54	5.06	614.29	− 2.44
33	0.50	0.90	1.83	5.36	3.30	626.18	11.89
34	− 2.01	1.26	1.11	− 0.72	3.45	629.27	3.09
35	1.44	7.58	3.27	− 4.40	− 1.03	636.13	6.86
36	− 1.67	− 8.06	− 0.41	0.11	− 0.88	625.22	−10.91
37	H	− 4.37	− 8.58	− 0.85	2.70	614.12	−11.10
38	− 4.77	2.44	− 6.10	− 3.00	− 0.51	602.18	−11.94
39	−15.42	1.44	6.06	− 2.11	− 6.95	585.20	−16.98
40	− 8.06	− 2.33	− 5.73	1.51	9.55	580.14	− 5.06
41	− 2.33	− 4.66	5.73	4.81	2.73	586.42	6.28
42	0.89	1.44	− 2.92	5.66	4.99	596.48	10.06
43	− 3.14	− 4.59	− 1.74	− 4.32	− 5.14	577.55	−18.93
44	− 5.62	− 5.88	9.13	5.77	− 3.03	577.92	0.37
45	2.44	4.88	2.99	2.59	5.25	596.07	18.15
46	1.56	H	4.62	9.76	− 3.40	608.61	12.54
47	− 3.81	2.07	− 2.10	− 2.59	1.44	603.62	− 4.99
48	0.92	− 3.44	1.37	H	4.00	606.47	2.85
49	− 1.04	− 3.03	− 5.18	− 2.66	1.44	596.00	−10.47
50	− 2.51	3.62	7.51	0.55	5.73	610.90	14.90
51	1.04	− 0.22	0.96	− 1.92	7.02	617.78	6.88
52	− 2.22	− 0.74	0.60	− 2.11	− 0.08	613.23	− 4.55
53	H	0.15	2.37	0.44	− 0.30	615.89	2.66
TOTALS	−104.89	− 9.90	− 5.62	10.36	46.58		−63.47

1961 DAILY DOW POINT CHANGES
(Dow Jones Industrial Average)

WEEK #	MONDAY	TUESDAY	WEDNESDAY	THURSDAY	FRIDAY	WEEKLY DOW CLOSE	NET POINT CHANGE
					1960 Close: 615.89		
1	H	− 5.64	11.24	1.18	− 1.03	621.64	5.75
2	2.78	1.30	1.49	1.29	5.15	633.65	12.01
3	− 0.46	− 4.23	5.14	− 1.71	1.98	634.37	0.72
4	5.45	− 1.03	− 1.07	1.15	4.72	643.59	9.22
5	7.05	− 2.44	1.19	4.23	− 0.65	652.97	9.38
6	− 7.32	− 1.71	4.91	− 3.73	− 5.45	639.67	−13.30
7	− 2.63	5.87	5.98	2.97	− 0.19	651.67	12.00
8	1.98	− 1.25	H	2.02	1.18	655.60	3.93
9	4.84	1.64	0.95	6.36	2.18	671.57	15.97
10	2.89	− 7.32	− 0.99	− 2.82	0.23	663.56	− 8.01
11	0.88	− 3.36	1.80	7.50	6.10	676.48	12.92
12	2.36	− 0.11	0.65	− 3.93	− 2.97	672.48	− 4.00
13	− 1.45	− 1.45	6.83	0.22	H	676.63	4.15
14	0.96	1.14	− 1.41	2.02	4.34	683.68	7.05
15	8.38	2.05	− 3.95	1.86	1.70	693.72	10.04
16	3.00	− 6.12	− 4.39	− 1.97	1.02	685.26	− 8.46
17	−12.60	10.43	− 0.91	− 2.64	− 0.83	678.71	− 6.55
18	− 1.66	5.29	6.56	3.35	− 1.58	690.67	11.96
19	− 1.61	− 2.14	− 0.31	− 0.12	1.42	687.91	− 2.76
20	4.46	5.37	7.78	− 4.38	4.82	705.96	18.05
21	− 3.52	− 1.85	− 4.07	− 6.36	6.12	696.28	− 9.68
22	H	H	0.44	− 1.35	2.33	697.70	1.42
23	5.73	0.36	− 2.93	0.83	− 0.79	700.90	3.20
24	− 4.14	− 2.61	1.66	− 4.54	− 5.77	685.50	−15.40
25	− 4.82	7.19	− 1.78	− 0.47	3.04	688.66	3.16
26	− 7.50	2.72	0.71	− 2.64	2.01	683.96	− 4.70
27	5.85	H	2.96	1.50	− 1.54	692.73	8.77
28	0.43	1.31	−23.68	15.11	5.05	690.95	− 1.78
29	− 6.36	− 5.29	3.44	0.23	− 0.16	682.81	− 8.14
30	− 0.67	4.23	7.82	8.61	2.33	705.13	22.32
31	0.24	8.57	− 3.48	5.25	4.98	720.69	15.56
32	− 1.11	0.64	− 2.65	2.92	2.12	722.61	1.92
33	− 3.68	− 2.75	2.02	3.64	1.70	723.54	0.93
34	1.21	1.01	− 5.30	− 6.43	2.67	716.70	− 6.84
35	− 0.69	− 1.86	2.75	3.04	1.25	721.19	4.49
36	H	− 2.47	7.29	0.52	− 5.62	720.91	− 0.28
37	− 6.55	8.25	− 0.41	− 7.20	1.30	716.30	− 4.61
38	− 5.06	− 8.70	4.78	− 1.01	− 4.74	701.57	−14.73
39	− 9.71	1.34	7.93	− 0.85	0.93	701.21	− 0.36
40	− 1.38	− 1.17	4.65	5.18	− 0.24	708.25	7.04
41	− 2.83	1.25	− 1.05	− 0.12	− 2.19	703.31	− 4.94
42	− 0.16	− 1.17	2.22	0.65	0.77	705.62	2.31
43	− 6.64	− 1.74	3.48	− 0.04	− 1.94	698.74	− 6.88
44	2.35	2.83	− 0.08	2.99	2.43	709.26	10.52
45	5.34	H	9.14	− 1.46	2.55	724.83	15.57
46	3.60	4.13	1.78	− 1.01	− 3.80	729.53	4.70
47	0.56	− 0.77	1.10	H	2.18	732.60	3.07
48	− 0.61	− 3.92	− 0.89	− 5.58	7.20	728.80	− 3.80
49	2.42	0.09	− 1.22	− 3.64	1.78	728.23	− 0.57
50	4.33	1.46	0.89	− 3.97	− 1.54	729.40	1.17
51	− 1.69	− 5.30	0.16	− 2.47	0.77	720.87	− 8.53
52	H	2.22	8.34	0.08	− 0.37	731.14	10.27
TOTALS	−17.76	4.29	67.51	14.26	46.95		115.25

1962 DAILY DOW POINT CHANGES
(Dow Jones Industrial Average)

WEEK #	MONDAY .	TUESDAY	WEDNESDAY	THURSDAY	FRIDAY	WEEKLY DOW CLOSE	NET POINT CHANGE
					1961 Close: 731.14		
1	H	— 6.43	1.30	— 3.48	— 7.69	714.84	—16.30
2	— 5.86	— 1.34	— 1.62	4.65	1.06	711.73	— 3.11
3	— 2.23	— 4.21	— 7.88	— 1.38	4.69	700.72	—11.01
4	1.26	— 3.44	— 0.37	— 1.65	— 4.33	692.19	— 8.53
5	— 2.27	4.17	5.91	2.54	4.01	706.55	14.36
6	— 0.41	4.25	5.34	1.09	— 2.55	714.27	7.72
7	0.65	— 0.60	— 0.65	3.60	— 0.81	716.46	2.19
8	— 2.10	3.19	— 4.53	H	— 3.48	709.54	— 6.92
9	— 3.32	3.00	— 1.17	3.76	— 0.81	711.00	1.46
10	— 1.01	— 1.82	— 1.54	7.12	0.69	714.44	3.44
11	0.24	1.90	4.37	2.59	— 1.27	722.27	7.83
12	— 1.89	— 0.72	— 3.04	0.08	— 0.24	716.46	— 5.81
13	— 5.79	— 3.39	4.97	— 0.97	— 4.33	706.95	— 9.51
14	— 1.53	— 4.82	— 3.72	4.00	— 1.25	699.63	— 7.32
15	— 6.67	2.50	— 0.56	— 9.23	2.23	687.90	—11.73
16	— 3.84	4.37	2.58	3.24	H	694.25	6.35
17	0.36	— 1.61	— 9.31	— 5.01	— 6.48	672.20	—22.05
18	— 6.87	5.91	— 1.28	5.53	— 4.29	671.20	— 1.00
19	— 0.21	— 7.09	— 9.20	— 7.47	— 6.60	640.63	—30.57
20	— 5.57	9.16	— 1.32	— 4.25	0.91	650.70	10.07
21	— 2.11	—12.25	— 9.82	— 3.96	—10.68	611.88	—38.82
22	—34.95	27.03	H	9.40	— 2.31	611.05	— 0.83
23	—17.37	1.28	8.95	— 1.71	— 0.59	601.61	— 9.44
24	— 6.44	—14.23	— 6.90	—11.04	15.18	578.18	—23.43
25	— 3.97	— 2.60	— 8.53	—12.59	—11.30	539.19	—38.99
26	— 2.42	— 1.01	1.22	20.37	3.93	561.28	22.09
27	12.47	5.73	H	4.39	— 7.70	576.17	14.89
28	4.65	5.19	3.05	1.21	— 0.08	590.19	14.02
29	— 2.09	—10.25	— 6.61	1.92	4.02	577.18	—13.01
30	0.29	— 3.35	0.55	4.94	5.39	585.00	7.82
31	6.44	6.49	— 6.57	2.47	2.55	596.38	11.38
32	— 3.14	— 4.89	2.59	0.25	1.13	592.32	— 4.06
33	2.97	6.61	4.86	— 0.05	3.31	610.02	17.70
34	2.84	— 4.22	6.90	0.46	— 2.26	613.74	3.72
35	— 1.17	— 7.32	— 2.01	— 0.92	6.86	609.18	— 4.56
36	H	— 6.73	— 3.31	1.67	0.05	600.86	— 8.32
37	1.17	1.96	2.35	— 2.35	1.85	605.84	4.98
38	1.79	— 0.54	n/c	— 5.44	— 9.87	591.78	—14.06
39	— 8.87	5.31	9.74	— 4.36	4.86	578.98	—12.08
40	— 7.03	6.78	— 0.21	3.89	4.18	586.59	7.61
41	— 0.50	1.09	0.96	— 1.67	n/c	586.47	— 0.12
42	3.22	— 0.34	— 1.67	— 6.53	— 7.86	573.29	—13.18
43	— 4.69	—10.54	18.62	— 5.82	— 1.84	569.02	— 4.27
44	10.33	9.63	0.79	7.36	7.45	604.58	35.56
45	5.90	H	5.27	— 6.61	6.99	616.13	11.55
46	8.28	— 1.30	7.37	— 1.34	1.84	630.98	14.85
47	— 4.77	6.73	4.31	H	7.62	644.87	13.89
48	— 2.81	5.99	3.80	0.76	— 3.31	649.30	4.43
49	— 2.89	5.07	2.51	— 2.26	0.37	652.10	2.80
50	— 7.02	0.08	2.17	— 2.13	2.89	648.09	— 4.01
51	— 2.60	— 5.35	6.86	1.55	— 2.14	646.41	— 1.68
52	1.30	H	3.93	— 1.08	0.87	651.43	5.02
53	0.67				(Year's Close)	652.10	0.67*
TOTALS	**—88.44**	**13.03**	**9.97**	**— 4.46**	**— 9.14**		**—79.04**

*Partial Week

1963 DAILY DOW POINT CHANGES
(Dow Jones Industrial Average)

WEEK #	MONDAY	TUESDAY	WEDNESDAY	THURSDAY	FRIDAY	WEEKLY DOW CLOSE	NET POINT CHANGE
					1962 Close: 652.10		
1		H	− 5.31	10.63	4.81	662.23	10.13*
2	− 0.09	7.74	− 1.88	1.51	2.09	671.60	9.37
3	4.14	− 0.38	− 6.36	3.98	− 0.46	672.52	0.92
4	2.72	0.29	2.05	− 0.59	2.72	679.71	7.19
5	3.18	0.84	− 5.15	4.27	0.34	683.19	3.48
6	− 1.18	− 0.71	1.22	− 3.43	0.83	679.92	− 3.27
7	− 5.18	1.88	5.10	3.14	1.21	686.07	6.15
8	2.89	− 2.13	− 4.77	− 0.42	H	681.64	− 4.43
9	− 7.03	0.67	− 4.48	− 7.86	− 3.22	659.72	−21.92
10	7.32	0.12	0.92	3.35	1.00	672.43	12.71
11	1.59	1.18	2.46	− 3.93	2.60	676.33	3.90
12	− 2.77	− 1.50	5.06	− 1.55	2.26	677.83	1.50
13	0.34	2.21	4.35	− 2.26	0.05	682.52	4.69
14	3.34	− 1.59	6.24	6.61	5.31	702.43	19.91
15	3.60	n/c	− 1.68	4.10	H	708.45	6.02
16	2.93	− 0.46	− 0.67	− 2.09	3.52	711.68	3.23
17	− 0.67	3.97	2.76	0.59	− 1.17	717.16	5.48
18	− 2.05	2.59	1.97	1.42	− 3.01	718.08	0.92
19	− 4.31	− 1.22	5.99	3.43	1.33	723.30	5.22
20	− 0.29	− 3.17	4.50	− 1.50	1.97	724.81	1.51
21	− 4.63	3.86	− 1.20	− 1.46	− 0.85	720.53	− 4.28
22	− 2.28	− 0.30	4.55	H	4.46	726.96	6.43
23	− 0.69	0.22	− 0.56	0.94	− 4.46	722.41	− 4.55
24	− 5.92	1.89	4.98	− 1.93	0.60	722.03	− 0.38
25	− 3.82	0.69	0.94	− 0.99	1.93	720.78	− 1.25
26	− 2.36	− 2.10	− 7.33	− 2.96	0.85	706.88	−13.90
27	− 5.53	7.59	4.42	H	3.09	716.45	9.57
28	− 5.79	3.43	− 1.97	− 2.36	− 2.06	707.70	− 8.75
29	− 4.42	− 1.16	− 2.40	− 3.82	− 2.01	693.89	−13.81
30	− 5.15	− 0.90	3.04	− 3.17	1.67	689.38	− 4.51
31	1.33	5.71	− 0.99	− 0.56	2.96	697.83	8.45
32	4.72	4.51	− 3.14	0.26	4.21	708.39	10.56
33	1.88	0.86	3.82	3.60	0.77	719.32	10.93
34	− 0.51	− 1.54	− 1.55	2.75	4.67	723.14	3.82
35	1.03	− 4.29	5.19	1.33	2.92	729.32	6.18
36	H	2.70	0.90	5.06	− 2.61	735.37	6.05
37	− 2.45	4.51	2.91	− 0.08	− 0.13	740.13	4.76
38	− 1.67	1.67	− 2.27	5.36	0.38	743.60	3.47
39	− 3.17	5.53	− 2.27	− 6.74	1.03	737.98	− 5.62
40	− 5.19	5.54	− 0.39	6.31	0.81	745.06	7.08
41	− 1.20	0.04	− 4.07	0.73	1.20	741.76	− 3.30
42	0.08	0.35	6.26	2.32	− 0.17	750.60	8.84
43	1.71	− 5.10	− 0.73	5.32	3.81	755.61	5.01
44	3.78	1.11	− 5.31	0.04	− 1.50	753.73	− 1.88
45	− 4.51	H	− 5.19	1.63	5.15	750.81	− 2.92
46	2.96	− 3.56	0.90	− 4.07	− 7.04	740.00	−10.81
47	− 5.15	1.80	5.41	− 9.41	−21.16	711.49	−28.51
48	H	32.03	− 2.52	H	9.52	750.52	39.03
49	1.39	− 0.09	3.69	8.35	− 3.61	760.25	9.73
50	− 1.17	0.17	− 2.04	0.22	2.74	760.17	− 0.08
51	1.47	4.74	0.83	− 3.35	− 1.78	762.08	1.91
52	− 3.78	− 1.44	H	3.35	2.74	762.95	0.87
53	− 3.05	3.05			(Year's Close) 762.95		n/c*
TOTALS	**−43.61**	**81.85**	**16.23**	**26.07**	**30.31**		**110.85**

*Partial Week

1964 DAILY DOW POINT CHANGES
(Dow Jones Industrial Average)

WEEK #	MONDAY	TUESDAY	WEDNESDAY	THURSDAY	FRIDAY	WEEKLY DOW CLOSE	NET POINT CHANGE
					1963 Close: 762.95		
1			H	3.13	1.60	767.68	4.73*
2	1.83	2.22	2.73	2.09	− 2.22	774.33	6.65
3	− 1.21	1.37	0.22	1.42	− 0.44	775.69	1.36
4	− 2.66	3.41	4.87	1.55	0.18	783.04	7.35
5	2.30	2.44	− 5.18	0.84	1.90	785.34	2.30
6	− 0.62	− 1.42	− 0.26	3.37	5.18	791.59	6.25
7	− 2.88	3.45	2.66	− 0.40	0.14	794.56	2.97
8	1.63	− 0.79	− 0.49	2.08	H	796.99	2.43
9	0.13	− 0.53	2.79	− 2.34	3.10	800.14	3.15
10	2.61	2.97	− 1.02	− 0.93	2.26	806.03	5.89
11	1.15	2.21	4.48	0.35	2.00	816.22	10.19
12	0.26	1.68	2.09	− 0.89	− 4.43	814.93	− 1.29
13	− 1.33	− 2.17	1.73	2.75	H	815.91	0.98
14	− 0.62	− 2.00	2.79	4.79	2.12	822.99	7.08
15	1.77	− 1.99	1.42	− 2.84	0.40	821.75	− 1.24
16	− 0.44	1.64	2.48	0.22	1.68	827.33	5.58
17	− 2.79	1.91	− 2.88	− 1.91	− 6.77	814.89	−12.44
18	− 3.02	4.83	− 3.89	− 2.04	6.33	817.10	2.21
19	6.73	2.80	1.55	1.99	− 1.60	828.57	11.47
20	− 1.50	0.31	− 1.60	− 1.33	1.78	826.23	− 2.34
21	− 4.92	− 4.03	2.83	− 0.31	1.07	820.87	− 5.36
22	− 0.62	− 1.33	− 0.98	2.62	H	820.56	− 0.31
23	− 2.00	− 4.78	− 1.99	− 9.31	3.55	806.03	−14.53
24	− 5.72	5.23	1.99	3.72	− 1.86	809.39	3.36
25	4.17	4.60	5.19	0.63	1.27	825.25	15.86
26	1.32	− 3.87	4.31	− 0.47	3.51	830.99	5.74
27	− 0.05	0.56	6.56	3.41	H	841.47	10.48
28	2.77	0.70	0.51	− 0.32	2.38	847.51	6.04
29	− 1.96	− 1.92	1.17	2.67	3.88	851.35	3.84
30	− 1.96	− 2.44	0.70	− 1.17	− 0.84	845.64	− 5.71
31	− 4.59	− 3.70	1.32	0.70	1.73	841.10	− 4.54
32	− 0.75	− 7.58	0.28	− 9.65	5.76	829.16	−11.94
33	0.19	− 1.27	6.00	4.44	0.29	838.81	9.65
34	1.40	2.62	− 1.07	− 3.05	− 0.09	838.62	− 0.19
35	− 1.31	− 5.11	− 2.99	6.04	3.84	839.09	0.47
36	− 0.61	5.52	1.08	0.94	2.29	848.31	9.22
37	H	3.60	3.66	3.93	7.63	867.13	18.82
38	− 0.89	− 3.70	1.64	4.49	− 3.55	865.12	− 2.01
39	6.46	0.89	− 0.52	1.03	1.73	874.71	9.59
40	0.75	0.28	− 0.37	− 3.37	0.65	872.65	− 2.06
41	4.50	− 2.01	− 1.36	1.12	3.18	878.08	5.43
42	− 0.51	− 1.36	− 1.03	− 6.74	5.10	873.54	− 4.54
43	2.67	5.29	− 1.78	− 2.71	0.61	877.62	4.08
44	− 0.61	− 1.03	− 4.82	0.70	1.22	873.08	− 4.54
45	2.43	H	− 1.69	− 0.28	3.33	876.87	3.79
46	− 2.30	− 3.93	2.95	1.03	− 0.51	874.11	− 2.76
47	5.99	5.29	6.32	− 3.00	2.01	890.72	16.61
48	− 1.43	− 1.68	− 5.21	H	− 0.28	882.12	− 8.60
49	− 6.69	−11.00	2.73	3.63	0.14	870.93	−11.19
50	3.06	− 3.30	− 6.88	− 0.67	1.20	864.34	− 6.59
51	− 3.69	− 3.20	2.63	3.49	5.16	868.73	4.39
52	1.01	0.62	− 2.34	0.14	H	868.16	− 0.57
53	− 1.15	− 4.83	6.51	5.44	(Year's Close)	874.13	5.97*
TOTALS	− 3.70	−14.53	39.84	21.96	67.61		111.18

*Partial Week

1965 DAILY DOW POINT CHANGES
(Dow Jones Industrial Average)

WEEK #	MONDAY	TUESDAY	WEDNESDAY	THURSDAY	FRIDAY	WEEKLY DOW CLOSE	NET POINT CHANGE
					1964 Close: 874.13		
1	− 4.35	6.08	3.82	4.68	− 1.76	882.60	8.47
2	0.62	2.67	0.96	0.33	3.97	891.15	8.55
3	4.06	1.06	− 0.96	− 2.05	0.33	893.59	2.44
4	2.87	1.38	1.68	1.43	1.91	902.86	9.27
5	0.82	0.09	2.53	− 2.24	− 2.49	901.57	− 1.29
6	− 3.68	3.35	− 8.32	−11.04	6.59	888.47	−13.10
7	− 3.15	− 3.97	1.58	0.76	1.92	885.61	− 2.86
8	H	6.35	5.88	2.06	3.58	903.48	17.87
9	− 3.72	2.15	− 1.15	− 3.01	− 1.77	895.98	− 7.50
10	0.86	− 2.77	− 1.68	4.12	3.82	900.33	4.35
11	− 0.48	− 0.95	0.47	− 2.82	− 0.76	895.79	− 4.54
12	0.33	2.57	1.87	− 2.22	− 6.68	891.66	− 4.13
13	− 3.84	1.23	n/c	1.28	3.05	893.38	1.72
14	− 0.15	− 1.33	1.04	4.96	3.39	901.29	7.91
15	5.07	1.65	4.85	− 0.95	H	911.91	10.62
16	0.85	− 0.80	− 1.25	4.35	1.35	916.41	4.50
17	0.45	1.30	0.70	− 0.15	3.60	922.31	5.90
18	− 0.20	6.11	4.00	1.30	− 1.00	932.52	10.21
19	− 1.05	− 0.55	3.25	4.70	0.75	939.62	7.10
20	− 8.95	− 0.05	1.50	− 4.85	− 5.26	922.01	−17.61
21	− 7.80	6.79	− 3.84	− 3.94	4.82	918.04	− 3.97
22	H	− 9.51	− 4.47	− 4.84	1.65	900.87	−17.17
23	1.28	−13.10	− 9.21	− 3.35	5.21	881.70	−19.17
24	−12.99	5.86	3.50	4.99	− 3.89	879.17	− 2.53
25	− 5.05	1.31	− 5.21	−12.46	− 3.40	854.36	−24.81
26	−13.77	10.81	16.63	3.56	3.57	875.16	20.80
27	H	− 1.98	− 2.41	7.08	1.64	879.49	4.33
28	− 1.53	− 0.99	6.26	− 2.25	− 0.55	880.43	0.94
29	− 0.17	−11.47	− 3.78	− 3.24	2.20	863.97	−16.46
30	3.29	− 3.73	4.39	6.31	7.51	881.74	17.77
31	0.11	− 0.65	2.68	− 2.25	0.88	882.51	0.77
32	− 2.74	− 0.88	2.58	0.49	6.86	888.82	6.31
33	2.31	3.13	0.11	− 2.58	− 1.87	889.92	1.10
34	− 2.85	0.05	3.73	5.33	− 0.22	895.96	6.04
35	− 0.33	− 2.53	0.50	6.80	7.57	907.97	12.01
36	H	2.14	3.57	3.79	1.48	918.95	10.98
37	1.97	− 4.33	6.36	8.23	− 2.19	928.99	10.04
38	2.19	− 4.66	5.10	− 4.17	2.09	929.54	0.55
39	8.34	− 2.03	− 3.46	− 1.81	− 0.93	929.65	0.11
40	1.21	7.84	− 1.86	− 2.42	3.90	938.32	8.67
41	4.33	− 1.53	− 0.11	− 3.51	3.18	940.68	2.36
42	5.16	1.92	0.71	1.81	2.14	952.42	11.74
43	− 4.28	8.18	3.18	− 0.39	1.71	960.82	8.40
44	− 1.86	H	2.17	0.72	− 2.39	959.46	− 1.36
45	− 5.51	− 2.23	− 0.50	2.06	3.01	956.29	− 3.17
46	− 0.39	0.61	0.06	− 6.07	2.22	952.72	− 3.57
47	− 6.34	2.56	n/c	H	− 0.78	948.16	− 4.56
48	− 1.23	− 0.22	0.89	− 3.01	1.51	946.10	− 2.06
49	− 6.57	11.80	− 4.73	2.95	3.17	952.72	6.62
50	− 1.17	2.51	4.68	0.39	− 1.28	957.85	5.13
51	− 5.63	7.24	6.40	0.50	H	966.36	8.51
52	− 6.57	− 1.83	2.34	3.39	5.57	969.26	2.90
TOTALS	−70.23	36..65	57.03	2.75	68.93		95.13

1966 DAILY DOW POINT CHANGES
(Dow Jones Industrial Average)

WEEK #	MONDAY	TUESDAY	WEDNESDAY	THURSDAY	FRIDAY	WEEKLY DOW CLOSE	NET POINT CHANGE
						1965 Close: 969.26	
1	− 0.72	0.72	12.36	3.84	0.67	986.13	16.87
2	− 0.72	1.44	− 2.89	1.73	1.61	987.30	1.17
3	2.45	4.45	− 3.06	− 3.34	0.34	988.14	0.84
4	3.28	0.22	− 0.72	− 0.56	− 5.01	985.35	− 2.79
5	− 1.84	− 7.62	6.40	− 1.06	5.12	986.35	1.00
6	3.34	1.34	4.12	− 4.34	− 1.78	989.03	2.68
7	− 1.34	− 6.12	0.83	− 7.13	− 0.05	975.22	−13.81
8	− 8.74	H	− 6.35	− 9.47	2.34	953.00	−22.22
9	− 1.11	−13.70	− 6.18	4.34	− 4.01	932.34	−20.66
10	−14.58	2.22	9.86	− 0.61	− 1.28	927.95	− 4.39
11	−10.86	− 6.01	4.95	3.29	3.56	922.88	− 5.07
12	6.29	5.35	− 5.52	− 0.39	1.34	929.95	7.07
13	2.67	− 3.23	− 9.63	5.01	6.52	931.29	1.34
14	6.57	6.85	0.55	0.50	H	945.76	14.47
15	− 3.34	− 5.18	1.12	7.12	2.29	947.77	2.01
16	− 5.79	− 0.34	9.64	3.45	− 4.90	949.83	2.06
17	0.72	− 3.34	− 2.67	− 7.13	− 3.73	933.68	−16.15
18	− 1.73	−10.18	− 6.91	−15.09	3.06	902.83	−30.85
19	−16.03	8.68	− 0.05	− 9.86	− 9.46	876.11	−26.72
20	− 8.58	− 3.39	14.36	− 5.51	3.90	876.89	0.78
21	5.57	5.95	2.01	1.33	5.29	897.04	20.15
22	H	−12.97	− 0.44	− 0.90	5.13	887.86	− 9.18
23	− 6.18	− 4.35	2.01	3.28	9.13	891.75	3.89
24	5.85	5.57	− 2.06	− 3.95	− 2.90	894.26	2.51
25	− 1.50	2.22	6.02	− 4.57	0.73	897.16	2.90
26	− 8.19	− 8.07	− 9.30	− 1.50	6.96	877.06	−20.10
27	H	− 1.79	13.59	2.78	2.40	894.04	16.98
28	− 0.95	− 6.90	− 4.79	6.40	1.56	889.36	− 4.68
29	− 0.95	− 4.34	− 9.58	− 0.50	− 4.84	869.15	−20.21
30	−16.32	− 0.66	4.06	− 2.17	− 6.68	847.38	−21.77
31	−12.20	− 2.61	9.13	9.80	0.89	852.39	5.01
32	− 3.34	− 4.23	6.29	− 0.62	2.62	840.53	−11.86
33	− 5.68	−11.02	− 4.24	− 8.85	− 6.12	804.62	−35.91
34	−12.59	− 1.89	9.41	− 7.18	−11.81	780.56	−24.06
35	−13.53	8.69	12.69	3.68	− 4.40	787.69	7.13
36	H	− 5.35	− 4.95	− 2.51	0.67	775.55	−12.14
37	15.04	4.89	10.75	8.07	n/c	814.30	38.75
38	− 3.45	− 4.84	−12.42	4.18	− 6.80	790.97	−23.33
39	1.73	1.39	−13.14	− 8.29	1.56	774.22	−16.75
40	−16.26	5.23	− 7.74	− 5.84	− 5.29	744.32	−29.90
41	10.19	4.12	19.54	− 5.24	− 1.22	771.71	27.39
42	7.18	12.98	− 6.52	− 1.67	3.62	787.30	15.59
43	0.45	5.34	8.02	8.46	− 1.61	807.96	20.66
44	− 0.89	2.56	− 2.34	− 2.95	0.72	805.06	− 2.90
45	− 2.84	H	7.69	6.96	2.22	819.09	14.03
46	− 5.34	1.56	5.56	− 4.84	− 6.63	809.40	− 9.69
47	−11.24	− 3.18	1.84	H	6.52	803.34	− 6.06
48	− 2.18	− 5.90	− 3.67	− 1.84	− 0.28	789.47	−13.87
49	2.12	5.84	10.58	4.79	0.22	813.02	23.55
50	7.52	3.84	1.28	− 8.80	− 2.00	807.18	− 5.84
51	− 8.19	− 4.40	2.84	4.24	− 2.57	799.10	− 8.08
52	H	− 6.90	− 3.62	− 2.23	− 0.66	785.69	−13.41
TOTALS	−126.23	−54.74	56.13	−45.69	−13.04		−183.57

1967 DAILY DOW POINT CHANGES
(Dow Jones Industrial Average)

WEEK #	MONDAY	TUESDAY	WEDNESDAY	THURSDAY	FRIDAY	WEEKLY DOW CLOSE	NET POINT CHANGE
					1966 Close: 785.69		
1	H	0.72	4.73	14.37	3.23	808.74	23.05
2	4.73	0.67	8.35	7.46	5.18	835.13	26.39
3	— 1.89	10.41	3.84	— 1.05	0.72	847.16	12.03
4	0.56	n/c	— 7.13	— 1.89	5.34	844.04	— 3.12
5	4.07	1.78	— 1.50	4.73	4.34	857.46	13.42
6	— 2.34	— 2.61	8.46	— 3.45	— 1.79	855.73	— 1.73
7	— 2.39	3.56	— 1.11	— 4.23	— 0.72	850.84	— 4.89
8	— 2.96	— 3.78	H	2.67	0.56	847.33	— 3.51
9	—10.69	2.73	4.12	3.22	— 0.11	846.60	— 0.73
10	— 4.40	— 0.44	1.56	0.83	4.35	848.50	1.90
11	— 3.68	— 0.55	9.79	14.43	1.28	869.77	21.27
12	0.66	— 3.84	3.96	6.12	H	876.67	6.90
13	— 2.95	1.56	— 4.18	— 1.11	— 4.01	865.98	—10.69
14	— 6.01	— 0.78	2.00	0.06	— 7.91	853.34	—12.64
15	—10.91	5.23	— 3.01	4.18	10.91	859.74	6.40
16	6.85	6.41	0.94	4.68	4.56	883.18	23.44
17	4.35	3.67	— 2.17	5.79	2.23	897.05	13.87
18	— 4.12	— 1.28	5.12	5.18	4.01	905.96	8.91
19	3.67	— 9.74	— 5.79	2.11	— 6.18	890.03	—15.93
20	— 7.62	3.39	— 3.56	— 4.90	— 2.79	874.55	—15.48
21	— 3.50	— 2.34	— 6.29	8.29	— 0.39	870.32	— 4.23
22	— 5.34	H	—12.42	12.42	— 1.67	863.31	— 7.01
23	—15.54	14.94	6.48	4.01	1.69	874.89	11.89
24	4.04	7.22	— 5.54	2.65	1.74	885.00	10.11
25	— 0.46	— 3.93	— 2.95	— 1.97	1.68	877.37	— 7.63
26	— 5.26	— 2.72	— 0.52	— 6.93	— 1.68	860.26	—17.11
27	— 0.57	H	5.25	— 0.92	5.03	869.05	8.79
28	6.47	3.93	— 0.75	— 0.17	3.52	882.05	13.00
29	0.69	13.35	7.23	5.37	0.87	909.56	27.51
30	— 5.03	— 3.24	1.85	n/c	— 1.61	901.53	— 8.03
31	2.71	8.73	9.30	— 0.29	1.79	923.77	22.24
32	— 3.40	2.08	4.27	— 1.50	— 4.57	920.65	— 3.12
33	— 4.33	2.83	— 3.47	2.55	0.81	919.04	— 1.61
34	— 6.77	— 4.79	— 2.37	— 6.65	— 4.39	894.07	—24.97
35	0.64	0.05	— 1.04	7.57	— 0.11	901.18	7.11
36	H	2.95	2.83	1.21	— 0.63	907.54	6.36
37	2.08	2.13	12.02	5.67	4.04	933.48	25.94
38	5.26	— 8.67	— 0.28	0.69	3.87	934.35	0.87
39	8.73	— 5.90	— 4.04	— 3.76	— 2.72	926.66	— 7.69
40	— 5.66	3.47	— 3.18	5.84	1.61	928.74	2.08
41	4.57	— 6.70	— 6.36	— 7.05	4.97	918.28	—10.46
42	— 9.65	— 4.16	— 0.87	0.23	— 6.99	896.73	—21.44
43	— 2.08	— 6.47	— 1.45	4.16	— 2.71	888.18	— 8.55
44	— 1.56	— 6.88	—12.66	— 2.25	— 8.21	856.62	—31.56
45	— 1.33	H	— 5.72	7.40	5.84	862.81	6.19
46	— 3.07	— 7.34	2.78	4.56	2.37	862.11	— 0.70
47	— 4.33	13.17	3.07	H	3.58	877.60	15.49
48	4.51	2.77	— 1.73	— 7.34	3.35	879.16	1.56
49	4.34	4.62	4.16	— 0.06	— 4.97	887.25	8.09
50	— 5.20	— 0.75	1.04	1.10	— 2.83	880.61	— 6.64
51	1.04	— 0.29	5.54	1.45	— 0.98	887.37	6.76
52	H	0.75	6.82	2.89	7.28	905.11	17.74
TOTALS	—73.07	35.93	25.41	98.37	32.78		119.42

1968 DAILY DOW POINT CHANGES
(Dow Jones Industrial Average)

WEEK #	MONDAY	TUESDAY	WEDNESDAY	THURSDAY	FRIDAY	WEEKLY DOW CLOSE	NET POINT CHANGE
					1967 Close: 905.11		
1	H	1.73	— 2.71	— 4.74	1.85	901.24	— 3.87
2	7.68	— 0.63	— 4.34	— 4.16	— 0.81	898.98	— 2.26
3	— 6.24	— 5.60	— 3.36	— 0.98	— 2.48	880.32	—18.66
4	— 8.61	— 6.94	— 2.54	2.02	0.81	865.06	—15.26
5	— 1.39	— 4.10	— 4.10	5.89	2.20	863.56	— 1.50
6	— 2.43	0.12	— 1.33	— 9.60	—10.28	840.04	—23.52
7	H	— 8.27	5.61	1.85	— 2.89	836.34	— 3.70
8	2.31	4.45	6.13	H	0.57	849.80	13.46
9	— 8.03	4.91	— 1.96	— 4.22	— 0.06	840.44	— 9.36
10	— 9.88	— 3.53	10.18	— 0.99	— 0.98	835.24	— 5.20
11	7.80	0.18	— 0.99	—11.32	6.64	837.55	2.31
12	2.54	— 7.10	— 2.14	— 5.72	0.92	826.05	—11.50
13	1.22	4.27	5.03	— 1.45	5.55	840.67	14.62
14	20.58	2.71	5.15	3.41	— 6.71	865.81	25.14
15	18.61	H	8.21	13.06	H	905.69	39.88
16	4.50	— 3.41	1.39	1.04	—11.56	897.65	— 8.04
17	— 5.66	5.49	0.98	7.11	0.46	906.03	8.38
18	2.31	3.88	0.98	4.85	1.16	919.21	13.18
19	— 4.68	5.37	— 1.04	— 7.51	1.56	912.91	— 6.30
20	— 2.95	— 1.90	— 0.24	— 4.10	— 4.74	898.98	—13.93
21	— 4.79	2.13	0.47	— 3.64	2.13	895.28	— 3.70
22	— 3.68	5.18	— 1.57	H	3.79	899.00	3.72
23	6.38	11.25	— 9.21	2.71	4.75	914.88	15.88
24	— 1.50	4.57	H**	— 4.09	— 0.24	913.62	— 1.26
25	—10.17	— 3.25	H	— 1.92	2.65	900.93	—12.69
26	0.90	— 0.42	H	— 2.65	— 0.96	897.80	— 3.13
27	— 1.45	0.49	6.67	H	H	903.51	5.71
28	9.09	7.82	H	2.40	— 0.36	922.46	18.95
29	1.26	— 2.52	H	— 3.25	— 4.03	913.92	— 8.54
30	—13.60	— 2.22	H	—12.63	3.00	888.47	—25.45
31	— 5.11	— 0.36	H	— 4.93	— 6.80	871.27	—17.20
32	1.26	4.39	H	— 6.55	— 0.72	869.65	— 1.62
33	11.37	3.66	H	— 5.17	6.38	885.89	16.24
34	1.79	0.99	H	— 0.37	4.04	892.34	6.45
35	3.79	— 2.48	H	0.68	1.68	896.01	3.67
36	H	4.35	6.59	10.57	3.73	921.25	25.24
37	3.73	— 5.60	H	— 3.73	1.56	917.21	— 4.04
38	4.16	1.68	H	0.93	0.44	924.42	7.21
39	6.03	7.83	H	— 5.04	0.56	933.80	9.38
40	1.99	6.53	H	7.15	3.48	952.95	19.15
41	3.73	— 0.44	H	— 6.46	— 0.19	949.59	— 3.36
42	0.37	5.35	H	3.60	8.58	967.49	17.90
43	n/c	— 4.35	H	— 6.46	4.60	961.28	— 6.21
44	— 3.55	— 6.65	H	1.31	— 3.98	948.41	—12.87
45	— 2.18	H	3.24	1.18	8.33	958.98	10.57
46	H	5.22	3.23	— 3.54	1.99	965.88	6.90
47	— 2.18	3.05	H	— 1.62	1.93	967.06	1.18
48	4.29	8.14	— 3.17	H	8.76	985.08	18.02
49	— 1.74	1.87	H	— 7.52	0.55	978.24	— 6.84
50	1.12	— 1.67	H	— 0.56	4.16	981.29	3.05
51	— 4.97	— 5.41	H	4.23	— 8.15	966.99	—14.30
52	—13.24	— 1.43	H	1.93	— 1.74	952.51	—14.48
53	— 7.40	— 1.36			(Year's Close)	943.75	— 8.76*
TOTALS	3.38	37.97	25.16	—59.00	31.13		38.64

*Partial Week
**Volume deluge forces Wednesday closings

1969 DAILY DOW POINT CHANGES
(Dow Jones Industrial Average)

WEEK #	MONDAY	TUESDAY	WEDNESDAY	THURSDAY	FRIDAY	WEEKLY DOW CLOSE	NET POINT CHANGE
					1968 Close: 943.75		
1			H	3.98	4.16	951.89	8.14*
2	−15.23	−10.94	− 4.47	6.21	− 1.93	925.53	−26.36
3	− 2.42	5.22	3.42	6.84	− 3.05	935.54	10.01
4	− 4.29	− 1.43	4.35	6.03	− 1.61	938.59	3.05
5	− 1.12	0.93	− 0.31	4.04	3.92	946.05	7.46
6	0.80	− 1.74	0.87	0.69	1.18	947.85	1.80
7	H	1.12	0.12	3.61	− 0.75	951.95	4.10
8	−14.23	− 6.90	− 5.72	− 8.45	H	916.65	−35.30
9	−12.68	− 4.17	5.97	− 2.74	2.18	905.21	−11.44
10	3.42	10.88	3.60	− 9.57	− 2.36	911.18	5.97
11	5.96	3.79	− 3.41	−10.38	− 2.86	904.28	− 6.90
12	− 0.25	3.35	4.73	8.02	− 0.13	920.00	15.72
13	− 2.92	n/c	6.22	7.58	4.60	935.48	15.48
14	H**	− 2.40	− 2.16	− 3.62	H	927.30	− 8.18
15	− 8.52	4.39	6.80	2.92	0.57	933.46	6.16
16	− 0.82	− 0.70	− 8.45	0.63	0.70	924.82	− 8.64
17	− 7.31	1.08	− 0.95	3.56	2.80	924.00	− 0.82
18	1.08	9.02	16.08	− 0.96	7.95	957.17	33.17
19	1.78	3.11	− 2.46	4.08	− 2.07	961.61	4.44
20	− 3.75	5.11	5.88	− 3.69	2.14	967.30	5.69
21	− 8.28	− 9.76	2.52	− 1.74	− 2.59	947.45	−19.85
22	− 0.51	− 8.28	− 1.74	0.64	H	937.56	− 9.89
23	− 4.39	− 2.39	− 1.94	1.87	− 5.94	924.77	−12.79
24	− 6.72	− 5.56	− 7.89	−12.02	2.26	894.84	−29.93
25	− 3.68	− 5.43	1.36	− 4.72	− 6.21	876.16	−18.68
26	− 5.30	6.34	− 3.10	− 3.82	− 0.52	869.76	− 6.40
27	3.43	2.71	4.79	5.43	H	886.12	16.36
28	− 2.91	−12.86	− 8.73	−13.83	4.46	852.25	−33.87
29	− 9.11	− 2.01	8.21	3.75	− 7.17	845.92	− 6.33
30	H	−11.90	− 6.07	− 1.42	− 8.47	818.06	−27.86
31	−11.83	− 4.27	1.62	11.89	11.12	826.59	8.53
32	− 4.01	− 1.35	4.65	0.39	− 1.81	824.46	− 2.13
33	− 4.63	− 6.87	− 3.83	4.10	7.65	820.88	− 3.58
34	6.80	6.01	− 0.47	1.65	2.38	837.25	16.37
35	− 5.81	− 7.92	1.26	3.63	8.31	836.72	− 0.53
36	H***	1.06	− 2.11	−10.37	− 5.80	819.50	−17.22
37	− 7.66	3.83	12.34	− 2.24	− 1.52	824.25	4.75
38	6.20	1.19	− 5.08	5.01	− 1.18	830.39	6.14
39	1.38	3.04	− 0.13	− 4.76	− 5.74	824.18	− 6.21
40	− 6.14	− 4.95	− 6.20	4.95	− 3.43	808.41	−15.77
41	0.99	− 3.17	− 4.03	1.59	3.17	806.96	− 1.45
42	12.34	13.13	− 2.37	8.71	− 2.71	836.06	29.10
43	3.17	7.65	13.47	− 4.62	6.53	862.26	26.20
44	− 1.98	− 4.42	− 7.52	2.17	5.48	855.99	− 6.27
45	− 1.45	− 1.06	0.60	1.12	5.28	860.48	4.49
46	2.57	− 3.30	− 3.76	− 6.14	− 0.59	849.26	−11.22
47	− 6.73	2.64	− 5.21	− 8.78	− 8.05	823.13	−26.13
48	−10.23	− 5.61	3.23	H	1.78	812.30	−10.83
49	− 7.26	− 3.69	− 7.99	3.17	− 3.50	793.03	−19.27
50	− 7.99	− 1.25	0.20	− 0.46	3.16	786.69	− 6.34
51	− 2.64	−10.22	− 3.90	13.86	6.07	789.86	3.17
52	− 3.89	− 2.18	10.36	H	3.50	797.65	7.79
53	− 5.28	2.31	5.68		(Year's Close) 800.36		2.71*
TOTALS	**−152.05**	**−48.82**	**18.33**	**17.79**	**21.36**		**−143.39**

*Partial Week
**Former President Eisenhower Funeral
***First Americans on The Moon

1970 DAILY DOW POINT CHANGES
(Dow Jones Industrial Average)

WEEK #	MONDAY	TUESDAY	WEDNESDAY	THURSDAY	FRIDAY	WEEKLY DOW CLOSE	NET POINT CHANGE
					1969 Close: 800.36		
1				H	8.84	809.20	8.84*
2	2.11	− 7.65	− 1.85	0.26	− 3.96	798.22	−11.09
3	− 7.59	− 2.51	− 0.85	− 2.12	− 2.44	782.60	−15.51
4	− 6.53	1.78	4.42	3.83	−10.56	775.54	− 7.06
5	− 6.66	− 4.89	− 5.15	−10.49	− 4.29	744.06	−31.48
6	2.38	11.02	− 2.97	− 4.23	2.51	752.77	8.71
7	2.91	− 9.05	10.07	− 1.72	− 2.31	753.30	0.53
8	0.40	− 6.27	9.37	1.12	− 0.46	757.46	4.16
9	H	− 3.04	13.86	− 3.83	13.14	777.59	20.13
10	2.64	7.19	0.73	− 0.60	− 3.43	784.12	6.53
11	− 5.81	1.39	− 1.58	− 1.65	− 4.36	772.11	−12.01
12	− 7.06	2.37	0.53	− 2.97	− 1.32	763.66	− 8.45
13	− 0.06	10.16	16.37	0.92	H	791.05	27.39
14	− 6.40	0.92	6.47	0.33	− 0.53	791.84	0.79
15	− 0.66	0.46	0.00	0.86	− 2.04	790.46	− 1.38
16	− 4.56	− 5.34	2.04	− 6.73	0.07	775.94	−14.52
17	− 0.07	− 3.36	− 9.90	−12.02	− 3.30	747.29	−28.65
18	−12.14	−10.82	13.06	− 1.32	− 2.44	733.63	−13.66
19	−19.07	− 4.82	8.65	4.68	− 5.34	717.73	−15.90
20	− 7.66	− 5.48	−10.75	− 9.05	17.43	702.22	−15.51
21	0.59	−11.41	−14.85	−11.30	− 3.08	662.17	−40.05
22	−20.81	−10.20	32.04	20.95	16.29	700.44	38.27
23	9.92	− 0.75	4.25	− 7.33	−11.50	695.03	− 5.41
24	5.20	− 0.07	− 5.81	− 9.93	− 0.21	684.21	−10.82
25	3.15	18.90	− 1.58	8.01	7.74	720.43	36.22
26	− 4.32	−18.00	− 5.82	1.30	− 5.75	687.84	−32.59
27	− 4.93	0.62	4.11	1.50	H	689.14	1.30
28	−13.48	− 6.30	12.73	10.68	7.33	700.10	10.96
29	2.12	0.82	8.62	11.78	11.64	735.08	34.98
30	− 1.17	−11.84	2.60	8.01	− 2.46	730.22	− 4.86
31	− 0.14	1.37	4.11	− 0.83	− 0.61	734.12	3.90
32	−11.16	2.94	− 1.09	− 1.99	2.88	725.70	− 8.42
33	−11.78	− 1.37	− 1.91	− 3.29	3.49	710.84	−14.86
34	− 1.78	7.60	7.33	5.61	15.81	745.41	34.57
35	14.17	− 0.61	1.50	− 0.68	6.02	765.81	20.40
36	− 1.23	− 6.43	− 1.51	8.63	5.88	771.15	5.34
37	H	1.99	− 6.71	− 5.68	1.09	761.84	− 9.31
38	− 4.72	− 6.57	3.76	3.36	0.82	758.49	− 3.35
39	− 6.57	− 4.45	6.91	4.93	2.46	761.77	3.28
40	− 2.80	1.91	− 0.20	n/c	5.48	766.16	4.39
41	10.54	5.75	1.23	− 6.64	− 8.35	768.69	2.53
42	− 4.45	− 4.18	2.67	5.14	− 4.52	763.35	− 5.34
43	− 6.85	2.33	0.82	− 1.78	1.51	759.38	− 3.97
44	− 2.95	− 1.98	1.51	− 2.40	2.05	755.61	− 3.77
45	2.40	10.06	2.74	0.75	0.41	771.97	16.36
46	5.69	− 0.28	2.12	−11.50	− 8.21	759.79	−12.18
47	0.34	0.34	− 6.23	1.58	5.75	761.57	1.78
48	5.95	5.21	1.98	H	6.64	781.35	19.78
49	12.74	0.20	8.35	5.89	7.53	816.06	34.71
50	2.60	− 3.56	0.14	5.82	4.86	825.92	9.86
51	− 2.74	− 3.56	− 0.55	3.08	0.62	822.77	− 3.15
52	− 1.23	1.23	0.34	5.27	H	828.38	5.61
53	2.53	11.09	− 0.68	− 2.40	(Year's Close) 838.92		10.54*
TOTALS	**−99.00**	**−47.14**	**116.07**	**1.81**	**66.82**		**38.56**

*Partial Week

1971 DAILY DOW POINT CHANGES
(Dow Jones Industrial Average)

WEEK #	MONDAY	TUESDAY	WEDNESDAY	THURSDAY	FRIDAY	WEEKLY DOW CLOSE	NET POINT CHANGE
					1970 Close: 838.92		
1	— 8.35	5.20	2.20	— 0.14	— 0.82	837.01	— 1.91
2	0.20	6.98	— 3.08	2.20	2.39	845.70	8.69
3	2.12	1.65	0.48	4.79	6.57	861.31	15.61
4	4.31	1.17	— 5.96	4.31	3.36	868.50	7.19
5	9.31	— 3.22	1.64	— 1.44	1.78	876.57	8.07
6	5.55	— 2.33	1.30	4.25	3.49	888.83	12.26
7	H	1.23	— 2.19	— 2.81	— 6.50	878.56	—10.27
8	— 9.58	1.02	5.62	6.36	— 3.15	878.83	0.27
9	3.70	0.48	— 0.62	8.97	6.64	898.00	19.17
10	0.62	0.48	— 3.22	3.56	— 1.10	989.34	0.34
11	9.86	6.44	— 0.62	2.81	— 3.91	912.92	14.58
12	— 2.32	— 1.71	— 9.52	1.44	2.67	903.48	— 9.44
13	n/c	— 0.09	0.98	— 0.49	— 0.84	903.04	— 0.44
14	2.03	7.66	5.76	1.90	H	920.39	17.35
15	6.25	0.64	5.27	5.62	2.04	940.21	19.82
16	8.64	— 4.43	— 3.09	— 0.70	7.16	947.79	7.58
17	— 3.79	3.09	3.73	— 2.67	— 6.40	941.75	— 6.04
18	— 9.34	6.04	1.47	— 2.53	— 0.42	936.97	— 4.78
19	— 4.42	4.70	0.21	— 1.12	— 0.28	936.06	— 0.91
20	—14.76	— 2.74	1.48	3.37	— 1.54	921.87	—14.19
21	— 8.72	— 6.46	— 0.28	— 0.63	2.03	907.81	—14.06
22	H	5.84	5.97	1.68	0.85	922.15	14.34
23	0.91	— 8.05	— 2.55	3.50	0.51	916.47	— 5.68
24	— 8.76	— 0.51	1.39	— 2.34	—17.09	889.16	—27.31
25	—12.63	— 2.11	5.03	— 2.19	— 0.58	876.68	—12.48
26	— 3.58	9.20	8.84	1.89	— 2.84	890.19	13.51
27	H	2.11	3.58	5.11	0.81	901.80	11.61
28	1.60	—11.02	— 1.17	— 2.34	— 0.36	888.51	—13.29
29	— 2.12	5.91	— 1.46	— 4.16	1.10	887.78	— 0.73
30	1.09	— 8.17	— 8.69	—10.59	— 2.99	858.43	—29.35
31	6.49	—14.89	— 5.11	4.53	1.16	850.61	— 7.82
32	— 7.96	— 3.06	6.79	12.63	— 2.99	856.02	5.41
33	32.93	10.95	—13.73	— 5.40	0.14	880.91	24.89
34	11.47	11.75	4.24	— 2.27	2.05	908.15	27.24
35	— 6.72	— 3.36	0.95	1.61	12.12	912.75	4.60
36	H	3.72	4.46	— 5.04	— 4.89	911.00	— 1.75
37	— 1.61	— 7.74	3.21	— 1.75	5.11	908.22	— 2.78
38	— 3.07	— 1.75	— 9.85	— 2.27	— 1.97	889.31	—18.91
39	— 5.84	0.95	— 0.59	3.36	6.79	893.98	4.67
40	1.68	— 4.52	9.41	1.25	— 7.89	893.91	— 0.07
41	— 1.97	1.61	— 4.75	—10.44	— 3.51	874.85	—19.06
42	— 2.41	— 4.01	—12.78	— 0.80	— 2.48	852.37	—22.48
43	— 3.87	— 3.14	— 8.98	1.24	1.38	839.00	—13.37
44	—13.14	2.12	14.60	0.59	— 2.78	840.39	1.39
45	— 2.85	0.37	—11.76	—11.24	— 1.97	812.94	—27.45
46	— 2.41	8.18	3.43	— 6.79	— 4.68	810.67	— 2.27
47	— 7.52	— 5.18	0.66	H	17.96	816.59	5.92
48	13.14	1.61	14.67	2.78	10.80	859.59	43.00
49	— 3.87	1.68	— 2.55	— 2.70	4.60	856.75	— 2.84
50	2.04	— 3.65	8.62	7.63	2.41	873.80	17.05
51	11.21	3.31	— 3.46	— 3.69	H	881.17	7.37
52	0.30	8.51	3.68	— 4.59	1.13	890.20	9.03
TOTALS	**—16.16**	**22.46**	**13.66**	**6.25**	**25.07**		**51.28**

1972 DAILY DOW POINT CHANGES
(Dow Jones Industrial Average)

WEEK #	MONDAY	TUESDAY	WEDNESDAY	THURSDAY	FRIDAY	WEEKLY DOW CLOSE	NET POINT CHANGE
					1971 Close: 890.20		
1	— 0.90	2.93	12.20	4.06	1.88	910.37	20.17
2	— 2.41	4.14	— 1.28	— 5.64	1.50	906.68	— 3.69
3	4.44	6.10	— 2.26	— 4.66	— 2.86	907.44	0.76
4	—10.62	— 2.10	— 5.57	10.68	6.55	906.38	— 1.06
5	— 4.21	— 0.38	4.06	— 2.70	3.53	906.68	0.30
6	— 2.71	3.16	11.59	2.56	— 3.69	917.59	10.91
7	— 6.69	3.61	8.43	— 0.91	— 4.51	917.52	— 0.07
8	H	— 4.06	— 1.58	0.82	10.09	922.79	5.27
9	1.50	3.84	7.30	— 1.66	8.66	942.43	19.64
10	7.75	— 3.31	— 1.28	— 2.78	— 2.94	939.87	— 2.56
11	—11.21	5.34	3.31	— 0.60	6.17	942.88	3.01
12	— 1.73	— 7.15	— 0.07	10.76	— 2.41	942.28	— 0.60
13	— 2.56	— 2.71	— 3.99	7.68	H	940.70	— 1.58
14	0.22	2.49	11.14	4.89	3.16	962.60	21.90
15	— 4.52	4.52	4.36	— 1.43	2.19	967.72	5.12
16	— 1.13	2.33	— 4.14	1.51	— 2.49	963.80	— 3.92
17	— 6.32	—10.99	0.45	— 0.97	8.20	954.17	— 9.63
18	—11.89	— 7.08	— 1.73	3.84	3.92	941.23	—12.94
19	— 3.39	—12.72	5.95	3.76	7.00	941.83	0.60
20	0.37	— 2.93	1.88	10.08	10.31	961.54	19.71
21	3.77	— 3.01	3.16	3.61	2.18	971.25	9.71
22	H	— 0.07	—10.46	n/c	0.67	961.39	— 9.86
23	— 7.00	— 2.93	— 7.38	— 2.78	— 6.85	934.45	—26.94
24	2.26	1.58	8.50	— 0.82	— 0.91	945.06	10.61
25	— 3.23	6.39	3.39	— 0.90	— 6.02	944.69	— 0.37
26	— 8.28	— 1.13	— 4.44	— 4.59	2.78	939.03	—15.66
27	— 0.37	H	4.81	8.66	— 4.07	938.06	9.03
28	— 5.79	— 6.40	— 2.18	— 6.70	5.27	922.26	—15.80
29	— 7.30	— 3.24	4.97	— 6.24	10.00	920.45	— 1.81
30	14.91	— 0.91	— 1.88	— 5.72	— 0.15	926.70	6.25
31	— 1.96	5.72	10.69	6.55	4.06	951.76	25.06
32	1.36	— 0.68	— 1.28	1.73	11.29	964.18	12.42
33	9.33	— 3.54	— 5.72	— 2.86	4.44	965.83	1.65
34	1.36	6.32	— 3.16	—11.97	0.98	959.36	— 6.47
35	— 2.41	— 2.25	3.16	5.87	6.32	970.05	10.69
36	H	— 0.68	— 5.94	— 0.98	— 1.21	961.24	— 8.81
37	— 6.24	— 8.96	3.84	— 2.33	— 0.23	947.32	—13.92
38	— 1.96	— 2.18	— 2.93	— 0.76	3.54	943.03	— 4.29
39	— 7.30	0.83	10.69	7.90	— 1.88	953.27	10.24
40	n/c	1.20	— 3.16	—10.01	4.06	945.36	— 7.91
41	3.39	3.09	— 5.42	— 8.96	— 7.00	930.46	—14.90
42	— 8.80	4.82	5.86	— 0.22	10.69	942.81	12.35
43	8.50	1.20	— 1.13	— 0.82	— 4.14	946.42	3.61
44	n/c	9.10	13.02	4.52	11.06	984.12	37.70
45	0.68	H	— 1.06	4.52	7.00	995.26	11.14
46	1.81	6.09	— 4.74	5.27	1.88	1005.57	10.31
47	— 0.53	8.21	7.29	H	4.67	1025.21	19.64
48	— 7.45	1.58	— 0.53	— 0.60	5.72	1023.93	— 1.28
49	3.09	— 4.07	4.59	5.72	— 0.07	1033.19	9.26
50	3.08	— 3.08	— 2.71	— 5.42	2.18	1027.24	— 5.95
51	—13.99	— 4.07	— 4.36	— 4.82	4.21	1004.21	—23.03
52	H	2.49	0.98	H	12.34	1020.02	15.81
TOTALS	—85.08	— 3.55	65.24	16.14	137.07		129.82

*Former Present Truman Funeral

1973 DAILY DOW POINT CHANGES
(Dow Jones Industrial Average)

WEEK #	MONDAY	TUESDAY	WEDNESDAY	THURSDAY	FRIDAY	WEEKLY DOW CLOSE	NET POINT CHANGE
					1972 Close:	1020.02	
1	H	11.66	12.12	− 3.99	7.68	1047.49	27.47
2	0.37	− 0.75	− 1.05	5.64	−12.34	1039.36	− 8.13
3	−13.77	− 1.28	4.81	n/c	− 2.93	1026.19	−13.17
4	− 7.38	− 0.15	−14.07	H	− 1.05	1003.54	−22.65
5	− 7.08	− 3.53	6.09	−13.24	− 4.97	980.81	−22.73
6	− 2.41	1.51	−11.59	− 1.13	12.27	979.46	− 1.35
7	12.11	5.19	−16.85	− 6.78	6.10	979.23	− 0.23
8	H	4.36	− 9.25	− 2.56	−11.89	959.89	−19.34
9	− 6.10	− 5.87	7.15	− 5.42	11.67	961.32	1.43
10	5.57	12.11	0.98	− 3.54	− 4.21	972.23	10.91
11	− 2.48	6.32	2.78	− 9.03	− 6.77	963.05	− 9.18
12	−10.99	− 2.63	−11.06	−13.17	− 2.49	922.71	−40.34
13	5.19	17.01	3.09	11.14	− 8.13	951.01	28.30
14	−14.83	− 8.43	− 2.70	− 1.59	7.61	931.07	−19.94
15	16.48	12.94	6.92	− 3.38	− 4.67	959.36	28.29
16	− 2.63	− 3.31	4.89	4.89	H	963.20	3.84
17	− 7.83	−14.60	−10.23	7.22	−15.57	922.19	−41.01
18	− 0.76	− 0.22	11.13	13.33	8.20	953.87	31.68
19	− 3.16	5.87	− 7.53	− 9.71	−11.36	927.98	−25.89
20	−18.29	7.75	− 0.30	− 5.42	−16.55	895.17	−32.81
21	− 8.66	5.95	2.56	29.42	6.40	930.84	35.67
22	H	− 5.27	−16.70	− 7.46	− 7.45	893.96	−36.88
23	− 8.05	14.90	− 2.63	11.44	10.38	920.00	26.04
24	− 4.89	11.89	−11.51	−12.57	−14.37	888.55	−31.45
25	−13.47	6.47	3.16	−11.06	6.17	879.82	− 8.73
26	−10.69	10.31	5.19	10.01	− 2.93	891.71	11.89
27	−11.14	− 6.40	H	0.15	− 4.21	870.11	−21.60
28	7.15	11.06	19.87	− 6.25	−15.95	885.99	15.88
29	11.59	0.45	7.37	1.28	4.22	910.90	24.91
30	2.25	5.57	14.30	1.51	2.18	936.71	25.81
31	− 2.94	− 7.37	−14.22	− 2.04	− 1.27	908.87	−27.84
32	3.91	− 0.83	− 9.93	− 0.53	9.11	892.38	−16.49
33	− 9.18	−12.49	3.46	− 1.43	− 0.90	871.84	−20.54
34	− 4.44	− 9.56	− 5.94	12.56	− 0.97	863.49	− 8.35
35	7.22	1.36	11.36	− 0.90	5.04	887.57	24.08
36	H	7.82	3.69	1.96	− 2.41	898.63	11.06
37	− 7.30	− 5.57	− 4.44	− 0.75	5.79	886.36	−12.27
38	6.63	− 1.73	19.11	10.16	7.37	927.90	41.54
39	8.81	3.84	8.95	3.77	− 6.17	947.10	19.20
40	1.73	7.97	7.75	− 8.65	15.35	971.25	24.15
41	6.40	− 3.46	−13.62	15.50	2.56	978.63	7.38
42	−11.59	0.37	− 4.89	− 2.78	3.99	963.73	−14.90
43	− 3.16	5.94	5.34	2.64	12.57	987.06	23.33
44	− 2.26	−16.26	−11.96	− 7.75	−13.55	935.28	−51.78
45	−15.88	− 6.32	7.00	12.57	−24.24	908.41	−26.87
46	−10.76	− 6.62	−21.15	4.67	16.78	891.33	−17.08
47	−28.67	−17.76	10.08	H	− 0.98	854.00	−37.33
48	−29.05	− 7.22	22.05	− 4.67	−12.86	822.25	−31.75
49	−15.73	− 3.31	−14.90	25.81	23.93	838.05	15.80
50	13.09	−16.96	−23.45	−10.30	15.22	815.65	−22.40
51	− 4.53	18.37	0.08	− 1.46	− 9.38	818.73	3.08
52	− 3.92	H	22.75	13.45	− 2.99	848.02	29.29
53	2.84				(Year's Close)	850.86	2.84*
TOTALS	−192.68	29.09	− 5.94	41.56	−41.19		−169.16

*Partial Week

1974 DAILY DOW POINT CHANGES
(Dow Jones Industrial Average)

WEEK #	MONDAY	TUESDAY	WEDNESDAY	THURSDAY	FRIDAY	WEEKLY DOW CLOSE	NET POINT CHANGE
					1973 Close: 850.86		
1		H	4.46	25.37	− 0.46	880.23	29.37*
2	− 3.38	−15.07	−26.99	−11.68	18.37	841.48	−38.75
3	− 1.30	6.22	9.69	16.07	−16.69	855.47	13.99
4	− 0.84	8.84	7.53	− 7.92	− 3.69	859.39	3.92
5	− 6.38	− 0.69	10.00	− 6.77	−11.61	843.94	−15.45
6	−22.44	− 0.86	3.98	3.84	− 8.06	820.40	−23.54
7	−16.50	2.73	0.24	3.05	10.40	820.32	− 0.08
8	H	− 0.78	11.50	15.80	9.15	855.99	35.67
9	− 4.61	8.13	3.91	− 2.89	− 8.61	851.92	− 4.07
10	1.26	19.24	7.43	−10.79	8.99	878.05	26.13
11	10.40	− 1.33	4.54	− 1.88	− 1.95	887.83	9.78
12	−13.61	− 6.65	4.77	3.13	2.66	878.13	− 9.70
13	2.89	2.66	−12.51	−16.82	− 7.67	846.68	−31.45
14	− 3.20	3.13	11.42	0.86	−11.35	847.54	0.86
15	− 7.58	6.88	− 3.13	1.10	H	844.81	− 2.73
16	− 1.02	17.44	6.18	2.51	−10.02	859.90	15.09
17	− 1.33	−12.59	−13.61	− 4.69	6.96	834.64	−25.26
18	0.78	1.33	17.13	− 2.82	− 5.16	845.90	11.26
19	− 1.02	2.27	3.84	14.78	−15.33	850.44	4.54
20	− 4.85	2.27	− 1.80	−10.72	−16.50	818.84	−31.60
21	− 6.42	− 2.89	− 6.96	2.66	11.42	816.65	− 2.19
22	H	− 2.35	−18.93	8.21	− 1.41	802.17	−14.48
23	19.09	7.43	1.49	15.17	8.37	853.72	51.55
24	5.95	− 7.59	− 3.52	3.52	− 8.99	843.09	−10.63
25	− 9.86	− 2.97	− 4.15	− 5.32	− 5.40	815.39	−27.70
26	0.94	12.52	−11.89	−13.30	− 1.25	802.41	−12.98
27	3.83	−15.56	2.19	H	− 1.10	791.77	−10.64
28	−21.20	1.72	−10.17	− 2.50	27.61	787.23	− 4.54
29	− 0.62	−10.64	9.00	4.22	− 1.25	787.94	0.71
30	2.42	7.36	8.05	−10.09	−11.11	784.57	− 3.37
31	−13.68	− 5.32	− 8.14	− 6.33	1.48	752.58	−31.99
32	7.82	13.38	23.78	−12.67	− 7.59	777.30	24.72
33	−10.01	−10.88	−15.87	− 2.66	− 6.34	731.54	−45.76
34	− 9.70	5.01	−15.26	− 6.96	−17.83	686.80	−44.74
35	1.33	−16.59	− 4.93	− 9.77	21.74	678.58	− 8.22
36	H	−15.25	−15.33	22.76	7.12	677.88	− 0.70
37	−14.94	− 4.77	− 3.45	−12.98	−14.55	627.19	−50.69
38	12.59	9.00	3.13	22.14	− 3.29	670.76	43.57
39	− 7.04	− 9.62	− 4.15	−11.97	−16.03	621.95	−48.81
40	−14.08	3.05	− 3.29	−13.92	− 3.05	584.56	−37.39
41	23.00	− 4.93	28.39	17.06	10.09	658.17	73.61
42	15.33	−15.10	−16.11	9.15	3.44	654.88	− 3.29
43	14.94	− 6.96	−17.83	− 8.77	− 0.07	636.19	−18.69
44	− 2.35	25.50	13.69	− 7.51	− 0.24	665.28	29.09
45	− 8.05	17.52	− 5.63	2.81	− 4.77	667.16	1.88
46	5.48	−13.46	n/c	− 0.78	−10.79	647.61	−19.55
47	−22.69	−10.87	− 4.46	− 1.02	6.73	615.30	−32.31
48	− 3.36	5.32	2.03	H	− 0.63	618.66	3.36
49	−15.64	− 6.41	2.03	−11.58	− 9.46	577.60	−41.06
50	2.34	13.93	1.48	1.02	− 3.60	592.77	15.17
51	− 5.94	10.71	5.95	0.94	− 5.95	598.48	5.71
52	− 8.84	8.76	H	6.34	− 2.58	602.16	3.68
53	1.09	12.99			(Year's Close) 616.24		14.08*
TOTALS	−131.00	29.11	−20.28	−12.60	−89.85		−234.62

*Partial Week

1975 DAILY DOW POINT CHANGES
(Dow Jones Industrial Average)

WEEK #	MONDAY	TUESDAY	WEDNESDAY	THURSDAY	FRIDAY	WEEKLY DOW CLOSE	NET POINT CHANGE
					1971 Close: 616.24		
1			H	15.80	2.50	634.54	18.30*
2	2.66	3.99	— 5.79	9.86	13.53	658.79	24.25
3	— 4.61	— 5.48	4.69	2.35	—11.11	644.63	—14.16
4	2.82	— 5.55	10.71	4.15	9.85	666.61	21.98
5	26.05	2.11	11.19	— 9.54	7.27	703.69	37.08
6	7.75	— 3.37	9.78	— 3.68	— 2.26	711.91	8.22
7	— 3.52	— 0.79	7.43	11.89	7.28	734.20	22.29
8	H	— 2.90	5.09	8.99	4.39	749.77	15.57
9	—12.83	—17.76	8.92	3.05	7.90	739.05	—10.72
10	14.08	4.61	— 4.92	8.99	8.29	770.10	31.05
11	6.03	— 5.24	— 7.20	— 0.71	10.49	773.47	3.37
12	13.06	— 7.12	— 9.93	— 5.48	— 0.94	763.06	—10.41
13	—19.63	4.46	18.30	4.07	H	770.26	7.20
14	— 2.11	— 6.57	— 1.02	— 8.37	— 4.93	747.26	—23.00
15	— 4.38	6.34	18.77	13.30	8.21	789.50	42.24
16	17.45	8.13	0.63	3.75	—11.03	808.43	18.93
17	7.43	— 1.72	—11.65	1.17	8.14	811.80	3.37
18	— 1.80	— 6.96	18.30	9.62	17.52	848.48	36.68
19	7.12	—20.88	1.72	4.06	9.63	850.13	1.65
20	— 2.66	2.66	8.60	— 9.93	—11.19	837.61	—12.52
21	0.08	— 7.20	—11.81	0.23	12.99	831.90	— 5.71
22	H	— 5.79	— 9.07	— 2.04	17.29	832.29	0.39
23	14.32	— 0.47	— 6.18	2.19	— 2.51	839.64	7.35
24	— 9.54	— 7.98	2.43	— 5.24	5.16	824.47	—15.17
25	10.09	— 5.95	— 0.78	17.52	10.09	855.44	30.97
26	9.39	4.23	3.67	1.41	— 1.02	873.12	17.68
27	5.87	— 1.57	— 7.04	1.41	H	871.79	— 1.33
28	—10.71	— 3.29	14.08	n/c	— 0.78	871.09	— 0.70
29	4.77	5.95	— 9.70	— 7.83	— 1.87	862.41	— 8.68
30	— 7.67	— 7.98	—10.09	3.60	— 6.18	834.09	—28.32
31	— 6.26	— 2.97	6.80	— 0.15	— 5.01	826.50	— 7.59
32	— 8.45	— 7.90	3.52	2.12	1.95	817.74	— 8.76
33	6.02	4.78	— 7.98	— 3.52	8.60	825.64	7.90
34	— 2.89	—14.24	—15.25	— 1.57	13.07	804.76	—20.88
35	7.58	— 9.23	3.91	22.45	5.87	835.34	30.58
36	H	—11.65	8.60	6.02	— 2.34	835.97	0.63
37	4.14	—12.36	—10.09	— 5.00	— 3.37	809.29	—26.68
38	— 6.10	— 8.06	3.92	15.56	15.18	829.79	20.50
39	— 9.39	— 0.55	6.34	— 5.95	— 1.64	818.60	—11.19
40	—13.37	—11.35	— 9.72	10.39	18.66	813.21	— 5.39
41	6.45	— 3.15	7.40	0.63	— 0.63	823.91	10.70
42	13.86	— 2.52	1.97	0.63	— 5.67	832.18	8.27
43	10.07	4.57	2.75	5.59	—14.64	840.52	8.34
44	— 2.04	12.98	—12.83	0.79	— 3.38	836.04	— 4.48
45	—10.32	4.41	6.14	4.65	— 5.12	835.80	— 0.24
46	— 0.32	3.07	13.70	— 1.02	2.44	853.67	17.87
47	2.99	— 1.42	— 7.00	— 4.73	— 2.75	840.76	—12.91
48	4.88	9.76	3.15	H	2.12	860.67	19.91
49	— 4.33	—13.14	—17.71	3.62	—10.31	818.80	—41.87
50	2.83	2.52	9.84	— 1.26	0.08	832.81	14.01
51	3.78	7.71	1.97	5.82	— 7.71	844.38	11.57
52	— 5.75	5.12	8.19	H	7.87	859.81	15.43
53	— 3.15	— 4.25	N/C		(Year's Close)	852.41	— 7.40*
TOTALS	59.74	—129.96	56.75	129.66	119.98		236.17

* Partial Week

1976 DAILY DOW POINT CHANGES
(Dow Jones Industrial Average)

WEEK #	MONDAY	TUESDAY	WEDNESDAY	THURSDAY	FRIDAY	WEEKLY DOW CLOSE	NET POINT CHANGE
					1975 Close: 852.41		
1				H	6.30	858.71	6.30*
2	19.12	12.99	7.87	9.29	3.15	911.13	52.42
3	11.26	− 9.45	16.69	− 5.12	5.12	929.63	18.50
4	14.09	6.14	− 3.62	− 2.76	10.47	953.95	24.32
5	7.56	− 3.70	− 6.46	17.40	6.53	975.28	21.33
6	− 3.93	1.26	4.01	−11.81	− 9.91	954.90	−20.38
7	2.28	11.57	3.15	− 5.12	− 8.42	958.36	3.46
8	H	− 7.79	9.52	15.67	12.04	987.80	29.44
9	− 2.52	8.27	1.02	−15.74	− 6.22	972.61	−15.19
10	2.75	9.76	− 6.29	− 8.19	2.28	972.92	0.31
11	15.82	4.96	1.58	8.03	−15.67	987.64	14.72
12	−13.14	8.97	2.52	− 6.14	H	979.85	− 7.79
13	2.44	13.14	13.78	− 7.08	1.33	1003.46	23.61
14	− 6.06	− 5.27	7.32	− 5.35	− 2.52	991.58	−11.88
15	12.51	− 2.44	−15.43	− 9.13	− 8.81	968.28	−23.30
16	2.99	12.99	− 9.61	5.83	H	980.48	12.20
17	7.63	15.35	7.56	− 3.31	− 7.00	1000.71	20.23
18	2.05	− 7.25	5.20	1.42	− 5.28	996.85	− 3.86
19	− 6.53	3.38	− 7.24	3.07	6.69	996.22	− 0.63
20	11.26	− 0.87	− 0.94	− 4.57	− 8.50	992.60	− 3.62
21	− 4.96	1.81	− 0.55	8.37	− 6.52	990.75	− 1.85
22	−19.22	0.16	− 3.06	3.06	9.66	975.23	−15.52
23	H	− 2.10	2.80	− 2.13	− 9.90	963.90	−11.33
24	− 5.81	1.88	− 1.88	6.30	14.41	978.80	14.90
25	12.44	− 5.32	2.70	14.57	− 1.31	1001.88	23.08
26	5.57	− 9.82	− 1.07	7.21	− 3.93	999.84	− 2.04
27	− 2.46	3.27	2.13	− 7.94	5.00	999.84	n/c
28	H	− 8.03	− 0.65	0.82	11.13	1003.11	3.27
29	8.10	− 5.15	− 0.90	− 7.70	− 4.25	993.21	− 9.90
30	− 2.38	− 2.54	1.15	1.64	− 0.17	990.91	− 2.30
31	0.60	− 7.38	− 2.80	− 2.04	5.35	984.64	− 6.27
32	− 2.38	8.07	1.95	− 5.60	− 0.68	986.00	1.36
33	− 2.54	9.97	− 6.64	0.33	3.07	990.19	4.19
34	2.58	6.57	− 4.33	−11.13	− 9.81	974.07	−16.12
35	− 2.58	− 8.56	7.90	−10.39	3.49	963.93	−10.14
36	4.99	4.82	12.21	− 1.16	4.32	989.11	25.18
37	H	7.48	− 3.65	− 6.07	1.49	988.36	− 0.75
38	− 5.07	− 4.65	0.67	8.64	7.15	995.10	6.74
39	− 0.59	20.28	− 0.74	− 3.25	− 1.49	1009.31	14.21
40	3.82	−18.20	− 3.74	− 1.00	−10.30	979.89	−29.42
41	− 1.91	−11.22	− 7.07	5.40	−12.71	952.38	−27.51
42	−11.56	− 8.47	15.95	−12.38	1.08	937.00	−15.38
43	9.56	3.41	4.90	− 9.97	− 6.15	938.75	1.75
44	− 0.75	10.14	7.98	− 3.49	12.30	964.93	26.18
45	1.16	H	− 9.56	3.91	−17.37	943.07	−21.86
46	− 9.39	− 2.91	− 6.73	7.39	− 3.74	927.69	−15.38
47	7.73	− 0.08	2.74	12.05	− 1.33	948.80	21.11
48	7.07	− 6.57	1.66	H	5.66	956.62	7.82
49	− 6.57	− 2.83	2.18	− 2.74	3.91	950.55	− 6.07
50	11.22	− 1.08	2.57	7.48	2.41	973.15	22.60
51	1.09	6.39	3.16	− 2.49	− 2.24	979.06	5.91
52	− 6.65	5.96	6.15	1.08	H	985.62	6.56
53	10.47	3.96	− 5.15	4.16	5.56	1004.65	19.03
TOTALS	**81.16**	**61.32**	**50.89**	**−26.80**	**−14.33**		**152.24**

*Partial Week

1977 DAILY DOW POINT CHANGES
(Dow Jones Industrial Average)

WEEK #	MONDAY	TUESDAY	WEDNESDAY	THURSDAY	FRIDAY	WEEKLY DOW CLOSE	NET POINT CHANGE
					1976 Close: 1004.65		
1	− 4.90	−11.88	− 9.81	1.83	3.24	983.13	−21.52
2	3.74	−10.22	− 8.40	7.90	− 3.99	972.16	−10.97
3	− 4.91	− 4.82	6.24	− 9.64	3.40	962.43	− 9.73
4	1.17	2.32	− 7.39	− 3.99	2.99	957.53	− 4.90
5	− 3.16	3.99	− 5.57	− 5.65	0.75	947.89	− 9.64
6	− 1.58	− 4.07	− 8.40	4.08	− 6.40	931.52	−16.37
7	6.81	5.99	3.98	− 4.57	− 3.49	940.24	8.72
8	H	− 0.33	− 1.66	− 5.65	0.83	933.43	− 6.81
9	2.99	8.31	− 2.66	6.57	4.82	953.46	20.03
10	1.66	− 3.08	− 9.14	3.83	0.99	947.72	− 5.74
11	10.64	6.65	2.99	− 3.16	− 3.82	961.02	13.30
12	− 7.48	− 2.58	− 8.64	− 6.65	− 6.81	928.86	−32.16
13	− 2.75	5.90	−10.80	− 2.08	8.23	927.36	− 1.50
14	−11.80	0.58	− 1.41	4.15	H	918.88	− 8.48
15	5.22	13.06	1.02	8.82	0.76	947.76	28.88
16	− 5.00	− 3.99	3.82	− 6.79	− 8.73	927.07	−20.69
17	−12.47	1.02	8.14	3.56	− 0.42	926.90	− 0.17
18	4.32	2.97	6.53	2.72	− 6.70	936.74	9.84
19	− 3.65	3.05	− 9.24	− 1.36	2.80	928.34	− 8.40
20	4.16	3.98	5.43	− 5.43	− 6.02	930.46	2.12
21	−13.40	− 4.66	− 9.16	4.83	− 9.24	898.83	−31.63
22	H	− 0.17	7.89	− 3.40	9.08	912.23	13.40
23	− 9.16	5.60	4.32	− 3.14	0.94	910.79	− 1.44
24	1.61	10.17	− 5.00	2.88	n/c	920.45	9.66
25	3.82	4.33	− 2.29	− 0.94	4.33	929.70	9.25
26	− 5.60	− 8.48	− 2.29	2.97	− 3.65	912.65	−17.05
27	H	0.94	− 5.86	1.78	− 1.52	907.99	− 4.06
28	− 2.46	− 2.12	− 0.42	H*	2.96	905.95	− 2.04
29	4.65	8.67	1.21	1.30	1.64	923.42	17.47
30	− 9.18	− 6.06	−19.75	1.56	0.08	890.07	−33.35
31	1.74	− 4.42	− 1.39	2.17	0.52	888.69	− 1.38
32	− 9.27	n/c	7.62	− 9.61	− 6.33	871.10	−17.59
33	3.03	− 4.85	− 4.59	− 0.43	− 0.78	863.48	− 7.62
34	3.81	− 1.73	− 2.69	− 8.75	1.30	855.42	− 8.06
35	8.67	− 5.20	2.60	3.37	7.45	872.31	16.89
36	H	0.96	3.12	− 8.23	−11.09	857.07	−15.24
37	− 2.69	0.18	4.15	2.08	− 3.98	856.81	− 0.26
38	− 5.29	0.26	−10.82	− 1.82	n/c	839.14	−17.67
39	2.51	− 5.80	− 1.13	5.37	7.02	847.11	7.97
40	4.85	− 9.96	− 4.68	4.76	− 1.73	840.35	− 6.76
41	− 0.09	− 7.88	− 8.40	− 5.81	3.47	821.64	−18.71
42	− 1.30	0.17	− 8.31	2.60	− 6.50	808.30	−13.34
43	− 5.98	− 0.78	11.87	5.20	4.07	822.68	14.38
44	− 4.33	−11.44	− 6.06	1.82	7.27	809.94	−12.74
45	6.50	− 0.17	2.16	14.12	13.34	845.89	35.95
46	− 7.53	4.42	− 5.72	− 5.20	3.90	835.76	−10.13
47	0.35	6.41	0.78	H	1.12	844.42	8.66
48	− 4.85	−12.30	2.43	− 3.99	− 1.73	823.98	−20.44
49	− 2.95	−14.12	0.52	− 0.52	8.32	815.23	− 8.75
50	0.52	− 0.52	7.45	− 4.77	− 2.59	815.32	0.09
51	− 7.37	− 1.73	7.71	7.88	8.06	829.87	14.55
52	H	− 0.17	n/c	0.69	0.78	831.17	1.30
TOTALS	**−66.38**	**−43.60**	**−79.70**	**− 2.74**	**18.94**		**−173.48**

*Massive New York power failure, exchanges do not open

1978 DAILY DOW POINT CHANGES
(Dow Jones Industrial Average)

WEEK #	MONDAY	TUESDAY	WEDNESDAY	THURSDAY	FRIDAY	WEEKLY DOW CLOSE	NET POINT CHANGE
					1977 Close: 831.17		
1	H	−13.43	− 4.16	− 8.66	−11.43	793.49	−37.68
2	− 8.93	− 3.03	− 5.63	2.25	− 2.42	775.73	−17.76
3	− 3.99	7.28	7.28	− 7.63	− 1.73	776.94	1.21
4	− 6.24	0.87	0.87	− 9.10	0.78	764.12	−12.82
5	8.32	− 2.52	4.42	1.04	− 4.42	770.96	6.84
6	− 2.34	10.23	3.81	− 4.85	− 1.82	775.99	5.03
7	− 1.56	− 9.27	− 3.47	− 8.40	− 0.60	752.69	−23.30
8	H	− 3.38	− 0.26	1.90	5.29	756.24	3.55
9	− 7.89	− 6.23	1.21	3.12	0.86	747.31	− 8.93
10	− 4.59	4.07	4.08	− 0.87	8.58	758.58	11.27
11	1.38	2.60	− 3.98	4.24	5.89	768.71	10.13
12	5.11	−11.00	− 5.28	− 1.04	H	756.50	−12.21
13	− 3.29	5.63	2.94	− 2.16	− 2.26	757.36	0.86
14	− 6.32	4.33	7.71	0.87	5.63	769.58	12.22
15	4.07	− 3.47	− 3.89	8.92	19.92	795.13	25.55
16	14.99	− 6.85	4.77	6.50	− 1.74	812.80	17.67
17	13.26	7.53	3.38	−10.05	10.40	837.32	24.52
18	7.01	− 4.15	−11.35	− 4.42	4.68	829.09	− 8.23
19	− 4.51	− 2.51	0.09	12.04	6.50	840.70	11.61
20	6.06	7.54	4.07	− 7.45	− 4.07	846.85	6.15
21	8.57	−10.13	− 7.37	− 2.51	− 3.72	831.69	−15.16
22	H	2.51	6.41	0.09	6.84	847.54	15.85
23	16.29	2.68	− 4.59	0.17	− 2.86	859.23	11.69
24	− 2.51	0.26	− 2.42	−10.31	− 7.28	836.97	−22.26
25	1.65	− 8.58	− 5.11	2.77	− 4.68	823.02	−13.95
26	−10.74	5.03	2.60	1.73	− 2.69	818.95	− 4.07
27	− 6.06	H	− 7.10	1.38	5.29	812.46	− 6.49
28	4.33	4.50	3.64	− 0.17	15.07	839.83	27.37
29	− 0.78	−10.05	11.70	− 2.08	− 5.20	833.42	− 6.41
30	− 1.82	7.97	7.62	3.38	5.72	856.29	22.87
31	5.98	− 1.56	22.78	3.38	1.56	888.43	32.14
32	− 3.38	4.16	2.42	− 6.15	5.37	890.85	2.42
33	− 2.68	− 1.04	7.45	5.54	− 3.29	896.83	5.98
34	− 7.88	3.46	4.59	0.35	− 1.82	895.53	− 1.30
35	−10.65	− 4.68	0.52	− 3.90	2.51	879.33	−16.20
36	H	7.28	9.18	− 2.08	14.03	907.74	28.41
37	n/c	− 1.30	− 6.84	−12.56	− 8.49	878.55	−29.19
38	− 8.40	− 8.58	− 4.41	3.98	1.30	862.44	−16.11
39	− 0.09	5.81	− 7.97	1.12	4.51	865.82	3.38
40	5.54	− 3.46	6.06	2.51	3.55	880.02	14.20
41	13.17	− 1.56	9.79	− 4.68	0.35	897.09	17.07
42	−21.92	− 8.83	− 6.67	−13.26	− 8.40	838.01	−59.08
43	1.65	− 7.11	− 2.34	− 9.09	−15.07	806.05	−31.96
44	5.80	−19.40	35.34	−10.83	6.15	823.11	17.06
45	− 8.23	−14.81	7.54	− 3.64	3.12	807.09	−16.02
46	−15.08	− 6.75	0.34	8.58	3.55	797.73	− 9.36
47	7.88	− 1.56	2.95	H	3.12	810.12	12.39
48	3.72	− 9.70	−14.03	8.92	12.47	811.50	1.38
49	− 4.67	13.68	1.39	− 5.81	− 4.24	811.85	0.35
50	5.80	− 2.68	− 5.11	2.68	− 7.19	805.35	− 6.50
51	−17.84	2.34	3.81	1.13	13.68	808.47	3.12
52	H	7.54	− 7.45	− 2.60	− 0.95	805.01	− 3.46
TOTALS	−31.81	−70.32	71.33	−65.71	70.35		−26.16

1979 DAILY DOW POINT CHANGES
(Dow Jones Industrial Average)

WEEK #	MONDAY	TUESDAY	WEDNESDAY	THURSDAY	FRIDAY	WEEKLY DOW CLOSE	NET POINT CHANGE
						1978 Close: 805.01	
1	H	6.41	5.97	8.75	4.59	830.73	25.72
2	− 2.59	3.29	− 6.50	3.12	8.23	836.28	5.55
3	12.39	−13.08	− 1.39	4.94	− 1.65	837.49	1.21
4	1.04	8.32	− 0.44	8.23	5.11	859.75	22.26
5	− 3.98	− 3.99	−12.56	1.65	− 6.24	834.63	−25.12
6	−10.65	− 1.13	− 6.84	2.86	3.46	822.33	−12.30
7	2.51	5.37	− 0.43	− 0.69	− 2.08	827.01	4.68
8	H	7.54	n/c	− 5.98	− 5.29	823.28	− 3.73
9	− 2.16	−14.12	1.82	7.02	− 0.09	815.75	− 7.53
10	11.61	− 0.78	7.71	10.56	− 1.99	842.86	27.11
11	1.82	2.25	− 1.56	1.65	5.80	852.82	9.96
12	4.77	− 7.28	7.45	3.55	− 1.56	859.75	6.93
13	− 4.93	16.54	− 5.11	0.52	− 4.59	862.18	2.43
14	− 6.93	13.08	1.47	7.80	− 1.91	875.69	13.51
15	− 1.99	5.02	− 7.01	− 1.21	H	870.50	− 5.19
16	−10.05	− 2.52	2.34	− 5.02	1.73	856.98	−13.52
17	3.12	6.76	0.60	− 6.49	− 4.33	856.64	− 0.34
18	− 1.74	0.61	n/c	2.08	−10.05	847.54	− 9.10
19	−14.12	1.47	3.73	− 9.70	1.64	830.56	−16.98
20	− 5.54	0.86	2.60	14.47	− 1.04	841.91	11.35
21	0.52	2.94	− 7.97	0.26	− 1.38	836.28	− 5.63
22	H	− 3.73	−10.39	0.17	− 1.12	821.21	−15.07
23	0.69	9.44	4.16	1.47	− 1.82	835.15	13.94
24	2.43	7.71	− 3.12	0.17	0.96	843.30	8.15
25	− 3.90	n/c	0.43	3.81	5.46	849.10	5.80
26	− 4.85	− 6.59	2.86	2.52	− 1.06	841.98	− 7.12
27	− 7.94	1.54	H	0.17	10.41	846.16	4.18
28	6.83	− 2.65	− 6.48	− 7.00	− 3.33	833.53	−12.63
29	1.37	− 6.40	0.08	− 1.28	0.77	828.07	− 5.46
30	− 2.56	4.27	9.73	0.25	n/c	839.76	11.69
31	− 1.02	7.68	3.92	− 2.39	− 1.79	846.16	6.40
32	− 2.39	11.26	3.33	− 4.86	8.78	867.06	20.90
33	8.20	1.45	9.13	− 1.80	− 0.68	883.36	16.30
34	3.16	− 0.51	− 0.17	− 5.46	− 0.18	880.20	− 3.16
35	5.21	− 0.77	0.26	− 1.20	3.93	887.63	7.43
36	H	−15.02	− 6.48	1.19	6.83	874.15	−13.48
37	2.73	− 7.17	1.19	− 0.17	8.37	879.10	4.95
38	2.21	− 7.16	2.30	17.24	0.25	893.94	14.84
39	− 8.10	0.34	0.17	1.11	− 8.88	878.58	−15.36
40	− 5.63	12.37	− 0.17	4.95	7.51	897.61	19.03
41	−13.57	−26.45	− 8.27	− 4.70	− 5.63	838.99	−58.62
42	− 7.93	− 1.54	1.20	− 0.60	−15.44	814.68	−24.31
43	− 5.55	− 2.30	1.53	− 2.90	3.84	809.30	− 5.38
44	− 0.68	15.19	− 8.11	4.44	− 1.20	818.94	9.64
45	− 6.31	− 6.15	− 9.81	0.94	8.87	806.48	−12.46
46	15.45	− 7.85	2.47	4.78	− 5.63	815.70	9.22
47	− 0.43	− 6.05	− 1.80	H	4.35	811.77	− 3.93
48	16.98	− 2.90	4.61	1.28	− 9.39	822.35	10.58
49	− 2.73	5.29	3.50	6.66	− 1.88	833.19	10.84
50	0.68	− 0.17	1.97	0.42	6.66	842.75	9.56
51	1.87	− 5.97	0.26	4.43	− 4.43	838.91	− 3.84
52	0.25	H	− 1.02	1.96	− 1.19	838.91	n/c
53	− 0.17				(Year's Close)	838.74	− 0.17*
TOTALS	−27.82	4.72	−18.84	73.97	1.70		33.73

*Partial Week

1980 DAILY DOW POINT CHANGES

(Dow Jones Industrial Average)

WEEK #	MONDAY	TUESDAY	WEDNESDAY	THURSDAY	FRIDAY	WEEKLY DOW CLOSE	NET POINT CHANGE
					1979 Close: 838.74		
1		H	−14.17	− 4.26	8.53	828.84	− 9.90*
2	3.16	19.71	− 1.62	8.87	− 0.43	858.53	29.69
3	5.04	5.03	− 3.41	− 1.62	3.58	867.15	8.62
4	5.63	− 6.57	11.35	2.39	− 3.84	876.11	8.96
5	2.39	− 4.10	7.51	− 6.06	5.63	881.46	5.37
6	− 6.39	1.53	5.21	3.66	10.24	895.73	14.25
7	− 6.14	9.39	4.86	−10.07	− 8.79	884.98	−10.75
8	H	− 8.96	10.84	−18.34	0.25	868.77	−16.21
9	− 8.96	4.44	− 9.13	− 0.68	8.70	863.14	− 5.63
10	− 8.79	2.13	−11.60	−16.81	− 7.51	820.56	−42.58
11	− 1.62	7.51	− 6.91	− 9.98	2.13	811.69	− 8.87
12	−23.04	12.97	− 0.68	−11.86	− 3.93	785.15	−26.54
13	−19.71	2.39	− 5.71	− 2.14	17.67	777.65	− 7.50
14	8.10	− 1.28	3.33	− 3.67	H	784.13	6.48
15	−15.79	6.66	10.92	5.55	0.08	791.55	7.42
16	− 6.65	− 1.54	−12.11	− 2.39	− 5.46	763.40	−28.15
17	− 4.27	30.72	− 0.60	7.85	6.48	803.58	40.18
18	1.88	5.63	5.97	− 8.27	2.13	810.92	7.34
19	5.38	− 0.26	5.21	− 6.06	− 9.39	805.80	− 5.12
20	− 0.60	11.69	2.73	2.91	4.35	826.88	21.08
21	4.01	1.62	− 1.45	11.86	11.18	854.10	27.22
22	H	3.66	2.56	−14.07	4.60	850.85	− 3.25
23	− 3.50	− 3.58	14.25	0.68	2.82	861.52	10.67
24	− 0.85	3.32	8.71	− 0.09	3.76	876.37	14.85
25	1.36	1.54	2.64	−11.01	− 1.19	869.71	− 6.66
26	4.10	3.49	10.24	− 4.09	− 1.62	881.83	12.12
27	−13.91	4.35	3.75	12.89	H	888.91	7.08
28	9.30	− 0.86	− 0.08	−11.35	5.21	891.13	2.22
29	14.42	− 4.01	2.90	10.66	8.88	923.98	32.85
30	4.69	− 1.37	1.28	− 2.47	− 8.02	918.09	− 5.89
31	7.34	6.48	4.27	− 0.86	− 3.84	931.48	13.39
32	− 0.42	− 1.28	8.45	12.71	3.75	954.69	23.21
33	9.39	−11.69	− 3.16	13.40	4.09	966.72	12.03
34	−18.09	− 8.78	5.46	9.72	3.16	958.19	− 8.53
35	− 1.96	− 2.82	−10.32	−12.71	2.21	932.59	−25.60
36	H	8.19	12.38	− 4.35	− 7.85	940.96	8.37
37	−12.38	6.15	3.75	2.82	− 4.78	936.52	− 4.44
38	1.11	8.27	15.36	− 4.78	7.26	963.74	27.22
39	10.83	−12.54	2.73	− 8.79	−15.87	940.10	−23.64
40	−18.17	10.49	7.00	2.82	8.44	950.68	10.58
41	15.02	− 5.03	3.32	− 5.03	− 8.28	950.68	n/c
42	9.22	2.30	10.24	−13.74	− 2.56	956.14	5.46
43	4.70	− 6.40	0.68	−15.61	4.09	943.60	−12.54
44	−11.86	0.85	− 3.41	−11.43	6.74	924.49	−19.11
45	12.71	H	15.96	−17.75	− 2.99	932.42	7.93
46	1.37	10.24	20.90	17.49	3.93	986.35	53.93
47	− 0.09	11.69	− 6.91	9.13	−10.24	989.93	3.58
48	−11.18	3.93	7.00	H	3.66	993.34	3.41
49	−23.69	4.95	− 2.13	− 1.79	−14.25	956.23	−37.11
50	−22.53	0.34	−17.83	− 7.76	8.70	917.15	−39.08
51	− 5.55	6.49	10.41	1.70	7.00	937.20	20.05
52	21.59	− 0.51	4.77	H	3.33	966.38	29.18
53	− 5.80	1.45	1.96		(Year's Close)	963.99	− 2.39*
TOTALS	**−89.40**	**138.02**	**137.67**	**−112.78**	**51.74**		**125.25**

*Partial Week

1981 DAILY DOW POINT CHANGES
(Dow Jones Industrial Average)

WEEK #	MONDAY	TUESDAY	WEDNESDAY	THURSDAY	FRIDAY	WEEKLY DOW CLOSE	NET POINT CHANGE
					1980 Close: 963.99		
1				H	8.79	972.78	8.79*
2	19.88	12.03	—23.80	—15.19	2.99	968.69	— 4.09
3	0.08	— 3.67	1.37	3.50	3.32	973.29	4.60
4	— 2.30	—20.31	— 4.43	— 5.81	— 0.25	940.19	—33.10
5	— 1.28	10.58	— 6.91	6.31	— 1.62	947.27	7.08
6	—15.02	9.13	0.60	4.78	5.54	952.30	5.03
7	— 5.12	1.45	— 6.14	— 5.89	— 5.03	931.57	—20.73
8	H	8.11	7.42	—13.74	2.73	936.09	4.52
9	9.14	0.87	8.30	12.41	7.77	974.58	38.49
10	3.41	—11.97	5.42	— 6.82	n/c	964.62	— 9.96
11	11.80	— 3.76	— 4.99	22.15	— 4.05	985.77	21.15
12	17.02	—10.26	1.53	— 7.48	6.22	992.80	7.03
13	11.43	— 8.10	19.09	— 9.46	—10.98	994.78	1.98
14	— 2.62**	11.71	10.27	— 5.13	— 1.90	1007.11	12.33
15	—12.87	— 1.35	0.54	5.40	1.44	1000.27	— 6.84
16	— 7.11	— 4.06	12.61	3.87	H	1005.58	5.31
17	10.36	—10.00	1.08	3.25	10.08	1020.35	14.77
18	3.70	— 7.12	—12.61	— 6.57	— 2.16	995.59	—24.76
19	—16.48	— 6.67	0.90	5.05	— 1.99	976.40	—19.19
20	—12.96	7.38	— 3.06	5.31	12.88	985.95	9.55
21	— 0.18	— 5.76	— 3.15	— 0.27	— 4.87	971.72	—14.23
22	H	12.24	9.18	1.11	— 2.50	991.75	20.03
23	6.21	—10.48	2.23	— 2.97	7.05	993.79	2.04
24	1.85	— 1.20	— 0.56	13.54	— 1.14	1006.28	12.49
25	5.71	— 8.66	3.23	—11.41	1.04	996.19	—10.09
26	— 1.99	12.46	— 7.33	— 2.56	— 3.90	992.87	— 3.32
27	— 8.28	— 7.71	— 9.22	— 8.47	H	959.19	—33.68
28	— 9.89	4.85	— 0.67	5.52	— 3.33	955.67	— 3.52
29	— 1.33	— 6.09	5.90	1.33	3.42	958.90	3.23
30	—18.36	— 6.08	— 9.80	3.90	8.18	936.74	—22.16
31	9.13	— 6.47	— 2.00	7.71	7.23	952.34	15.60
32	— 6.09	— 0.26	7.61	— 0.67	—10.37	942.54	— 9.80
33	1.14	5.62	— 4.09	— 0.86	— 7.42	936.93	— 5.61
34	—10.18	— 2.38	2.09	1.91	— 7.80	920.57	—16.36
35	—20.46	1.72	— 2.57	—10.18	3.14	892.22	—28.35
36	—10.75	1.24	1.52	—17.22	— 5.33	861.68	—30.54
37	H	—10.56	2.76	8.56	10.37	872.81	11.13
38	— 6.66	— 7.80	— 6.75	—11.51	— 3.90	836.19	—36.62
39	10.37	— 0.86	— 4.76	— 5.80	—11.13	824.01	—12.18
40	18.55	5.33	2.09	2.28	8.47	860.73	36.72
41	— 0.86	— 3.61	12.46	9.42	— 5.14	873.00	12.27
42	— 3.52	— 3.90	—14.93	5.61	— 4.57	851.69	—21.31
43	— 4.56	4.75	— 0.85	— 2.76	—10.28	837.99	—13.70
44	— 7.03	7.42	— 0.77	— 4.66	19.60	852.55	14.56
45	14.27	1.90	— 1.90	— 7.71	— 6.66	852.45	— 0.10
46	2.76	— 1.23	3.14	3.42	— 4.66	855.88	3.43
47	—10.85	5.14	— 6.09	0.67	8.18	852.93	— 2.95
48	— 1.14	18.45	7.90	H	7.80	885.94	33.01
49	3.04	1.24	— 7.61	1.24	8.84	892.69	6.75
50	— 5.70	— 5.24	6.47	3.81	— 5.52	886.51	— 6.18
51	—15.03	4.47	— 7.23	1.81	5.23	875.76	—10.75
52	— 2.66	— 1.14	— 2.29	3.71	H	873.38	— 2.38
53	— 3.04	— 2.09	4.85	1.90	(Year's Close)	875.00	1.62*
TOTALS	—64.47	—30.72	—13.95	—13.66	33.81		—88.99

*Partial Week
**NYSE closed at 3:17—attempted assassination of Reagan.

1982 DAILY DOW POINT CHANGES

(Dow Jones Industrial Average)

WEEK #	MONDAY	TUESDAY	WEDNESDAY	THURSDAY	FRIDAY	WEEKLY DOW CLOSE	NET POINT CHANGE
					1981 Close: 875.00		
1	7.52	−17.22	− 4.28	0.76	4.75	866.53	− 8.47
2	−16.07	− 2.76	− 8.75	3.33	5.32	847.60	−18.93
3	7.52	− 7.71	− 1.52	2.38	− 3.24	845.03	− 2.57
4	− 2.28	− 1.24	1.15	21.59	6.85	871.10	26.07
5	−19.41	0.86	− 7.52	2.00	4.00	851.03	−20.07
6	−17.60	− 2.86	6.09	− 1.99	− 0.86	833.81	−17.22
7	H	− 2.47	− 3.71	1.33	− 4.66	824.30	− 9.51
8	−13.04	1.72	13.79	− 0.95	− 1.43	824.39	0.09
9	4.00	− 2.57	−10.66	− 7.61	− 0.19	807.36	−17.03
10	−11.89	8.37	1.05	0.67	− 8.19	797.37	− 9.99
11	3.62	− 2.66	− 2.48	9.42	0.38	805.65	8.28
12	13.89	7.13	− 3.33	4.29	− 9.71	817.92	12.27
13	5.90	0.67	− 1.72	10.47	5.33	838.57	20.65
14	− 3.24	4.00	− 2.48	6.09	H	842.94	4.37
15	− 1.62	− 0.28	− 2.95	1.52	3.81	843.42	0.48
16	2.66	− 5.52	2.86	9.70	9.04	862.16	18.74
17	3.42	− 8.08	− 4.86	− 7.70	3.42	848.36	−13.80
18	0.67	5.42	n/c	8.75	6.00	869.20	20.84
19	− 8.28	4.95	− 0.10	− 6.66	− 1.33	857.78	−11.42
20	−12.46	− 4.47	− 4.95	− 3.42	3.42	835.90	−21.88
21	0.48	− 1.81	− 5.80	− 3.81	− 5.42	819.54	−16.36
22	H	− 4.57	1.91	− 0.38	−11.52	804.98	−14.56
23	− 0.95	− 1.80	− 6.66	3.14	11.03	809.74	4.76
24	− 7.89	− 0.58	− 4.37	− 5.42	− 2.86	788.62	−21.12
25	1.33	9.71	13.51	− 2.76	− 7.33	803.08	14.46
26	8.85	0.28	− 0.28	− 8.66	− 6.28	796.99	− 6.09
27	H	1.91	0.76	5.32	9.14	814.12	17.13
28	10.75	− 0.67	4.19	− 1.05	1.33	828.67	14.55
29	− 2.57	7.33	− 1.24	− 0.19	− 1.43	830.57	1.90
30	− 5.13	− 2.67	−10.94	0.38	− 3.61	808.60	−21.97
31	13.51	− 5.71	−12.94	− 7.61	−11.51	784.34	−24.26
32	− 3.99	− 1.05	− 2.09	− 0.29	11.13	788.05	3.71
33	4.38	38.81	− 1.81	9.14	30.72	869.29	81.24
34	21.88	−16.27	9.99	7.52	− 8.94	883.47	14.18
35	9.83	8.01	− 6.26	14.35	15.73	925.13	41.66
36	H	−10.85	1.47	− 3.22	− 5.71	906.82	−18.31
37	11.87	4.32	7.45	− 2.66	−10.86	916.94	10.12
38	− 0.64	18.49	− 7.18	− 1.84	− 6.25	919.52	2.58
39	1.38	− 1.57	−13.06	−10.02	11.49	907.74	−11.78
40	− 4.13	3.58	37.07	21.74	20.88	986.85	79.11
41	25.94	− 9.11	11.40	−18.21	− 3.77	993.10	6.25
42	26.12	− 5.42	20.32	2.86	− 5.52	1031.46	38.36
43	−36.33	10.94	0.28	−15.36	0.73	991.72	−39.74
44	13.98	16.38	43.41	−15.27	1.56	1051.78	60.06
45	−14.34	22.81	−15.73	10.21	−14.81	1039.92	−11.86
46	−18.49	−13.43	19.50	4.60	−10.85	1021.25	−18.67
47	−21.25	− 9.01	9.01	H	7.36	1007.36	−13.89
48	− 4.51	36.43	− 8.19	2.02	− 1.75	1031.36	24.00
49	24.29	1.29	− 9.85	−19.13	− 9.20	1018.76	−12.60
50	5.52	−14.90	−16.74	− 2.39	21.25	1011.50	− 7.26
51	− 6.99	25.75	4.78	10.03	H	1045.07	33.57
52	25.48	−11.68	0.73	−12.23	− 0.83	1046.54	1.47
TOTALS	21.69	70.22	28.27	14.75	36.61		171.54

1983 DAILY DOW POINT CHANGES
(Dow Jones Industrial Average)

WEEK #	MONDAY	TUESDAY	WEDNESDAY	THURSDAY	FRIDAY	WEEKLY DOW CLOSE	NET POINT CHANGE
					1982 Close: 1046.54		
1	− 19.50	19.04	− 1.19	26.03	5.15	1076.07	29.53
2	16.28	− 8.56	− 0.18	− 9.66	6.90	1080.85	4.78
3	3.96	− 5.16	−11.59	2.76	−17.84	1052.98	−27.87
4	−22.81	11.86	− 4.04	25.66	1.10	1064.75	11.77
5	10.95	−15.91	2.85	2.02	13.25	1077.91	13.16
6	9.19	−11.77	− 7.91	20.33	− 1.25	1086.50	8.59
7	10.60	− 4.00	− 5.67	1.48	3.91	1092.82	6.32
8	H	−12.42	16.54	24.87	− 0.87	1120.94	28.12
9	− 8.32	18.09	4.35	3.00	2.90	1140.96	20.02
10	0.78	−21.96	12.86	−11.70	− 3.20	1117.74	−23.22
11	− 3.29	10.07	− 8.52	0.97	0.77	1117.74	n/c
12	7.55	− 2.32	17.90	5.03	− 5.81	1140.09	22.35
13	− 6.77	− 2.13	12.10	−13.26	H	1130.03	−10.06
14	− 2.42	− 7.45	− 6.67	4.16	7.06	1124.71	− 5.32
15	17.12	3.49	11.32	8.61	6.09	1171.34	46.63
16	11.90	− 8.70	16.93	− 3.20	8.03	1196.30	24.96
17	− 9.09	22.25	− 1.06	11.12	6.68	1226.20	29.90
18	−21.87	3.68	4.64	7.07	12.87	1232.59	6.39
19	− 4.36	1.45	− 9.96	− 5.32	4.35	1218.75	−13.84
20	−15.77	2.81	− 2.23	−12.19	− 1.35	1190.02	−28.73
21	10.54	18.48	9.97	− 5.52	− 7.35	1216.14	26.12
22	H	−16.16	2.23	9.23	1.60	1213.04	− 3.10
23	1.20	−19.33	− 9.41	3.50	7.11	1196.11	−16.93
24	24.44	6.71	10.02	11.02	− 6.11	1242.19	46.08
25	− 3.01	8.22	− 1.71	− 3.90	− 0.10	1241.69	− 0.50
26	−12.22	−20.24	4.61	8.12	3.30	1225.26	−16.43
27	H	−16.73	12.12	−10.21	− 3.21	1207.23	−18.03
28	8.31	−17.02	− 0.70	6.51	−12.02	1192.31	−14.92
29	− 2.41	7.22	30.74	1.51	1.80	1231.17	−38.86
30	1.70	10.82	−13.22	−14.12	−17.13	1199.22	−31.95
31	− 5.01	− 6.21	9.82	−14.73	0.20	1183.29	−15.93
32	−20.23	5.21	7.71	− 1.59	8.44	1182.83	− 0.46
33	10.67	− 3.05	16.05	−14.02	1.73	1194.21	11.38
34	8.94	−10.26	− 8.64	0.81	7.01	1192.07	− 2.14
35	2.04	1.93	20.12	− 9.35	8.64	1215.45	23.38
36	H	23.27	5.39	2.03	− 6.40	1239.74	24.29
37	−10.67	− 4.98	5.38	−14.43	10.67	1225.71	−14.03
38	8.23	15.25	− 5.90	14.23	− 1.93	1255.59	29.88
39	5.18	−12.80	− 6.00	− 1.83	− 7.01	1233.13	−22.46
40	− 1.83	5.39	13.51	18.60	3.35	1272.15	39.02
41	12.50	−19.51	− 5.49	1.73	2.14	1263.52	− 8.63
42	5.18	−17.89	− 4.06	4.77	− 2.64	1248.88	−14.64
43	0.10	3.46	− 8.64	− 1.73	−18.59	1223.48	−25.40
44	1.72	4.07	8.03	−10.17	− 8.84	1218.29	− 5.19
45	− 3.45	0.10	17.58	3.35	14.33	1250.20	31.91
46	3.87	− 6.10	3.35	3.35	− 3.65	1251.02	0.82
47	17.78	7.01	− 0.20	H	1.83	1277.44	26.42
48	− 7.62	17.38	−11.18	− 0.92	− 9.86	1265.24	−12.20
49	5.29	− 1.22	4.47	−11.89	− 1.83	1260.06	− 5.18
50	1.53	− 5.70	− 9.24	− 9.86	5.38	1242.17	−17.89
51	2.44	− 2.64	13.01	− 1.32	− 3.15	1250.51	8.34
52	H	13.21	− 0.51	− 3.05	− 1.52	1258.64	8.13
TOTALS	39.34	−39.75	149.68	47.90	14.93		212.10

1984 DAILY DOW POINT CHANGES

(Dow Jones Industrial Average)

WEEK #	MONDAY	TUESDAY	WEDNESDAY	THURSDAY	FRIDAY	WEEKLY DOW CLOSE	NET POINT CHANGE
					1984 Close:	1258.64	
1	H	— 5.90	16.31	13.19	4.40	1286.64	28.00
2	— 0.42	— 7.74	— 1.16	1.99	— 9.21	1270.10	—16.54
3	— 2.51	3.87	— 2.09	— 3.35	— 6.91	1259.11	—10.99
4	—14.66	— 1.57	—10.99	— 2.20	0.31	1230.00	—29.11
5	— 8.48	— 0.94	— 8.27	1.57	—16.85	1197.03	—32.97
6	—22.72	6.18	—24.19	— 3.56	7.96	1160.70	—36.33
7	—10.57	13.71	— 5.13	— 3.77	— 6.07	1148.87	—11.83
8	H	— 9.53	— 5.13	0.42	30.47	1165.10	16.23
9	14.86	—22.82	— 2.51	4.81	12.04	1171.48	6.38
10	— 6.28	—12.67	— 8.90	3.46	— 7.33	1139.76	—31.72
11	15.60	9.42	1.26	1.36	16.96	1184.36	44.60
12	—12.98	4.39	— 4.92	—14.97	— 1.04	1154.84	—29.52
13	— 1.89	1.36	20.31	— 3.87	— 5.86	1164.89	10.05
14	—11.73	— 4.40	— 0.20	—18.01	1.67	1132.22	—32.67
15	1.68	4.40	— 7.33	26.17	— 7.01	1150.13	17.91
16	10.15	4.29	— 8.06	1.57	H	1158.08	7.95
17	— 8.58	13.40	0.63	11.72	— 6.18	1169.07	10.99
18	1.68	12.25	3.56	— 5.03	—16.22	1165.31	— 3.76
19	1.25	9.74	—10.78	1.67	—10.05	1157.14	— 8.17
20	— 6.07	— 0.21	2.30	—10.89	— 8.48	1133.79	—23.35
21	— 8.48	— 8.69	— 2.82	—10.37	3.67	1107.10	—26.69
22	H	— 5.86	1.35	2.26	19.50	1124.35	17.25
23	7.22	— 6.68	8.95	— 1.40	— 1.19	1131.25	6.90
24	—15.64	— 5.08	n/c	—12.92	—10.71	1086.90	—44.35
25	22.75	6.18	15.80	— 4.42	3.86	1131.07	44.17
26	— 0.55	— 7.73	— 6.07	9.83	5.85	1132.40	1.33
27	— 2.32	— 4.20	H	— 9.72	— 1.99	1122.57	— 9.83
28	11.48	— 7.17	—18.33	— 3.98	5.30	1109.87	—12.70
29	6.96	6.07	—11.26	— 8.72	— 1.55	1101.37	— 8.50
30	— 4.75	—10.05	10.38	10.60	7.07	1114.62	13.25
31	— 4.64	5.30	19.33	31.47	36.00	1202.08	87.46
32	0.88	1.66	— 8.51	27.94	— 5.96	1218.09	16.01
33	1.99	— 5.97	—15.13	10.16	2.76	1211.90	— 6.19
34	5.08	22.75	— 7.95	0.66	4.09	1236.53	24.63
35	— 8.61	4.19	— 5.19	— 3.64	1.10	1224.38	—12.15
36	H	—12.03	— 3.32	9.83	—11.48	1207.38	—17.00
37	— 4.86	— 4.53	2.32	27.94	9.27	1237.52	30.14
38	— 0.44	—10.82	—13.25	3.53	—14.80	1201.74	—35.78
39	3.32	2.10	4.96	4.64	—10.05	1206.71	4.97
40	— 7.73	— 7.62	— 8.50	4.53	— 4.86	1182.53	—24.18
41	— 4.64	— 2.76	2.10	5.85	7.62	1190.70	8.17
42	12.26	— 5.19	— 1.88	29.49	0.55	1225.93	35.23
43	— 8.73	— 4.19	3.42	— 5.41	— 6.07	1204.95	—20.98
44	— 3.54	15.90	— 9.93	9.71	— 0.44	1216.65	11.70
45	12.59	14.91	—10.93	— 4.53	— 9.72	1218.97	2.32
46	0.22	—12.59	0.33	— 0.77	—18.22	1187.94	—31.03
47	— 2.65	9.83	6.40	H	18.78	1220.30	32.36
48	— 7.95	7.84	—14.80	—11.93	— 4.52	1188.94	—31.36
49	— 6.52	2.65	—13.47	— 1.11	— 7.28	1163.21	—25.73
50	9.05	6.07	— 3.20	— 6.29	7.07	1175.91	12.70
51	0.88	34.78	— 3.53	— 4.75	— 4.31	1198.98	23.07
52	11.16	H	— 1.22	— 6.40	1.65	1204.17	5.19
53	7.40				(Year's Close)	1211.57	7.40*
TOTALS	**—40.48**	**44.70**	**—139.24**	**94.36**	**— 6.41**		**—47.07**

* Partial Week

1985 DAILY DOW POINT CHANGES
(Dow Jones Industrial Average)

WEEK #	MONDAY	TUESDAY	WEDNESDAY	THURSDAY	FRIDAY	WEEKLY DOW CLOSE	NET POINT CHANGE
					1984 Close:	1211.57	
1		H	−12.70	− 9.05	− 4.86	1184.96	−26.61*
2	5.63	1.11	11.04	20.76	− 5.41	1218.09	33.13
3	16.45	− 3.75	− 0.11	− 1.99	− 1.33	1227.36	9.27
4	34.01	− 1.87	15.23	− 4.30	5.63	1276.06	48.70
5	1.77	14.79	− 4.74	− 1.11	− 9.05	1277.72	1.66
6	12.36	− 4.85	− 4.64	9.49	−0.11	1289.97	12.25
7	−13.91	0.55	21.31	−10.04	− 5.86	1282.02	− 7.95
8	H	− 1.43	2.54.	− 4.09	− 3.20	1275.84	− 6.18
9	1.66	8.61	− 5.08	2.98	15.35	1299.36	23.52
10	− 9.83	2.32	−11.48	− 8.84	− 1.87	1269.66	−29.70
11	− 1.11	3.20	−10.05	− 1.65	−12.70	1247.35	−22.31
12	2.32	21.42	− 5.85	2.98	− 0.77	1267.45	20.10
13	− 7.51	− 0.22	5.19	− 4.20	6.07	1266.78	− 0.67
14	5.97	− 7.07	− 7.62	0.99	H	1259.05	− 7.73
15	− 6.07	0.88	6.08	3.75	1.99	1265.68	6.63
16	1.10	2.77	2.76	− 7.18	1.43	1266.56	0.88
17	n/c	12.15	− 0.22	6.29	− 9.60	1275.18	8.62
18	−15.46	− 1.66	−16.01	0.22	4.97	1247.24	−27.94
19	0.55	4.97	− 2.98	10.49	13.91	1274.18	26.94
20	3.32	− 4.20	0.22	4.53	7.29	1285.34	11.16
21	19.54	4.82	− 5.94	− 7.05	5.26	1301.97	16.63
22	H	− 0.45	1.46	2.80	9.63	1315.41	13.44
23	− 4.48	4.37	5.26	6.72	−10.86	1316.42	1.01
24	2.02	− 4.60	− 7.50	−16.24	10.86	1300.96	−15.46
25	− 2.57	6.38	− 7.39	2.35	24.75	1324.48	23.52
26	− 3.92	2.47	0.78	8.40	3.25	1335.46	10.98
27	1.68	− 3.13	− 7.62	H	8.06	1334.45	− 1.01
28	− 6.04	− 6.50	10.98	4.81	0.90	1338.60	4.15
29	− 3.14	12.43	10.08	− 7.05	8.62	1359.54	20.94
30	− 1.90	− 5.83	− 2.91	4.71	3.47	1357.08	− 2.46
31	−13.22	2.24	1.35	8.17	− 2.57	1353.05	− 4.03
32	− 6.16	−21.73	− 0.12	4.82	− 9.07	1320.79	−32.26
33	− 6.50	1.01	1.68	0.78	− 5.04	1312.72	− 8.07
34	− 0.22	11.20	5.83	−11.43	0.22	1318.32	5.60
35	− 0.67	4.82	8.62	4.04	− 1.12	1334.01	15.69
36	H	− 4.82	− 2.47	− 0.89	9.86	1335.69	1.68
37	3.58	− 5.82	−14.01	− 7.05	− 4.71	1307.68	−28.01
38	1.46	−10.98	2.24	6.39	− 8.85	1297.94	− 9.74
39	18.37	4.81	− 9.07	8.74	H**	1320.79	22.85
40	7.84***	12.32	− 7.28	− 0.56	− 4.37	1328.74	7.95
41	− 4.37	1.12	1.23	1.35	11.87	1339.94	11.20
42	14.79	− 3.92	17.69	0.79	− 0.45	1368.84	28.90
43	− 4.70	0.22	2.80	− 4.82	− 5.82	1356.52	−12.32
44	3.47	8.74	6.84	− 1.26	15.94	1390.25	33.73
45	− 0.57	6.99	6.77	− 3.90	4.82	1404.36	14.11
46	27.52	1.72	− 5.85	11.47	− 4.13	1435.09	30.73
47	4.93	− 1.03	0.23	23.05	2.06	1464.33	29.24
48	− 7.68	0.12	18.92	H	− 3.56	1472.13	7.80
49	−14.22	1.15	25.34	− 1.49	− 5.73	1477.18	5.05
50	19.84	2.18	12.50	− 0.46	23.97	1535.21	58.03
51	17.89	− 8.60	− 2.07	1.49	− 0.92	1543.00	7.79
52	−14.22	− 9.63	H	7.34	16.51	1543.00	n/c
53	7.46	− 3.79			(Year's Close)	1546.67	
TOTALS	**87.06**	**46.00**	**51.26**	**56.05**	**94.73**		**335.10**

*Partial Week
**Hurricane Gloria
***First day of 9:30 a.m. trading

INDEX